PRICING

Also by Nessim Hanna

PRINCIPLES OF MARKETING

Also by H. Robert Dodge

CASES IN MARKETING MANAGEMENT
INDUSTRIAL MARKETING
MARKETING RESEARCH
PROFESSIONAL SELLING
SALES MANAGEMENT

Pricing

Policies and Procedures

Nessim Hanna
Professor of Marketing
Northern Illinois University

and

H. Robert Dodge
Head, Department of Marketing
Eastern Michigan University

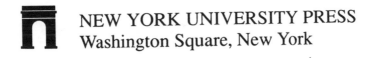
NEW YORK UNIVERSITY PRESS
Washington Square, New York

First published in the U.S.A. in 1995 by
NEW YORK UNIVERSITY PRESS
Washington Square
New York, N.Y. 10003

Library of Congress Cataloging-in-Publication Data
Hanna, Nessim.
Pricing : policies and procedures / Nessim Hanna and H. Robert
Dodge.
p.   cm.
Includes bibliographical references and index.
ISBN 0–8147–3517–7
1. Pricing. I. Dodge, H. Robert, 1929– . II. Title.
HF5416.5.H364 1995
658. 8'16—dc20   94–12862
                                                      CIP

Printed in Great Britain

Contents

vi   *Contents*

List of Tables

List of Figures

Preface

This is a book about pricing from essentially a marketing perspective. Rather that presenting formula-based schemes to arrive at prices for products, the emphasis is on meshing manufacturing and marketing strategies to maximize a firm's long-term profitability within the constraints of cost structure and the marketplace. It is argued that success for a firm is based on the premise that pricing decisions are in fact marketing decisions rather than accounting or finance decisions.

The paradox in pricing is the need to consider both the marketplace and the bottom line. Setting a price that adds profits may not produce sufficient sales. Conversely, a price that stimulates sales may not result in acceptable profitability. The risks of loss of market or reduced profitability are too great to rely on simplified methods such as the popular cost-plus that may set a price that is too high or too low.

Three important developments in the last few years have demonstratedly impacted marketing and in turn pricing. One is the concept of marketing as a philosophy of doing business with the objective of customer satisfaction. The implication is that customer satisfaction drives loyalty and in turn profitability. Customers view value of a product as the benefits received in relation to the price and costs of ownership.

The second development is the concept of the total product. The focus is now on what the product does for customers rather than what the product is. What a customer will pay for a product or service does not pertain solely to physical features or performance. It is the total package of features/benefits.

The third development that is just emerging is the movement away from a myopic fixation upon marketing activities such as pricing and the exchange process. Companies that are a success year in and year out concentrate on building customer relationships. Shelved are the traditionalistic approaches to pricing and their short-term impact.

The book begins by focusing on price as related to customer satisfaction and concepts of value and quality as interpreted by price. Crucial factors considered are effective cost information, customer valuation of the total product package, target market characteristics, and competitive dynamics. It continues by looking at price from the standpoint of the market, the useful and practical contributions of economic theory, and the link between costs and pricing. The remaining chapters consider pricing in special situations. Also included are chapters on the legal aspects of pricing and pricing as it pertains to international marketing ventures.

Many people have made important contributions to the writing and presentation of this book. The comments, suggestions and critiques of graduate students in the pricing course at Northern Illinois University provided valuable insight on the coverage, organization, and readability of the text. Carolyn Sabados, with the assistance of Marianne Markarewich, are owed a special thanks for typing the final manuscript. A thank-you is also due to Melody Dodge, who created the graphics for the book. Certainly neither of us could have completed the project without the encouragement of our respective families.

DeKalb, Illinois   NESSIM HANNA
Ypsilanti, Michigan   H. ROBERT DODGE

The authors and publishers are grateful to the original copyright-holders for permission to reproduce copyright material in the form of chapter-opening extracts and tabular and diagrammatic material. If any have been inadvertently omitted the publishers will be pleased to make the necessary arrangement at the first opportunity.

1 The Nature of the Pricing Process

> The fastest and most effective way for a company to realize its maximum profit is to get its pricing right. The right price can boost profit faster than increasing volume will; the wrong price can shrink it just as quickly. Without realizing it, however, many managers are leaving significant amounts of money – potential profit – on the table at the transaction level, the point where the product meets the consumer.
> (Michael V. Marn and Robert L. Rosiello, 'Managing Price, Gaining Profit', *The McKinsey Quarterly*, 1992, pp. 18–37)

Of all the decisions made by management, pricing is undoubtedly the most visible because of its direct impact on a firm's performance in the marketplace and overall level of profitablity. Whatever the nature of the business, success is measured by the extent revenues from sales exceed the costs of committed resources. Ideally, the price or prices set for a product or service will ensure the highest margin consistent with volume considerations, recognize customer evaluations of products/services, be responsive to competitive threats, and forestall competitive inroads.

The complexities and changes in the marketplace present formidable challenges to business and in turn marketing. Globalization, accelerated changes socially and demographically in customers, shifts in public policy, and technological changes have all contributed to making the marketplace a much more difficult place for any firm to do business. Illustrative of this are the pricing problems faced by Ford in marketing a world car. In the USA Ford may not break even over the lifetime of the car because it must be priced lower than the best-selling Taurus. In Europe, the car under a different name is the second most expensive Ford, producing a profit of from $2,000 to $3,000 per car.[1]

Added to this is the debate between customer satisfaction and the bottom line. Advocates of customer satisfaction feel that in maximizing customer satisfaction they can maintain or increase profitability through higher prices on products/services, greater customer loyalty, and reductions in the marketing costs associated with obtaining a new business. Opposed to this are those firms who believe that the market sets the price, so cutting internal cost will lead to higher profit margins and greater profitability. Resolution of this debate can come about through the premise that increases in quality resulting in increased customer satisfaction can lead to reduced costs through improving marketplace performance.

To make money we must reduce costs in producing a competitive product. There is a growing realization that the decision is not simply one of competing on price or differentiated product. Competitive advantages can be obtained in a number of ways in the ongoing interaction between the firm, the products/services of the firm, customers, and competition. Adding to the confusion is the obvious fact that success has been obtained with different approaches. For example, Fort Howard Paper, Dell Computer, and MCI have obtained a positional advantage with low prices while Maytag, John Deere, and Federal Express have successfully used differentiation and commanded a substantial premium over industry rivals.

Successful pricing bridges the gap between internal costs and external market demand to achieve a positional advantage. The optimum price for a product is one that meshes marketing and manufacturing strategies in the long-term probablility of the firm within the constraints of cost structure and marketplace. The strategic options for a firm are defined by (1) the cost structure of the firm; (2) the competitive status of the firm; (3) marketing strategies, particularly bases of competition; and (4) organizational capabilities.

CRITICAL FACTORS IN THE PRICING DECISION

The price of a product determines that product's contributions to profitability. The motivation in setting a high price is that it creates bigger margins, which in turn lead to increased profits. With low prices the opposite happens: margins are reduced and there is less contribution from that particular product. But, in setting too high a price or too low a price, a product's profitability can be reduced. Premium prices may deflate demand, resulting in less total profitability from sales of that product. Too high a price, as IBM found, can create an umbrella under which competitors can enter the market with lower prices and gain market share. Too low a price compared with what the market is willing to pay can create what is called an opportunity cost, which may be defined as the difference between the higher price, or the price the market would have paid for the product, and the lower price set by the firm.

Effective Cost Information

Marketing management needs to look carefully at the costs involved in the allocation of resources to create and define the product. This means not only manufacturing and distribution costs, but special marketing and technological costs.[2] In the case of manufacturing costs, companies still work with antiquated cost allocation systems that produce distortions in cost information. Overhead and support costs are allocated on the basis of direct labour, a major indicator of productive efforts at one time but no longer justifiable considering the rapidly increasing cost of factory support operations, marketing, distribution, product design and development, as well as other overhead functions.

One alternative to this is to assume all company's activities exist to support the production and delivery of products. All costs are therefore considered product costs and should be allocated accordingly.[3] Another approach to allocation of manufacturing costs is to distinquish between scale-related or volume costs and variety-related costs. Generally, scale-related costs decrease with volume while variety-related costs increase with the degree of variety. Generally, scale-related costs decline by 15–25 per cent per unit with a doubling of volume, while variety-related costs increase by 20–25 per cent with each doubling of variety.[4]

Customer Valuation

Rather than compete on price alone, marketers must think in terms of total value as perceived by the customer, or the combination of features and experiences that create a total customer perception of value (Figure 1.1). What a customer will pay for a product or service does not relate solely to physical features or performance. Rather, it is the total package including complementary features such as installation, delivery, technical support and after-sale service, as well as the symbolic features such as prestige and status that are perceived as delivering more value than competition at a pricing point. Price can also play an important psychological role in value positioning a product in the marketplace. Very likely the relative importance of the various features/benefits along with price will vary among market targets.

Unfortunately it is not always easy to measure customer perceptions. One reason is that differences between competitive offerings may be difficult to measure objectively. Another reason is that product or service qualities may be in a state of constant flux. Still another is the systematic distortion of product features/benefits by customers leading to a perception of value. To outcome

Figure 1.1   Conceptualization of providing total value to customers

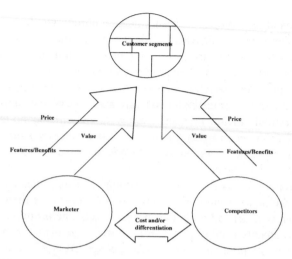

these problems, marketers must accept the criteria customers use judging product/service packages and monitor customers continuously.[5]

Market Targets

The total market for a product/service package can be segmented because of the differences between groups of customers. These differences may allow for product and pricing differentials whereby no market segment is buying the same product or paying the same price as another. This presents the possibility of higher profitability in that the firm can optimize its comparative value position in each market segment, with some segments willing to pay more than other for a version of a product/service package. The San Luis Sourdough Company, for example, uses a three-tier pricing system in selling to supermarkets and small speciality-food stores. The wholesale price for level 1 service (delivery) is 97 cents. If the customer wants the option of returning unsold day-old bread (level 2) the price increases to $1.02. Level 3 service of putting bread on customer's shelves, sticking a bar-code label on each bag and on the shelf, and accepting returns adds another 3 cents.[6]

A limitation on setting different prices is the Robinson-Patman Act, which makes it unlawful to discriminate in price between buyers of the same product. To avoid charges of price discrimination, it must be shown that the products are different, or, with the same product, that different costs are incurred in selling to different groups of customers and/or that the customers are not in direct competition with each other.

Competitive Dynamics

Competitor reactions have a significant impact on pricing to the extent they may keep a firm from making a price adjustment. The most common example is when a firm cuts the price of a product and competitors follow suit precipitating a 'price war' At the other end of the spectrum, the marketer considering a price increase needs to know whether competitors will follow suit and raise their price or hold their price, thereby creating a competitive differential. In the first case the marketer is surer of the price sticking but in the second there is a possibility of losing market share, particularly if the market is sensitive to price changes.

In addition to knowing competitor tendencies in regard to pricing adjustments, it is important to have some idea of the cost structures of competitors, as well as capacity utilization. Whether competitors will be able to take advantage will depend upon the relative size of the profit margin and on the excess capacity available. With this information, a marketer can estimate how much of a price increase is necessary to offset the loss of volume anticipated by the competition marketing at the original, now lower price. Assuming no change in product or market size, these relationships can be expressed as follows

$$X = \frac{(C_c (P_m))}{(V - C_c)}$$

where X is the price increase, in dollars; C_c is the excess capacity of competition; P_m is the present profit margin in dollars; and V is the present volume sold by all firms of size of total market.

To illustrate, suppose company A has a product that sells for $200 with a profit margin of $60. Suppose further that total market sales for company A and its competitors is 100,000, with company A selling 70,000 units and the competition 30,000 units. If the excess capacity of the competition totals 10,000 units, the question is: what price increase will offset losing sales equal to the competition's excess capacity? This is computed as

$$X = \frac{(10,000)(\$60)}{(70,000 - 10,000)}$$
$$= \frac{600,000}{60,000}$$
$$= \$10$$

or an increase of 5 per cent based on a price of $200.

Pricing Strategies

Price as an integral part of the marketing mix will contribute to the attainment of marketing objectives, which in turn are derived from objectives set forth for the firm as a whole. Focusing on gaining a competitive advantage, marketing management analyses the situation, sets specific functional objectives, and formulates strategies or ways of achieving these objectives. Of primacy in relating the capabilities of the firm to the marketplace are studying the market, determining market targets, and providing a product/ service package of superior value.

The decision confronting a marketer is: what pricing strategy is appropriate, indeed necessary, under different environmental conditions to reach a given objective? Development of rules such as following can be of help in formulating specific pricing strategies: [7]

1. *Scale* – Does the size of purchases merit pricing separately for individual customers?
2. *Consumer knowledge* – Are customers able to evaluate the value of a product in dollars and cents and recognize differences between price levels?
3. *Demand* – Does price play an important role in consumer pricing decisions?
4. *Information* – Can a marketer accurately determine price/value evaluations and levels of demand?
5. *Competitive Substitute* – Are there other products in the category that provide relatively close substitutes against which prices can be compared?
6. *Patronage* – Will customers favour competitors for non-price reasons?

It is vitally important that marketing management develop plans and in particular pricing plans that protect and ensure the integrity of the firm and its customers through consistent relationship. In regard to pricing, tactics that may be extremely profitable or advantageous in the short run are discarded in favour of long-run customer relationships. Thus the common practice of raising prices for products in short supply is replaced by a pricing aimed at customer loyalty; the implication is that in the long run customers will be lost to the firm with replacement costs running five times the retention costs.

With a knowledge of marketing objectives, costs, customers, and competitors, a marketer can relate pricing strategies to the other elements of the marketing mix to optimize effective interaction. The positive relationships between the elements of the marketing mix allow one element to reinforce another, thus producing a synergistic effect. An example would be the use of premium pricing with a high-quality, top-of-the-line product. Integration of elements is another way of exploiting the potentialities of the marketing mix. For example, the initial selling price of a product might be increased (front-end loading) to cover the 'free' servicing of the product during the first five years product life.

The concept of leverage considers the marginal responsiveness of the use of various elements of the marketing mix. The optimal state is for each element to be used to the best advantage in support of the entire marketing mix. As an example, suppose the marketing objective is to increase sales of a product and in turn market share. Suppose further that marketing management is considering the following three options:

1. Add special features to the product and reduce the price of the product (value pricing).
2. Increase advertising with no change in product or price.
3. Use rebates, discounts with no change in product or advertising.

Using the principle of leverage, marketing management would select the option that produced the greatest return per unit of investment. In making comparisons a price reduction is the same as an increase in advertising.

DEFINING PRICE

What is price? The answer depends upon whether the concept is viewed from the marketplace or from the standpoint of costs. Customers view price as a monetary expression of the value for dimensions of quality or features/benefits for a given product or service as compared with other products or services. This relationship can be expressed as follows

$$\text{Price} = \frac{\text{Quality}}{\text{Value}}$$

In other words, price is the payment for quality as interpreted by the valuation of the marketplace. From a psychological standpoint, price represents a quantitative estimate and/or subjective image of the benefits from a selective group of product features for a good or service. As such, psychological prices serve as expected prices or reference points in purchasing products.

The value set by the marketplace is for the benefits obtained from a bundle of features found in a particular product or service. This bundle will include physical or performance features that provide the basic functioning of the product, reliability of the product, convenience of use, flexibility of use and the aesthetics of appearance, as well as complementary features such serviceability and technical assistance, and symbolic features that may range from prestige and status to cleanliness and security. For example, in associating perceived quality, special features, prestige, and exclusiveness with higher price, it is no wonder that cars such as the Lexus, Infiniti and Mercedes-Benz have high price tags.

In viewing price from the standpoint of costs, management ignores the marketplace and concerns itself solely with covering costs incurred in manufacturing and distributing the product, plus a return on investment. Used extensively by smaller firms, cost-based pricing can be found in government-regulated industries such as public utilities and automobile insurance. In the case of a utility, cost of natural gas or electrical power is predicted on the costs incurred by the utility in providing the service to residence and places of business, plus a designated return on investment. Price changes are submitted to a government authority for approval. The governmental authority in this situation acts as a surrogate of the marketplace.

Pricing based largely on costs is likely to be found in markets that are price inelastic, such as petrol. Ups and downs in the retail price of petrol reflect the changes in the supply and demand of petrol at the wholesale level. An increase in the price of crude oil, for example, is passed through to the individual customer at the pump. It should be noted that market considerations, such as the times when many travellers will be on the road and the locations of the petrol stations on major highways, do impact the retail price of the product.

For most companies, regardless of industry, it is extremely risky to base prices strictly on costs and a desired rate of return. The obvious reason is that, by using only costs plus a return, the resulting price may be too high or too low in relation to the marketplace. Too high a price means sales volume will be less than it should be and a steady decline can be anticipated as members of the market seek lower cost substitues; too low a price results in the company not getting as much money as it could from the sale of its products. Thus, in either case, the company involved is not maximizing its profit potential because it fails to recognize market response to price measured in terms of volume.

When pricing is considered it is usually in terms of the free market and the interplay of costs and market responsiveness. Administrative prices, on the other hand, are set by andministrative action with seemingly no regard for the realities of the marketplace. While the term is outdated today, administrative pricing in the past was criticized as a tool of 'big business' to restrain trade and drive out smaller competitors.

When the value of a product is not reflected in the price, mechanism of supply and demand are not effective in setting price, and/or when there is a desire to control the sale of a product for the public good, government intervention is often favoured as a solution. Governments become involved in pricing directly and indirectly. Direct involvement includes government ownership of production or distribution facilities, and the use of subsidies. In several states, the state government controls the resale distribution of alcoholic beverages. Agricultural subsidies play a prominent role in pricing of agricultural products. Indirectly, the government affects pricing through regulatory board, research funding, subsidization of cultural and economic activities, and enactment of public policy.

PRICE STRUCTURES

A price structure is defined as a series of the price levels that represent how a product will be priced. These price levels allow flexibility in pricing by providing variations in price depending on product features, customer differences, and purchasing behaviour. For example, a price structure for vacuum cleaners might show different prices for each model, the type of customer; wholesale, retail, commercial, and the number purchased (quantity discount). Price structures vary from simple ones involving one product with a quantity discount to complex structures such as those found in the airline industry. Airlines, for example, set prices based on itinerary, time of day, class of service, length and period of stay, and timing of reservation.

Benefits from the use of a pricing structure include greater flexibility in pricing, rapid adjustment to competitive trends in the marketplace, and enhancement of market segmentation strategies through objective distinctions between customer types. Price structures are used by different types of firms in varying market conditions. So extensive is the use of price structures that very few examples remain of one price to all for one product. One example is a fixed-price dinner featured by an exclusive restaurant where all patrons pay the same price regardless of the main course selected.

The benefits of a price structure as opposed to a single price do not always carry over to the customer. To avoid a direct price for essentially similar products or services, airlines, car rental companies, and telephone companies complicate their true prices through the use of price structures and the use of such gimmicks as 'frequent flyer', 'frequent renter', and 'frequent caller'. So complicated and confusing is airline ticketing today that repeated calls to travel agencies may produce different prices for the same trip.

One of the primary reason in adopting of a pricing structure is to provide a ready response to competitive threats or market opportunities. Traditionally, discounts from list price have been used to respond to competition. A list price is quoted with a series of prices to a buyer. Suppose, as shown below, that the list price is $10 and the discount structure is 40–20–10–10–5. This gives the seller the option of quoting five different prices. The one problem with price discounts is the question of price discrimination. It is legal for a seller to meet competition, but pricing below competition is often judged to be illegal.

	List price	$10.00
less	40 per cent discount	4.00
	Price level	6.00
less	20 per cent discount	1.20
	Price level	4.80
less	10 per cent discount	0.48
	Price level	4.32
less	10 per cent discount	0.43
	Price level	3.89
less	5 per cent discount	0.20
	Price level	$ 3.69

The key to competitive response pricing is to identify the pertinent differences in serving various segments. Air fares are priced in terms of the competitive nature of the route rather than the cost structure that may include miles incurred in flying the route and delay times at airports in order to be more effective in serving customers. As a result, on more extensively travelled routes such as New York–Chicago, or New York–Los Angeles, the fares are lower than on comparable routes that are less frequently travelled and where there is less competition.

A pricing structure that recognizes the differences between customer segments will also allow for different customer evaluations of the product or service and different perceptions of value. Ideally, the pricing structure will allow for charging higher prices to one segment over another in line with each segment's evaluation of product value and the corresponding price members of the segment are willing to pay. For example, an open-air facility that features concerts that appeal to different types of customer will adopt different price schedules. Regardless of the type of concert, the ticket for a seat protected from the elements will bear a higher price tag than one where the purchaser will sit or stand in the open at some distance from the stage.

Another reason in setting up a pricing structure is to install customer incentives that are cost effective from the seller's perspective. Customers buying in case lots are quoted a lower price because the handling and shipping costs associated with less-than-case lots are not incurred by the seller in making a sale. Customers picking up orders instead of having them delivered in return for a price concession on the products involved is another example of trade-offs between the seller and buyer, whereby the buyer takes on the function of delivery in exchange for a lower price on the products involved. A less obvious example of cost sharing can be found in the pricing of options for a car. Usually a lower price is quoted for options when purchased in combination than if the same items were purchased separately. The reason for the car manufacturer offering a lower price is the resulting reduction in both production costs and complexity in production scheduling.

CONSTRAINTS ON PRICING PRACTICES

Although market valuations and costs of product are major pricing determinants, industry membership, structure of the marketplace, general economic conditions, and legal constraints (singularly or in combination) place constraints on the pricing practices of a firm. As an example, the more competitive the industry, the easier is the pricing decision. This has resulted in the increasing use of different forms of non-price competition such as advertising to position products and more recently customer satisfaction. 'Category-busting', where a retailer presents a bewildering array of product selection, is a technique that is used to take pressure off of pricing by providing greater selection and/or availability.

The accelerated rate of change that is often abrupt has overturned many of the traditional approaches to marketing and pricing in an industry. The major competitors are not the same, nor are the products, the way products are sold, or the people to whom they are marketed. The joint ventures of data processing, duplication, and transmission are just one example.

General economic conditions tend to amplify the advantages and disadvantages attached to a particular pricing option. It is difficult to resist increasing prices during times of prosperity and when consumer confidence is up, or lowering prices during periods of recession. However, to do either weakens the firm in terms of its relationship with marketplace. Competing in global markets implies that decision makers on selling prices must look at not just one set of economic conditions, but several different economic environments.

In developing pricing strategies those responsible for decisions must work within what seems at times a baffling legal framework. Once focused on preserving competition and preventing ruinous competition, the applicable legal framework has expanded to foreign trade, public policy, and national interests.

ETHICS IN PRICING

The process of setting a price for a product may produce a conflict with social values. The reason is that in setting a price, the marketer wants to achieve the best possible return over the long run. This may result in a higher or lower price than market forces dictate at a particular time. While high prices will provoke more comment than low prices, the motives of the seller will be questioned with both. High prices suggest excess profits and the seller making more money than he or she should on a reasonable basis. Low prices, on the other hand, suggest less value to the customer and a seller who may be trying to put something over on a customer. ·

At dispute is the difference between what the product costs to make and a selling price or profit. To put profits in a negative light, they are cited in absolute rather than relative terms. Some of the instances where pricing may be questioned are:

- The incremental prices in a product line do not seem justified in terms of value increases (proliferation of product models).
- The price of branded merchandise is considerably higher than generic merchandise (pharmacuticals).
- There is a disproportionately high price for replacement parts (foreign cars)
- The price of 'new' products is greater than the value of the change incorporated in the products (false obsolescence).

Questions arise about price when it is used as a false reference or appeal to increase sales. 'Original price', 'previously priced at', and 'comparable value' are examples of the use of price as a reference that misleads and often can be, and indeed may be, false. Using price in advertising to attract customers may be misleading and can also be illegal when the purpose is to sell them more expensive products ('bait and switch'). Unlike the ethical considerations of profit, those related to reference and bait prices are fairly straightforward; customers can stop buying from businesses using such tactics. One answer to the question of ethical pricing is a statement of principles.

REFERENCES

1. Alex Taylor III 'Ford's $6 Billion Baby', *Fortune*, vol. 127 (28 June 1993) pp. 76–81.
2. Robert J. Mayer 'Winning Strategies for Manufacturers in Mature Industries', *The Journal of Business Strategy*, vol. 8 (Fall 1987) pp. 25–30.
3. Robin Cooper and Robert S. Kaplan 'Measure Costs Right: Make the Right Decision', *Harvard Business Review*, vol. 66 (September–October 1988) pp. 96–105.
4. George Stalk Jr 'Time – The Next Source of Competitive Advantage', *Harvard Business Review*, vol. 66 (July–August 1988) pp. 41–51.
5. Y. K. Shetty 'Managing Product Quality for Profitability', *Sam Advanced Management Journal* (Autumm 1988) pp. 33–8.
6. Paul B. Brown 'You Get What You Pay For' *Inc.*, October 1990, pp. 155–6.
7. Hugh M. Cannon and Fred W. Morgan 'A Strategy Pricing Framework', *The Journal of Services Marketing*, vol. 4 (Spring 1990) pp. 19–30.

2 Market Interpretations of Price

One popular misconception about the sports economy is that ticket-buyers are picking up the tab for skyrocketing costs – including the extravagant salaries of stars. The truth according to economist Gerald Scully is that 'there is no relationship whatsoever between ticket prices and owners' costs'. Prices are set on the basis of what the market will bear. Owners can't pass along their costs until demand increases – that is until fans' perceptions of the games rise.

(*USA Today* © 1993; reprinted by permission.)

The concept of price is exceedingly complex, and the roles it can play are numerous. Two basic roles for price are allocation and information. The price of a product as an allocative mechanism determines who can buy the product, and how much can be purchased, or the total demand for the product. In an allocative role, prices can have a divisive impact in splitting a society into 'haves' and 'have-nots'. Effective pricing by increasing the total size of the potential market enables more consumers to be able to reap the benefits of society's organizational resources. Conversely, ineffective pricing may polarize the social classes and alienate the poor from the rest of society.[1] At the same time, price provides signals, and in effect positions a product as to its quality and the acquired social status in owning the product. Price is often a clear indicator of what the consumer may desire or want to be recognized for in a purchasing or use situation. Price, therefore, along with deals and promotional levels, can be a potent marketing stimulus in eliciting the response of purchasing behaviour.

PRICE AS PART OF THE MARKETING MIX

Price as an element of the marketing mix generates revenues to the firm. In contrast, the other elements of the marketing mix – product, promotion, and distribution – involve expenditures, although it can be argued that pricing below competition in an effort to increase sales is an implicit expenditure because it represents a loss of potential profit from the sale of an item. Competition forces firms to focus on and serve customers better than competitors through superior product offerings, more services, as well as more effective pricing schemes.[2] Effectiveness in pricing is viewed in terms of product positioning and total profitability over the life of the product.

Effective combinations of price and quality can produce a favourable strategic position and in turn higher profits (Table 2.1). Firms classified as having high relative quality with low relative price report the highest return on investment; they are followed closely by firms designated as having high relative quality and high relative price. Interestingly enough, the return on investment for high quality, high price firms tops that of low quality, low price firms by more than a two-to-one margin, or 34 per cent to 15 per cent. The poorest performers are medium-quality, medium-price firms, with only a 2 per cent return.

Table 2.1   Return on investment as a function of quality and price

	Relative quality			
Relative price	*Low (%)*	*Medium (%)*	*High (%)*	*Average (%)*
Low	15	11	36	21
Medium	9	2	16	9
High	17	18	34	23
Average	14	10	29	17

Source: Alex Miller and Bill Camp, 'Exploring Determinants of Success in Corporate Ventures', *Journal of Business Venturing*, vol. 1 pp. 87–105. © 1985, Elsevier Science Inc.; reprinted by permission.

Marketing management must weigh the behavioural aspects of price and then juggle all the elements of the marketing mix, including price in an effort to attain the goals set forth, principally those related to profitable sales growth. The elements of the marketing mix are synergistic; that is, the actions of the elements, taken together, increase each other's effectiveness. The result is that the combined effect of the marketing mix is greater than the effect had the elements been merely totalled as individual entities of the marketing effort. To accomplish this, each element must support and reinforce the other elements.

In using the marketing mix, the emphasis is on the fit of the elements, or, in other words, the relationship of the elements with one another as they impact the total marketing programme. These interrelationships or interactions can be thought of in terms of consistency, integration, and leverage.[3] Consistency is the logical and useful fit between elements. It is inconsistent, for example, to set a low price on a premium product or to distribute a premium product through low-quality retailers. Generally, premium products have excellent quality, are priced higher relative to competition, and selectively distributed through high-quality channel outlets.[4] Conversely, products that are less than premium have less quality and lower prices, and are mass-distributed.

Integration is the active, harmonious interaction among the elements of the marketing mix. For example, extensive advertising may be utilized with a high selling price because the added margin permits the extensive advertising that in turn creates the product positioning that justifies a higher price. Ralph Lauren, Cadillac, Pella Windows, and Perrier are national brands employing integration in this form. Integration of price with another element of the marketing mix is also found with promotional pricing, where lower prices are combined with advertising and merchandising, and up-front or front-load pricing, where initial prices include product plus extended customer service. Leverage in the marketing mix is obtained by using each element to the best advantage in support of the total mix. As an example, if promotion pricing in form of rebates is more effective at building market share than either heavy advertising or improved distribution, then it would be sensible to invest in price discounts through rebates. On the other hand, if price discounts result in diminishing returns, it would be sensible to shift the emphasis to another element that will bring greater returns per unit of investment. The investment in promotional pricing can be stated in terms of sales dollars not realized as a result of price discounts, rather than an expenditure of funds. Beer and soft drinks are examples of products where the price element is leveraged in the form of lower or promotional prices.

PRICE AS PURCHASING INFORMATION

The price of a product or service is subjected to different interpretations and utilization by consumers in making purchase decisions. Thus, what is seemingly a concrete, tangible aspect of a particular product or service may be intangible and highly subjective. The psychological aspects of price may be used in several ways by the customer. One is the use of price to signal characteristics of a product or service such as quality, value, and positional status. The makers of BMW cars believe that the luxury-performance market is shifting from cars representing what he or she has to what he or she is. That is, the brand of car, instead of signalling positional status or prestige now provides information as to how astute the buyer is in getting the most value for the money. The following formula helps in visualizing this

Features/benefits – Price (i.e. cost of obtaining) = Value

Obviously the greater the value, the more likely is the consumer to purchase the brand of product in question. Just as obviously the only part of the formula that is concrete is price. Therefore it behooves the seller to eliminate as much as possible of the subjectively surrounding features or benefits. This has been done by demonstrating quality and special features. So-called value pricing used extensively by car manufacturers involves keeping the same price or making a reduction for a model of a car that has a bigger package of features. Another psychological aspect is the use of price to sort products and services into groups or categories, while still another is the use of price to convey impressions about the product or service, notably that the potential buyer is getting a bargain at this price.

Whether or not price provides information to the purchaser depends upon the inferred relationship between price and the product or service, and also the reliability of that relationship. In other words, does the price of a product convey information about the product or service that can be depended upon? If the purchaser uses the psychological price he or she will tend to ignore non-price information pertaining to the product and make what is called a price-seeking choice to maximize expected quality. In such a case, the purchaser associates higher prices with better quality.

If quality is defined as the outcome of use of the product or performance, customers may infer quality from price for several reasons.[5] One reason is that past experience may be consistent with a positive price–quality relationship, or one where higher prices are synonymous with higher quality. Second is the rationalization that higher prices result from firms spending more to supply quality. Finally, consumers may trust the market and believe that higher prices are the result of others' willingness to pay more for a better quality.

Typically, both the strength of the relationship and its dependability will increase disproportionately from staples, where there is virtually an absence of either, through shopping goods, to positional goods such as those in the premium and luxury categories (Figure 2.1). Speciality goods are not considered, because they comprise a category where price does not seem to be a factor in the purchasing decision. With speciality goods the emphasis is on brand insistence, leading to price inelasticity.

Figure 2.1   Price as an informational indicator of quality

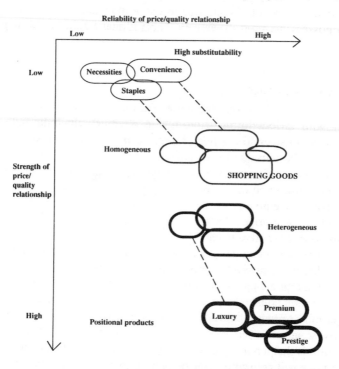

The two categories of shopping goods offer good examples of the value of price as an indicator of product quality. Price is usually a poor indicator of product quality for homogeneous shopping goods such as frozen foods and men's or women's undergarments. Consumers rely instead on use criteria, discount what they may feel is uncertain information on quality and decide only on the basis of price. For frozen foods this might be taste and freshness, while undergarments might be judged on fit and feel. On the other hand, consumers tend to feel that price is a better predictor, and are more confident in using price with heterogeneous shopping goods such as apparel, where distinctions are more evident to the customer. Usually the greater the variation between brands, the greater the tendency to pay a higher price as a payment for some identifiable product characteristic. Thus, with a stereo set, videotape recorder, or tennis racket, the association between higher price and definable product-associated characteristics is usually clearer than with towels, bedding, and china.

As the social importance of product choice increases, the relationships and their dependability of price as information increases proportionately. A higher price by excluding a large portion of the market defines status and differences in that some are able to possess the product and many more are not able to possess the product. Generally, positional products will have higher prices.

PRICE AS A MARKETING STIMULUS

Price, along with various forms of promotion, act to stimulate consumer response in terms of sales. The expected pattern is an increase in sales, with a cut in price or the introduction of a 'new' product or brand at a lower price. A major competitive tool in many industries is promotional pricing, involving short-term price cuts, cash-back deals or rebates, value pricing, or merchandising incentives that may include premiums or contests. The stimulative effect of a price discount is most obvious with homogeneous shopping goods that are advertised as 'loss leaders'.

Promotional pricing serves a dual purpose. The retailer, in offering for limited time at a discount a product such as coffee, soft drinks, or pet food, does so in anticipation of building increased store traffic, which in turn is likely to result in purchases other than of just the discounted product. The manufacturer of the product uses discounting of price level to build market share. In those situations where products or services are purchased frequently, the anticipation is that a portion of those who switched brands and bought at the lower price will not switch back to their original choice once the price is restored to higher levels.

Response to marketing stimuli such as price cuts is an approach used by marketers in identifying consumers and segmenting markets. Defining markets by those characteristics that identify price sensitive consumers ties segmentation strategy with a profit measure. Profit maximization through a plan of segmentation can be achieved by allocating resources based on incremental responses to the marketing stimulus, in this case price cuts. The take-home sales market for soft drinks is an example of a market that appears to be price sensitive. Off-price retailers have focused their marketing efforts on price-sensitive consumers.

CONSUMER INTERPRETATIONS OF PRICE

While People's Express and MCI made significant inroads and, some say, changed their respective industries by offering drastically discounted, no-frills service, competition was able to counter their low-price advantages by packaging price with other important product aspects, principally quality and customer service. What the managements of both companies overlooked is that consumers perceive differences in competitive offerings in terms of several important product characteristics, of which lower price is but one. They also forgot that price has more than economic meaning to the consumer. As a consequence, People's Express is out of business and MCI has had to make numerous changes to be competitive with AT&T's level of service and transmission quality.

Time Implications

As a general rule, individual and industrial customers alike consider delays in getting the product a time cost. As a consequence, products that are readily available will often command a premium price as a trade-off with time costs. As an example, Atlas Door is able to get a premium for its industrial doors because of its faster deliveries, so that only weeks rather than the industry norm of nearly four months are needed to respond to an order for a door that was out of stock or customized.[6] Another firm, Norwalk Furniture, has realized significant increases in sales and expanded their dealer network by significantly shortening delivery time for ordered furniture to three weeks, as compared with an industry standard of around two to three months. JIT policies of industrial customers have shifted the emphasis to time delivery of quality products as opposed to price.

Psychological Implications

As previously discussed, consumers tend to rely on price in differentiating between products and forming impressions of product quality. The result is that successful quality products must have higher prices than their counterparts with less quality. This is demonstrated by the experience of Wilson Sporting Goods in initially pricing its Sting tennis raquet. Even though the Sting graphite raquet looked and played like the Prince Graphite, its $100 lower price due to an innovation in manufacturing conveyed a significantly lessor degree of quality than the Prince, resulting in poor sales performance. In the light of this, the Sting was repositioned to appeal to buyers who wanted a graphite raquet but felt they could only afford an aluminium frame.

While customers will tend to pay more for higher quality, others pay more to avoid the perceived less-desirable consequences of purchasing a lower-priced brand that may be unsatisfactory. The assumption is that the lower-priced brand lacks certain qualities, features, or customers service benefits to which are attached certain risks. Not being able to judge quality differences accurately, customers in attempting to reduce risk will pay a higher price as a form of insurance. This view of premium price as an avoidance of risk takes on added significance with the broadening of the product concept and the accompanying shift in emphasis from the physical or performance features and/or benefits to customer service features and/or benefits. Typically, those firms recognized as having high levels of customer service can charge higher prices than those with less customer service.

It is also apparent that prices are often used to sort products or brands into categories, or what are called price lines. Prices can also be psychological maximum and minimum for a product. Because the consumer perceives these prices falling within the range to be 'fair' or 'normal' prices for a given item, price changes that push the price above or below these limits might be less effective than might otherwise be the case. It is even possible that the form a price takes can have psychological effects. This is evident in the retail use of odd–even pricing. Odd prices such as $9.95 or $1,299 convey the idea of a bargain, whereas even prices such as $10 and $1,300 give the impression of higher quality and the associated prestige and status associated with purchase and use of the product.

PRICE–QUALITY RELATIONSHIP

With more and more products to choose from, and a constant flow of new and more complex products, the job of judging which of the available alternatives to purchase has become exceedingly complicated and made shopping much more difficult. Comparing models of a product or brands of a product at differing price levels is all the more difficult because the customer lacks complete information relative to differences in quality. If it is possible to measure quality, then quality differences can be compared to price differences. Comparative value can be determined using the following formula.

$$C_V = \frac{(Q_H - Q_L)/Q_L}{(P_H - P_L)/P_L}$$

where C_V is the comparative value or the relative difference in value between a higher-priced product (H) and a lower-priced product (L), Q_H is the quality dimension of H, Q_L is the quality dimension of L, P_H is the price of H, and P_L the price of L.

To illustrate the use of the formula, suppose it is possible to obtain quality ratings for four comparable cars, similarly equipped. These quality ratings together with list prices are as follows:

Brand	Quality Rating	List Price ($)
M	67	22,790
S	63	22,167
N	59	20,094
P	56	17,602

Suppose still further that a prospective customer wishes to compare brands M and S. The comparative value for brands M and S is computed as follows

$$C_V = \frac{(67-63)/63}{(\$22,790-\$22,167)/\$22,167}$$

$$= \frac{4/63}{623/22,167}$$

$$= \frac{0.063492}{0.028105}$$

$$= 2.26$$

What a comparative value of 2.26 means that for every additional dollar that is spent in buying brand M rather than brand S, the comparable value increase is $2.26. The purchase of the higher-priced brand in this hypothetical example is much the better decision because the increase in relative quality is much greater than the increase in relative price. Comparative values for brand comparisons show that while the prospective purchaser would be getting more quality with the higher-priced of the two brands, in no comparison is it commensurate with the relative price difference (Table 2.2).

Table 2.2   Comparative values for comparisons between four brands of cars

Comparison between	Comparative value
M and P	0.666
S and N	0.657
M and N	0.528
S and P	0.428
N and P	0.378

Because consumers find it difficult to generalize a direct price–quality relationship, price as an indicator of information intervenes as consumers shop for 'value for the money'. The relationship between price and quality appears stronger for high-ticket items, which often involve service arrangements that are purchased rather infrequently, than for more frequently purchased products of lesser price. For example, it is likely that the market will see more of price–quality relationship with cars and major appliances than with hosiery, towels, and household cleaners. The biggest obstacle to the consumer is his or her inability to make clear-cut quality comparisons in the marketplace. The broadening of the product concept, plus the profusion of products and marketing institutions, has made it difficult to concentrate on price and quality to the exclusion of other marketing inputs.

Most consumers appear to understand that higher-quality brands will have higher prices, although the increase in quality is not likely to be proportional to the increase in price. Evidence of this willingness to spend more to get more was found in a 1985 Gallup survey.[7] On average, consumers are willing to pay about a third more to get a better-quality car, about 50 per cent more to get a better-quality dishwasher, almost two-thirds more for a higher-quality sofa, and over twice as much for a good-quality pair of shoes. Only a small proportion of consumers would resist paying more for higher quality in any of the five items:

	Percentage who would pay nothing extra for higher quality
Car	10
Dishwasher	4
TV	6
Sofa	4
Shoes	3

Nowhere is the link between price and quality quote so evident as with major household appliances such as refrigerators and cooking units. Between brands, and models of a brand, consumers understand the extra cost attached to quality enhancements. As a consequence, terms like top-of-the-line, competitive, and economy are used to describe brands and models. This can be contrasted with the bedding industry, where special orders by retailers make it all but impossible to make price–quality comparisons even with the same brand between stores.

Positional advantages can accrue to firms that are able to effectively combine price and an expanded concept of quality that will include special features, supplier reliability and customer service. No longer is it possible, even with highly technical products, to compete solely in terms of price and specifications. Again, using the appliance industry as an example, market leaders fortify their position in the marketplace by providing above average quality at less price than market indications would permit. As a general rule, the price–quality relationship is more pronounced in buying a high-priced item, where there is a risk of a poor choice, where perceived relationships exist between price, product, and place of purchase, or where existing relationships may be carried over to unfamiliar products and/or suppliers.

ACCEPTABLE PRICE LEVELS AND PRICE RANGES

Another psychological dimension of price as related to products and sometimes brands is its use by consumers to set price levels for products or to sort products into price ranges. Price level refers to the amount of money one would expect to pay for a level of quality in a particular product type, in other words, the minimum one must pay to obtain value in a type of product. Prices below this minimum will indicate a sacrifice in value for the product. Using the same logic, a price above a perceived level may indicate too costly a valuation of quality.

An acceptable price range extends the perception of value in a product to a series of prices with an upper and a lower boundary. Willingness to buy a product is higher within the range than above or below the range. While the acceptable price range tends to narrow the price differentials available in a product, it simplifies the purchasing process for the customer.

Using men's dress shirts as an example, suppose the psychological price range is from a low of $35 to a high of $60. What this range conveys to the consumer is a psychological fit of price to product. A shirt initially priced below $35 is not looked upon as a bargain. In all likelihood, the consumer will question the product because its price signals a warning that something is amiss, perhaps a defect in the product, or, in the case of a shirt, an out-of-date style. Thus, the consumer faces a risk in buying the low-priced shirt because of the undesirable consequences. A price above the range conveys an expensive product without a proportionate increase in quality. The consumer, in many cases, will feel no shirt is worth that much. While there is the possibility that some consumers will attain satisfaction from simply paying a higher price, the seller can expect to substantially narrow his or her potential market with a price above the acceptable range. Off-price retailing has been very effective in discounting nationally recognized brands whose initial prices are above the acceptable range. The discount will bring the brand to within the acceptable price range.

Acceptable price ranges are usually found with convenience and shopping goods classifications rather than with speciality or luxury types of products. In fact, one price rather than a price range was once associated with certain products and services. As an example, five cents and then ten were once the customary prices for candy bars and phone calls from a public telephone.

Besides price categorization of product types, price dimensions may be perceived for brands or groups of brands. These brand dimensions are usually in the form of a dividing price rather than a price range. A price above the dividing price signals the top of the line, while a price below indicates something less than the top of the line. Usually only one brand can occupy a top of the line position. Kitchen Aid in dishwashers, Pella in windows, Del Monte in canned goods, Lady Godiva in chocolate, and Häagen-Dazs in ice cream are examples of brands that have been and/or are still occupants of such a position.

Although only one brand will occupy the top of the line position, with sports cars, the country of origin seems to be a significant factor. European-made sports cars are generally considered to be top of the line and priced accordingly above an arbitrary price. American- and Japanese-made sports cars, on the other hand, are generally priced below the arbitrary price. Pricing an American or Japanese sports car above the arbitrary price is perceived as too high, while pricing a European sports car below the arbitrary price does not represent a bargain. Possible comments about prices above and below the dividing psychological price dimensions might be as follows:

American-made sports car priced above arbitrary price – 'If I had that kind of money to spend, I would spend it on a (name of a European sports car).'

European-made sports cars priced below arbitrary price – 'I wonder what they left off the car to sell for this price. I would rather have the top of the line (name of American or Japanese sports car) than a cheapened version of (name of European sports car).'

Understandably, acceptable price levels and ranges for products will lag behind the actual prices of products and brands in the marketplace. Undoubtedly, one of the best examples of this has been the price changes in candy bars, and what has been instituted in term of quality and size to draw attention away from price. The transition has seen prices move from five cents to ten, to twenty-five, to fifty cents, and now one dollar or more. Much of the appeal of off-price retailers may be attributed to their price falling within the psychological price ranges that have lagged behind the steady increase of actual prices.

PRICE LINES

A variation of acceptable price levels or ranges is what is called price lining. With price lining, price levels or price ranges are set up for a product type and individual brands priced accordingly. Using men's neckties as an example, one price line might be $15–20, a second at $25–30, another at $40–50, and still another $60 and higher. J. Crew and Wembley will price ties in the lower two price lines, while Countess Mara and Nieman-Marcus will concentrate on the upper two price lines. Sometimes only one price level will be used as is the case with Saks Fifth Avenue in using the upper level exclusively. Men's fragrances provide another example of a market that can be categorized by price levels (Table 2.3).

Table 2.3   Price lines for men's fragrances

Price line	Selected brands	Price
Expensive: Department store and exclusive men's store brands.	Belami, Equipage, Bijan, Coolwater Joop, Zino, Minotaure, DNA, Romeo Gigli, Safari, Vendetta, Eternity, Gucci, Escape, Obsession, Boss, Red, Egoiste, Perry Ellis, Laggerfeld, Drakkar Noir, Mackie, Armani, Kouros, Xeryus, Colours	$30–$75 2.2–4.2 oz
Mass prestige: Sold on selective basis.	Quorum, Paco Rabanne, Tsar, Polo, Tuscany, Aramis, 1877	$28 and above 2.2–4.2 oz
Higher price level: Sold on mass distribution basis.	Old Spice, English Leather, Benchmark, Diplomat	$8 to $20 3.0–4.0 oz
Popular: Sold through food and drug stores.	Mennen's Skin Bracer, Brut 33, Aqua Velva	Under $7 3.0 oz

By offering products at more than one price line, the seller can appeal to more segments of the market. More than one price line also offers the potential for trading up from one price line to the next higher. The risk is the possible lack of consistency caused by different prices and the resulting damage to the product image.

A convenient way to visualize price lines is to think in terms of four price levels that can be labelled economy, moderate, prestigious, and luxurious. These four levels can then be related to the portion of the market in which each will have the most appeal. This is shown in Figure 2.2. In this hypothetical market the moderate price level is by far the largest, followed in relative importance by prestigious, economy, and finally luxurious.

Figure 2.2　Potential market share for prices lines of a hypothetical product

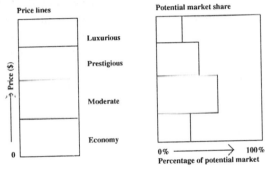

Closely akin to price lining is the perceptual fixing of a price to a certain type of product or service and the subsequent resistance of consumers to pay more than a certain amount of money for that product or service. A case in point is the price of a haircut. Price resistance was first encountered at $5. This has subsequently been raised to $10 with a repackaging and relabelling of the service as hair styling. Currently, many barber shops price regular haircuts below $10, say $7 or $8, and hair styling over $10. The fear with pricing over the resistance level is that consumers will seek alternative modes of satisfaction. The successive elevations of cinema prices and the leapfrogging of resistance levels has undoubtedly accelerated the shift to film video rentals and economy cinemas.

With acceptable prices and price ranges, sellers, in setting a price, are dealing with product valuation as perceived by consumers. Obviously, consumers will have different evaluations, yet are presented with one price in most situations at the retail level. In industrial and other organizational buying situations, it is far more common for the consumer to be presented several different prices as a result of negotiation. Typically, multiple prices are effective when differing consumer valuations can be determined by a particular characteristic of the purchasing process. However, there is the risk of confusing the consumer, as was the case when furniture retailers such as Levitz presented different prices depending upon the options selected for delivery and payment.

REFERENCE PRICES

The psychological dimensions of price are also present in reference prices. From the standpoint of the purchaser, a reference or expected price is recalled from memory as the basis for comparison of new prices. Whether or not a purchaser has a reference depends upon the amount of attention he or she pays to price, the memorability of the characteristics of price, and the use of price in making a purchase decision.[5] Sellers use the reference price (in this case, the original price of the product) to invite comparisons with the current discounted price. This is to help the purchaser determine savings in purchasing the product. Whether the reference price is reported accurately or inaccurately, believed or not believed by the consumer, it will have certain psychological implications in terms of product value. The consumer response will depend upon the size of the discount, the larger the discount in dollars, the greater the perception of a bargain and good buy.

ODD–EVEN PRICING

Odd–even pricing assumes that prices ending in an odd number increase consumer sensitivity, in that consumers react to these prices as indicating bargains. One reason is that consumers perceive odd prices as being substantially lower than even-priced items, even though the real difference is perceptually very small. Thus, an item priced at $3.99 is thought of as costing about $3 rather than $4. A rule of thumb in applying odd prices to merchandise is to have the price end in the number 5 or 9 below $50 and the number 5,6,7,8, or 9 above $50. By this rule, $25 would become $24.95 and $2,500 would become $2,499 or $2,495.

There is some indication that odd prices are distorted downward for some but not all products and in certain circumstances but not others. The appropriateness of odd pricing will therefore vary between products and buying situations. The perception of an odd price is a lower price, while an even price is more consistent with a quality connotation.

REFERENCES

1. A. Coskum Samli, M. Joseph Sirgy and H. Lee Meadow 'Measuring Contribution to Quality of Life', in A. Coskun Samli, ed. *Marketing and the Quality of Life Interface* (New York: Quorum Books, 1987) pp. 3–14.

2. Peter Reid Dickson 'Toward a General Theory of Competitive Rationality', *Journal of Marketing*, vol. **56** (January 1992) pp. 69–83.

3. Benson Shapiro 'Rejuvenating the Marketing Mix', *Harvard Business Review*, vol. 63 (September– October1985) pp. 28–34.

4. John A. Quelch 'Marketing the Premium Product', *Business Horizons,* vol. 30 (May–June 1987) pp. 38–45.

5. Gerald J. Tellis and Gary J. Gaeth 'Best Value, Price-Seeking and Price Aversion: The Impact of Learning on Consumer Choices', *Journal of Marketing*, vol. **54** (April 1990) pp. 34–45.

6. Joseph L. Bower and Thomas M. Hoot 'Fast-Cycle Capability for Competitive Power', *Harvard Business Review*, vol. **66** (November–December 1988) pp. 110–118.

7. *Consumer Perceptions Concerning the Quality of American Products and Services* (A study by the Gallup Organization for the American Society for Quality Control, 1985 Milwaukee, WI) pp. 12–13.

3 Pricing from the Standpoint of Economic Theory

> Few rational people would argue that there is not an affordability problem in the auto industry.
>
> It's not sticker shock. Consumers aren't saying 'I won't buy', they're saying 'I can't buy'.
>
> Something must be done. As factories prepare final 1994-model prices, they must face tough questions:
>
> Why isn't there a new car priced for the millions of Americans who now simply cannot afford to buy?
>
> Time has proved that rebates aren't the answer to the price problem. Specially equipped cars at an attractive and well-advertised price are popular, but they decimate the dealer discount and place a sometimes unrealistic limit on the dealer's profit potential.
>
> And widespread tampering with the dealer discount strikes terror in the heart of even the toughest manufacturer. But why can't factories solve the pricing dilemma?
>
> (Kevin E. Crain, 'Opinion', *Automotive News*, 5 July 1993, p. 12)

It is fairly obvious that a high price for a product tends to discourage a large portion of the market. Likewise, a low price typically encourages a large portion of the market to buy more of the product. It follows then that a high price tends to limit the potential market for a product, while a low price tends to expand the market. The quantity of any commodity that is produced and exchanged, and the price at which it sells, are determined primarily by conditions in the particular market for a product/service, given minimum quality differentiation between competing brands. In a competitive market, the principal forces that determine the price charged and the quantity produced and sold are contained in the prevailing conditions of supply and demand. The less competitive the market, the less the interaction of supply and demand.

DYNAMICS OF THE MARKETPLACE

The constant state of flux experienced in any given market is a result of heterogeneity to be found in both buyer demand and seller supply.[1] Buyer demand changes heterogeneously owing to: (1) some buyers being faster learners than others; (2) greater product interest in usage variances; and (3) some buyers having more discretionary income. The heterogeneous changes in supply arise from: (1) some sellers learning faster; (2) some having more resources; and (3) some prepared to take greater risks.

The resulting market imperfections present opportunities for both parties – buyer and seller. Quick response by the seller, typically in the form of information regarding competitive differentiation, can bring incremental profitability. However, in that the more profitable market segments will attract sellers, there will be an excess of supply over demand in these segments. This in turn forces sellers to consider innovative ways of better serving the buyer. Hence the need to consider price along with the other elements of the marketing mix in designing marketing strategies that maximize net customer satisfaction (gross customer satisfaction, *less* sacrifice or price of product/service).

THE CONCEPT OF DEMAND

Demand, as expressed in economic terms, is the relationship between the quantities of a product that will be purchased and the possible alternative prices for that product at a given time. This relationship is expressed graphically in term of a demand curve (Figure 3.1). The curve is based on three assumptions. The first is that the market is composed of those who are both desirous of the product in question and able to buy. One without the other is not relevant. For example, desire for a product such as a luxury good is not enough: it must be backed by the ability to buy the product in question.

Second, the general pattern of demand is an inverse relationship between quantity demanded and price changes. That is, the quantity demand increases with a decrease in price and conversely decreases with an increase in price. Finally, demand pertains to a given period of time. Over time, prices, products, and offers to buy will change, necessitating the need for new measurement of demand.

Inverse Relationship

The inverse relationship between price and quantity views buyer actions as deterministic. A decline in price brings about an increase in demand as individual buyers find they can buy more of the product with the same amount of money and new buyers enter the market. Suppose the product in question is a brand of car polish. At $10 per package a buyer is willing and

Figure 3.1   Example of a typical demand curve

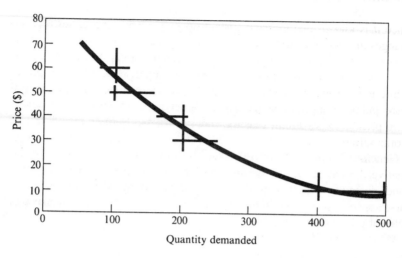

able to purchase two packages a year for a total outlay of $20. If the price of car polish is lowered, let's say to $5 per package, the buyer can spend the same amount ($20) to purchase more units of the product. The decline in price translates into an increase in the real income of the buyer to the extent he or she is able to purchase more units of the product. The tendency to purchase more car polish rather than some other type of product is called the 'income effect'.

As the price per unit declines and the prices of substitute product remain unchanged, the product in question becomes a more attractive buy to current users, as well as to users of competitive brands. With a lowering of the price of car polish, for example, the consumer may switch from competing brands of car polish or product used to keep their respective cars presentable. The 'substitution effect', or the substituting of a lower-priced product for a higher-priced product, leads to an increase in demand for the lower-priced product and a corresponding drop in demand for substitute products that are now less attractive at a higher price.

As the price per unit declines, the total market for the product increases with the entry of more potential buyers. Obviously more consumers will be in a position to buy car polish at $5 per package than at the original price of $10. Thus the total potential market is increased with a lowered price.

Elasticity of Demand

Once it is known that demand for a product is responsive or sensitive to changes in price, the next question is: what is the degree of responsiveness or sensitivity of price changes? A basic question for any business, regardless of size or type, is: can more money be made with a change in price? While the normal tendency is to think in terms of lowering price to sell more and make more money, the responsiveness, or in this case the lack of it, to price changes might be such that an increase in price results in lost profitability.

Generally, staples such as petrol, salt, milk, and plastic trash bags exhibit relatively little change in demand with a change in price. On the other hand, demand for luxury products such as fur coats and European sports cars, as well as services like air travel and long-distance phoning, reacts noticeably to change in price.

Measurement of the degree of responsiveness, or elasticity, is in terms of the coefficient of elasticity (E_D) using the following formula :

$$E_D = \frac{\text{Relative change (\%) in quantity demanded}}{\text{Relative change in price (\%)}}$$

$$= \frac{\%\Delta Q}{\%\Delta P} \text{ or } \frac{Q/Q_1}{P/P_1}$$

where Δ equals change.

Suppose for illustration that a particular product is initially priced at $60 and that demand at this price is 100 units. Suppose further that when the price is lowered to $54 per unit the demand is either 115 units, 110 units, or 105 units. When demand is 115 units, it is defined as elastic because the change in demand (15 per cent) is greater than the change in price (10 per cent), yielding a coefficient of elasticity greater than one:

$$E_D = \frac{15/100}{6/60} = \frac{0.15}{0.10} = 1.5$$

When demand for a product is proportional to the change in price, as it is at 110 units, the coefficient of elasticity is 1.0, signifying what is called unitary elasticity:

$$E_D = \frac{10/100}{6/60} = \frac{0.10}{0.10} = 1.0$$

If demand increases only 5 per cent to 105 units, then the coefficient of elasticity is less than 1.0 and demand is said to be inelastic:

$$E_D = \frac{5/100}{6/60} = \frac{0.15}{0.10} = 0.5$$

The profitability in making a pricing decision to lower or raise prices is influenced by the degree of elasticity. When demand is elastic, the rational decision is to lower price, because this results in more units being sold and an increase in total revenue. Price increases should be avoided if possible, because in the short run both units sold and total revenue are likely to drop. In situations where demand is inelastic and buyers are not as sensitive to price changes, an increase in price will produce greater total revenue, even though fewer units will be sold. With unitary elasticity, total revenue will remain the same with a price increase or decrease. However, a price increase is usually favoured because the number of units sold is greater, providing more opportunity to sell complementary products or related services. There is also the promotional effect of more units visible in the marketplace.

Changing Elasticity

In the previous examples, the coefficient of elasticity was determined for the change from one price to another. Using the price–quantity relationships depicted in Figure 3.1, the different elasticities for segments of the demand curve can be calculated. These are presented in Table 3.1.

Table 3.1   Elasticity changes along a demand curve

Quantity demanded	Price per unit ($)	Elasticity coefficient
60	70.00	
90	60.00	3.5
130	50.00	2.7
175	40.00	1.7
240	30.00	1.5
320	20.00	1.0
450	10.00	0.9

If we look at Table 3.1, it becomes obvious that the impact of a $10 decrease in price becomes less as the price is reduced from $70 per unit to $10 per unit. This is only logical, in that the relative change in price is increasing faster than the relative increase in quantity demanded. To illustrate, the change in price from $50 to $40 is 20 per cent, whereas the change from $40 to $30 is 25 per cent. At the same time, the increases in quantity demanded is about the same, i.e. 35 per cent between $50 and $40 and 37 per cent between $40 and $30.

From a practical standpoint price deductions are frequently stated in relative terms – 10 per cent, 20 per cent, etc. Thus the price levels would not be in $10 increments but $63, $56, $52.50, and $46.90 for discounts of 10, 20, 25, and 33 1/3 per cent respectively. Using the demand curve presented in Figure 3.1, the quantity demand and the coefficient of elasticity for each of the four discount levels is calculated as in Table 3.2.

Table 3.2   Quantity demanded and coefficient of elasticity

Percent reduction	Price level	Quantity demanded	Coefficient of elasticity
	$70.00	60	
10	$63.00	75	2.5
20	$56.00	113	4.4
25	$52.50	125	4.3
33 1/3	$46.90	156	4.8

It is apparent that the original price of $70 should be discounted, and that the most productive discount is 33 1/3 per cent. It is also apparent that a discount of 10 per cent is least productive, and that the minimum discount should at least be 20 per cent.

SUPPLY

Supply is analogous to demand. Supply, as expressed in economic terms, is a schedule of the quantities of a product that suppliers are willing to offer for sale at various prices during a particular time period, and assuming no changes in other elements of the marketing mix. With price an obvious incentive to produce and sell a product, the higher is the price per unit, the greater is the profit incentive to offer larger and larger quantities for sale. A typical supply curve, as illustrated in Figure 3.2, shows a direct relationship

Figure 3.2   Example of a typical supply curve

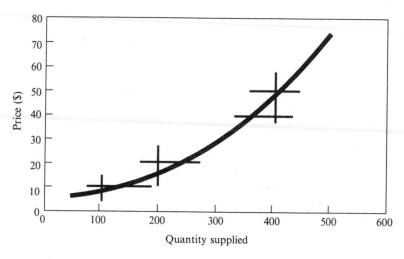

between price and supply quantity. At low prices suppliers are less willing to offer the product than at higher prices. As an illustration, at a price of $20 the supply is 230 units. This increases to 313 units when the price is raised to $30.

A shift in the supply curve whereby more or less of the product is offered at a particular price occurs as a result of changing costs or manufacturing technology (Figure 3.3). A shift to the left, as represented by the curve, *HH* means less of the product is offered at each designated price level as a result of cost increases. For example, when the price of crude oil increases, this pushes up the price of plastic resins made from petroleum derivatives. Conversely, lower costs or a breakthrough in manufacturing technology will shift the supply curve to the right. The resultant supply curve *LL* shows a willingness to supply more of the product at each price level.

Supply, Demand, and Market Equilibrium

If we assume competitive conditions, the price of a product as well as the quantity that will be bought and sold in the marketplace is determined by considering supply and demand simultaneously. Figure 3.4 shows the equilibrium price or the price at which quantity supplied and quantity demanded is the same. The quantity is 275 units at a price of $26 per unit.

At any other price there will be either a surplus or a shortage of the product. For example, at a price of $40 producers will supply 363 units, but

Figure 3.3   Example of shifts in the typical supply curve

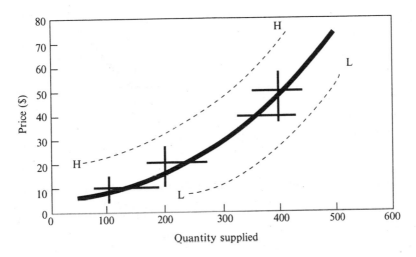

demand is only 188 units for a surplus of 175 units. On the other hand, at a price of $10 per unit the demand is for 438 units, but producers are willing to supply only 132 units, leaving a shortage of 306 units. With a surplus the pressure is on lowering price, while a shortage acts to push prices upward.

Figure 3.4   Determination of equilibrium of market price

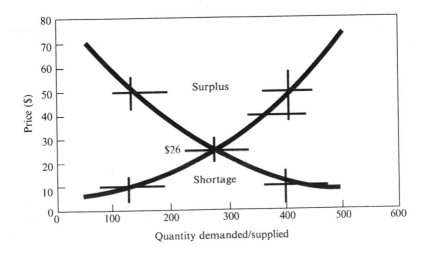

Pricing in a Market-oriented Economy

The efficiency of a market depends upon the extent to which market forces drive the market toward more efficient pricing equilibrium. The willingness of consumers to pay more for improved quality sets the upper boundary or limit for price increases. The opposite effects of reduced cost and reduced price levels sets its lower boundary or limit for price decreases. Within these boundaries, each market participant knows that offerings must be made more attractive in terms of increasing quality in the broadest sense and lowering of price as a reflection of lower costs. These seemingly conflicting goals force firms closer and closer to the limits of their respective capabilities.[2]

The attractiveness of quality improvements, marketing programmes, and/or lower prices reduce the competitiveness of other market participants and establish new pricing equilibrium. How extensive this remaking of the market is depends upon the innovator's current share of sales in the market and how radical is the implemented change. Much of the disequilibrium derives from the diffusion of information relative to the initiated change and the resulting responses of buyers and sellers.[3]

REFERENCES

1.   Peter Reid Dickson 'Toward a General Theory of Competitive Rationality', *Journal of Marketing*, vol. 56 (January 1992) pp. 69–83.
2.   Israel M. Kirzner *Competition and Entrepreneurship* (Chicago: University of Chicago Press, 1978).

4 Role of Costs in Pricing

> Our policy is to reduce the price, extend the operations, and improve the product. We first reduce the price to a point where we believe more sales will result. The new price forces costs down. Using costs to determine price may be scientific in the narrow sense, but not in the broad sense, because what earthly use is it to know the cost if it tells you, you cannot manufacture at a price at which the article can be sold? One of the ways of discovering what a cost ought to be is to name a price so low as to force everybody in the place to the highest point of efficiency.
>
> (From *My Life and Work* by Henry Ford and Samuel Crowther. Copyright © 1922 by Doubleday, a division of Bantam Doubleday Dell Publishing Group, Inc. Used by permission.)

The above passage from Henry Ford's autobiography portrays his basic philosophy in regard to pricing. This was to cut prices below the point warranted by existing costs so as to provide an incentive to expand production and sales, which, in turn, forced costs down. He contends that manufacturing improvements, forced by the low price, came about faster than if the normal practice of cost cutting were attempted *prior* to price cutting. What actually happened was that price cuts did lead to better sales, which, in turn, acted to force costs down and bring about manufacturing improvements, resulting in yet lower costs and prices – a vivid demonstration of a self-fulfilling prophecy.

In the period between 1910 and 1921, Ford cut the costs of producing the Model T by 75 per cent by modernizing manufacturing, integrating vertically to reduce the costs of purchased inputs, the further division of labour, and the elimination of model change. During the same time market share went from 10 per cent to 55 per cent.

IMPACT OF COSTS ON PRICING

While competitive environments, business organizational structures, and market response have changed dramatically, making pricing decisions more formidable and complex than those faced by Henry Ford, costs remain a major determinant. Mercedes-Benz, for example, treats cost management as synonymous with pricing in elaborating the four Ps (product, price, promotion, place) of marketing in strategy formulation. A watchful eye on costs and how they affect pricing and in turn margins is necessitated by two conditions. The first is global competition. No market is safe from competitive pressures that could dampen margins and negatively impact market share. Knowledge of the cost structure and the behaviour of costs, along with market information, provides the flexibility to respond to competitive threats more effectively than across-the-board price reductions.

Second, an almost constant stream of new ways to contain costs and become more cost effective has changed the bases of competition in practically every market. Louisiana Oil and Fire took all their salespeople off the road and made them telemarketers. The result was a 10 per cent reduction in selling expense with a doubling of sales volume. IBM has shifted its total reliance on a direct sales force and fixed-cost basis of selling to a selective use of variable-cost channels.

COST STRUCTURE PRICING

Knowledge of cost structure and behaviour lays the foundation for effective decisions regarding pricing. The basic question is: 'What price level will cover incurred costs and contribute to an adequate return on investment?' Other important questions are: 'What factors determine relative cost position?' 'What features/benefits of the product should we be pricing?' 'Should different prices be charged to different customers?'

Essential to effective pricing is the ability to recognize and identify all the elements of cost, fixed and variable, predictable and unpredictable, current or future, that may be part of the total process of developing, manufacturing, and marketing a product or products. Business history is filled with incidents where management has set a price, only to discover after it is too late that the price set is insufficient to cover total costs. The reasons are rarely improper cost calculations or allocations, but rather the elusive nature and subsequent undefinability of some types of costs.

While some costs can be easily detected, calculated, and allocated to the units of a product, others may either escape the attention of management or be of such a nature that the prediction of their probable impact on price is almost impossible to make with any degree of accuracy. Examples of the latter include the following:

1. Product liability costs arising from damages sustained by users of a product or service such as has been experienced with football helmets.
2. Recall costs due to unforeseen product malfunctioning or tampering and.

3. Costs of merchandise rendered unsaleable by non-competitive circumstances such as abrupt changes in the regulatory environment or natural disasters such as flooding.

Allocation of Costs

As markets become more complex, product lines proliferate, and competition becomes increasingly diverse, firms cannot afford allocation schemes that paint vague and inaccurate portrayals of their respective cost structure. Accurate cost information that allows decisions as product features, customer characteristics, and purchasing behaviour is essential.[1] No longer is it sufficient to know that prices will cover costs and yield a profit; today's overriding consideration is that cost advantages need to be reflected in pricing variations to gain competitive advantage.

Allocation of costs for the purpose of pricing is not a simple task. What complicates matters are the distortions resulting from sensible accounting choices made decades ago when most companies manufactured a narrow range of products and the costs of direct labour and materials (the most important production factors) could be traced easily to individual products.[2] One common error is to distribute indirect costs such as overheads on the basis of units sold. What often results is a distortion of costs, with lower-volume products consuming far less of the overhead than is actually the case.

Problems in allocation also arise from the use of antiquated bases such as direct labour. Direct labour, as an example, is becoming less and less a major determinant of product costs in many industries. In the electronics industry, Hewlett-Packard's direct labour costs are 23 per cent of the sales dollar. At BMW, total personnel costs are 20 per cent of net sales and about one-third the total expenditure for materials.

An approach that a number of firms favour is to allocate costs to activities. The theory behind such a system is that virtually all activities exist to support the production and delivery of today's products.[2] Further distinction in terms of before-sale and after-sale provides relevancy and realism to cost information. As an example, a marketing manager can compare the costs of quality enhancement in the factory with warranty costs after the sale and their respective impacts on pricing.

Another approach in allocating costs is on the basis of key determinants of competitive advantage in selling various customers or providing various products.[1] Although it is difficult to trace costs to customers and products, such information puts a business in a better position to create pricing that is profit-effective and at the same time customer-oriented. Features, quality, speed of delivery, and convenience are examples of possible categories of a customer-oriented classification scheme. As an illustration, suppose customers are divided into two groups – those that are price-sensitive and those that are service-sensitive.[1] Such a classification scheme as proposed will show where the costs are in servicing both types of customers. The guiding logic in such situations is that price-sensitive customers are often willing to assume certain aspects of service, while service-sensitive customers will pay more for better quality and extra service.

Forecasting Costs

Past costs are less important than current costs, and current costs are less important than what costs will be in the future. The challenge in making a pricing decision is to anticipate those categories of the cost structure that are more likely to change in the future. In the same manner that companies routinely forecast sales, they must forecast costs and integrate them into the cost structure where appropriate.

The starting point is the determination of the relative positions of the cost categories currently. The next two steps are first to forecast the changes in the relative cost positions and second to forecast the extent of change within each of the respective categories. In a hypothetical example, suppose the company has decided to outsource a substantial proportion of manufacturing to accommodate sales forecasts of smaller volumes for the present product line. At the same time, outsourcing will allow more flexibility in what products are produced. Risking oversimplification, what happens is that the relative costs of labour and overhead will diminish, with a corresponding increase in the cost of materials. Depending upon the actual expenditures, changes can also be expected in the relative positions of R&D, marketing, and general administration.

Once it is known what the cost structure should look like in the future, the next step is to apply the forecasted changes to determine the magnitude of the impact. In the previous example it is obvious that the impact of a raise in the hourly wage of manufacturing personnel will have less of an impact with the restructuring. If labour costs, for example, decrease in relative importance from 25 per cent to 10 per cent, then the impact of a forecast wage increase of 10 per cent would fall from 2.5 per cent to 1 per cent.

COST CONCEPTS

Looking at costs from the standpoint of their use in pricing, two questions must be asked. The first is: what type of costs are involved? We will see in yield pricing and value pricing that a simple distinction between fixed and variable costs can have significant importance to those making pricing decisions. The second question is: what costs have the greatest impact on customers? Those making pricing decisions must understand not only the types of costs and their behaviour, but also how customers evaluate the effects of incurred costs in terms of the total product. To explain the latter, the question that must constantly be asked is: do these features or benefits and/or services, individually or collectively, impact product value that can be reflected in pricing?

Fixed and Variable Costs

The most basic distinction that can be made is between fixed and variable costs. Fixed costs are the costs of being in business for a period of time and only vary from time period to time period. Fixed costs of a general nature include occupancy costs and investment in plant and multi-purpose equipment, as well as plant and general administrative overheads. When a capital investment is made for equipment to produce a specific item or for a specific programme such as the Aurora programme for Oldsmobile dealers (see Table 4.1) these fixed costs are considered specific. Obviously the more specific fixed costs are, the easier is the allocation task. R&D costs, for example, that relate to improvements and modifications of existing products should be allocated to those products that benefit from these efforts. Otherwise these costs will be spread over products that have no relationship to the R&D efforts.[2]

Table 4.1   Proposed requirements for selling the 1995 Aurora

What a dealer must do to sell the 1995 Aurora:

1. Clean-up, fix-up, paint-up: create an inviting shopping environment.
2. Commit to Oldsmobile's 'Retail Operating Standards'.
3. Undergo Aurora sales, service and management training. (Estimated cost for travel: $500 to $1,500.)
4. Commit to annual training curriculum. (Estimated annual cost for travel: $2,000 to $5,000.)
5. Buy Aurora image display. (Estimated cost: $3,000 to $4,000.)
6. Buy Aurora's essential tool package. (Estimated cost: $1,600.)
7. Buy Aurora's required parts package. (Estimated cost: $15,000 to $20,000.)
8. Attain at least 95 per cent of the June 1993 12-month average 'Par Excellence Delivery Rating' for dealers in area.
9. Attain at least 95 per cent of the June 1993 12-month average 'Customer Satisfaction Index' for dealers in area.

Total estimated cost: $22,000 to $32,000

Source: Phil Frame, 'Small Dealers Balk at Aurora Ante', *Automotive News*, 26 July, 1993, pp. 1 and 33.

Variable costs, on the other hand, have a direct relationship to the level of activity. Such costs can be called unit costs in that the costs are incurred for each unit produced or sold. An example is the materials and components that enter into each unit produced or the pre-delivery checks made on a product after it has been sold. For variable costs to be incurred, an event such as production or sale must occur, otherwise there are no variable costs.

Figure 4.1   Cost–volume relationships

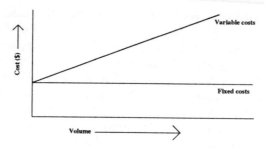

Incremental Costs

Incremental costs are an increase in either fixed costs or variable costs as a result of a managerial decision to change an existing policy or to add a new piece of equipment or install a new programme. Incremental costs could be called managerial costs, in that the change in level or rate results from a managerial decision. These decisions come about during the term for fixed costs, usually a year. For example, it may be decided to include more component parts as standard, thereby increasing per-unit variable costs.

The effect of incremental costs on pricing differs from that of either fixed or variable costs. The allocation of fixed costs plus variable costs provides a floor or least amount that can be charged for a product, given the truism that a business cannot survive selling products for less than they cost to make. More importantly, the makeup of fixed and variable costs is a basic informational source for cost management and subsequently pricing. Incremental costs, on the other hand, have an immediate and direct effect on the cost structure that may or may not be reflected in pricing.

STRUCTURAL FACTORS INFLUENCING COSTS

Obviously, some firms will enjoy cost advantages over others. One firm may be larger than another and able to spread costs over more units.

Another firm may have adopted a greater amount of technology and thus become more efficient. Still another firm may be more proficient and have greater expertness as a result of experience in producing and distributing a product. Whatever the reason or reasons, no two firms are likely to have the same cost structures, even with essentially the same product.

The more predominant structural factors affecting product costs can be grouped under several headings. These include economies associated with volume; economies of scope; core linkages; and balancing.

Economies Associated with Volume

In looking at the effect of volume on costs, it is necessary to consider the concepts of capacity, scale, and experience. The assumption is that product costs will fall as much as 25 per cent with each doubling of volume. The bases for this assumption are that with more volume there are smaller fixed costs per unit, as well as greater opportunities for workers to become more efficient at their respective tasks. Balanced against this are the standardizing of products, making it necessary to be more price competitive, and the reduction of flexibility, to accommodate the growing trend towards smaller markets.

Utilization of capacity, often confused with economies of scale, pertains to the spreading out of fixed costs over a large volume of product units. Economies of scale, on the other hand, relate to the ability to perform economic activities differently and more efficiently such as through technological additions at higher volumes of product. As an illustration, Xerox consolidated raw materials, which in turn simplified purchasing and pushed overhead rates from 9 per cent of total costs for raw materials to 3 per cent over a ten-year period. In terms of dollars and cents, Xerox now saves over $100 million annually on raw materials.

For firms with relatively burdensome fixed costs, such as motor manufacturers, metal fabricators, chemical companies, airlines, and hotels, increasing output spreads costs out over a greater number of units and so decreases, often dramatically, the fixed-cost burden per unit of product. The ratio of fixed costs to variable costs determines the degree of sensitivity to utilization of capacity. The higher the ratio, the greater the opportunity to achieve significant savings.

While the most obvious examples are in manufacturing, the effect of increasing volume can be seen in all parts of the firm. The potentiality of savings in purchasing is demonstrated by the Xerox example. In marketing, more units means lower advertising and selling costs per unit.

There are several reasons why utilization of capacity impacts product costs:

1. The variable costs accompanying increasing volume are relatively small or inconsequential in comparison with fixed costs. As an example, for one New York hotel the costs of construction and furnishing were estimated to be $187,000 per room. The housekeeping costs involved in maintaining a room when occupied as opposed to unoccupied are unconsequencial when compared with the write-off of these costs plus the fixed costs of operating the hotel on a daily basis. Still another example would be the in-flight service costs such as food and beverages for each passenger (variable cost) compared with the equipment, fuel, and personnel costs (substantially fixed in nature) in flying from one location to another.
2. The savings from purchasing needed materials, supplies, and services in quantity.
3. The savings from utilization of unproductive time; for example, manufacturing machinery will have less downtime.
4. More efficient utilization of manpower in all areas of the firm.

Economies of scale are attributable to reconceptualization of activities because of volume size. Large volumes, for example, may make it practical to install cost-saving technology and procedures that would not be possible at smaller volumes. Giant Foods Inc., a large grocery chain, found it feasible to install minicomputers in their pharmacies to attract even more business and to automate their warehouse complex, which further reduced operating costs and at the same time kept store shelves fully stocked, so increasing the probabilities of selling at greater volume. Without sufficient volume neither of these technologies would have been effective.

Scale sensitivity is also readily apparent with marketing and distribution activities such as product development, advertising, selling, packaging, and warehousing. For example, as a consequence of large size the sales force can become more specialized by customer and product type and reap the advantages of specialization such as greater selling proficiency.

There are limits to economies of scale. One is the growing heterogeneity of most markets. Stability in demand has been replaced by growing diversity, requiring an ever-increasing array of products. Shorter production runs, which requires setup time, more diverse inventories, and greater overhead all contribute to push costs upward at a rate of 20 to 35 per cent per unit each time variety doubles.[3] Another limit is the lack of growth in markets. Today's markets are for the most part saturated. One market entry has been replaced by several, each directed towards better serving the requirements of a small grouping of customers.

Experience economies are cost reductions from increases in accumulated volume of output. Experience economies result from learning by doing. The more experience a firm has in terms of volume, the more it learns how to perform efficiently. Within the manufacturing operation, schedules are improved and labour becomes more efficient with experience gained through increases in volume. Learning improvements can also lead to sustainable cost reductions in other areas of the firm such as marketing and distribution. A good example is setting up a warehousing system. The Boston Consulting Group have argued that experience–cost economies affect not just production labour costs but costs related to capital, administration, and marketing.

The experience curve concept holds that unit costs at any one time are a function of accumulated volume and an experience rate. Each time output doubles, costs decline by a certain percentage. This percentage decline varies from one activity to another and from one industry to another. Figure 4.2 shows a typical experience curve.

For the hypothetical example in Figure 4.2, unit costs are shown to drop by 15 per cent between 100 and 200 units and by another 15 per cent between 200 and 400 units. Theoretically this same 15 per cent drop would occur between 400 and 800, 800 and 1,600, and so on. However, some studies have shown a diminishing rate of cost reduction.

The sources of the experience effect are varied and include such factors as labour efficiency (as the assigned tasks are repeated over and over again) and work specialization (as the worker becomes more proficient in performing a single-facet operation as opposed to a multi-faceted one). Unlike cost reductions from capacity utilization, cost reductions resulting from experience are a result of concerted effort by management. The rate of learning will vary directly with the amount of management attention directed toward achieving it.

Economies of Scope

While capacity utilization and economies of scale improve the economy of present activities and justify special-purpose machinery, economies of scope bring efficiencies based on variety rather than volume. Economies of scope exist where the same piece of machinery can produce multiple products more cheaply in combination than separately. The emphasis shifts from specialized machinery and equipment that push costs down through long product runs to specialized software capable of shifting productive equipment to short runs of many different product designs. Again, total volume must be high enough to support such additional technology.

Figure 4.2   A typical experience curve (15 per cent reduction)

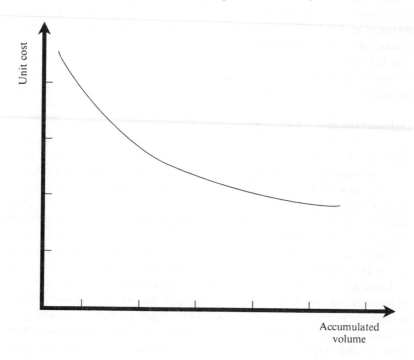

Core Linkages

Core linkages are relationships between activities where the way one is performed materially impacts the cost of performing the other. For example, the purchase of a higher-quality processed material may reduce both processing time and scrap to the extent that overall total costs are reduced. Savings from core linkages result from coordination and optimization.

Core linkages with suppliers are receiving a lot of attention currently as ways of achieving substantial cost benefits. One programme is just-in-time inventory, while another is quality assurance. By coordinating deliveries by suppliers, a firm eliminates the need for and the costs associated with maintaining an inventory. Quality assurance programmes undertaken by suppliers eliminate the need for inspection upon receipt and reduce scrap. In regard to the latter, one large electronics firm reduced its scrap from 11 million tonnes a year to less than 2 million tonnes with the installation of a quality assurance requirement for its suppliers.

Core linkages between divisions of a firm or between facilities can also reduce costs. For example, it may be possible to allocate activities to divisions and/or facilities in such a way as to take advantage of capacity utilization, and of economies of scale and scope, as well as of experience. One US company has shifted all of its labour-intensive production work to its subsidiary in Mexico, where the labour costs are averaging less than $2 an hour compared with $12 or more an hour in the USA.

Outsourcing and Balancing

More and more businesses are discovering they don't have to produce the entire product themselves to obtain the desired quality and control costs. As a result, portions of the production job are being outsourced or shifted to smaller-sized satellite plants. Normally a business will retain longer production runs and shift by outsourcing and balancing shorter production runs. It is not uncommon for the larger firm to provide the machinery and equipment to be used by the smaller firm. Flexibility-related costs may be reduced by leverage and the adjustment of volume to capacity.

While it is most frequently encountered in production, outsourcing can be found in marketing. A firm may contract out its sales function to another firm selling complementary products to the same customer. For example, a firm producing one type of frozen foods contracts out its selling function to a firm producing and selling other types. In that the selling cost is spread out over more products, the firm assuming the sales of the product becomes more efficient. In turn, part of this saving may be passed along to the outsourcing firm, making this arrangement less costly than one with a middleman. One definite saving in using another manufacturer's sales force emanates from having to deal with only firm rather than several middlemen, each in a different geographical market.

A variation of outsourcing is the shifting of the inventory management function to suppliers. Instead of reacting to purchase orders, suppliers make shipments based on demand information supplied them by their customer. For example, Wal-Mart no longer has the responsibility to manage its own inventory. Instead, suppliers such as Procter & Gamble ship on the basis of information supplied to them on sales of their products.

REFERENCES

1. Andrew A. Stern 'The Strategic Value of Price Structure', *The Journal of Business Strategy*, vol. 7 (Fall 1986) pp. 22–32.

2. Robin Cooper and Robert S. Kaplan 'Measure Costs Right: Make the Right Decisions', *Harvard Business Review*, vol. 66 (September–October 1988) pp. 96–103.

3. George Stalk, Jr. 'Time – The Next Source of Competitive Advantage', *Harvard Business Review*, vol. 88 (July–August 1988) pp. 41–51.

5 Cost-oriented Pricing

> In setting rates for public utilities, the Illinois Commerce Commission (ICC) traditionally allowed an immediate 100 per cent cost recovery for any new utility plant. Allocation of fully distributed costs to the rates gave the image of fairness and equality. A rate structure allowing for full recovery of costs is determined for each customer class and then phase-in rates are plugged in. This method was workable and effective because inflation, interest, and construction costs were low and stable and electricity demand was steady.
>
> (Illinois Commerce Commission, *Phase-in: An Alternative Regulatory Approach* (Springfield, Ill.: Sunset Monographs, 1985) pp. 1–15)

The above passage from ICC shows that utility rates are a product of cost, with costs allocation a major determinant in arriving at a particular rate. However, even in such rate-setting procedure cost allocation is not done equally across the board, but rather is based on the type of electric user. Rates are reached by dividing customers into classes on the basis of related use.

There are three basic approaches to pricing: cost-oriented, demand-oriented, and competition-oriented. Even though these pricing approaches are discussed separately, seldom if ever will a manager or group of managers use one approach exclusively. Rather, most of the approaches taken to pricing will utilize a combination of the three, with the degree of emphasis on one or the other varying with the specifics of the particular company.

COST-ORIENTED PRICING

Cost-oriented pricing is the most elementary pricing method. It involves the calculation of all the costs that can be attributed to a product, whether variable or fixed, and then adding to this figure a desirable markup, as determined by management.

The simplicity of this method is that it requires no other effort beyond consulting the accounting or financial records of the firm. There is no necessity to study market demand, consider competition, or look into other

51

factors that may have a bearing on price. Cost is considered the uppermost, most important determinant in the firm's pricing effort, which is then directed towards covering these costs and realizing the desired profitability.

Another important advantage of cost-oriented pricing is the cost justification defence of price discrimination as iterated in the Robinson-Patman Act. The defendant (seller) can justify that the price difference is the cost due to the different quantity sold and/or different method (therefore different cost) of transportation. Therefore, a proper accounting for costs can be shown to prove and justify price differences based on cost. The concept of cost and cost savings is an important justification also of quantity discounts, in that cost savings per unit sold arise due to economies corresponding to transportation costs.

Because of the simplicity of this method, retailers, wholesalers, and some manufacturers use it to determine their prices. In the case of retailers, for example, the purchase price of the product is added to the product's share of the operating expenses and a desirable margin, determined by the type of product under consideration, is then added to arrive at the selling price.

In construction contracting, defence contracting, public utilities, monopsony buying (where the buyer is a large, knowledgeable entity), as well as in service industries, the use of cost-oriented methods is widespread. The cost-oriented approach, in addition to its simplicity, can deliver the desired results in a relatively short period of time. Since this method does not require going beyond the physical boundaries of the firm, an astute accountant or a financial analyst can, within a reasonable short period of time arrive at the necessary cost figures.

WEAKNESSES OF THE COST-ORIENTED APPROACH

Despite the simplicity and speed with which prices can be determined under the cost approach, there are a number of inherent weaknesses that limit its practicality.

Ignoring Marketing Environment

The price an individual is willing to pay for a product may bear little relationship to the cost of manufacturing that product. Studies of consumer behaviour have produced considerable evidence that contradicts the assumptions made by the classical economists, in that the consumer as a wholly rational buyer may knowingly select a product or service at a higher price, even though lower-priced substitutes may be available. This is particularly true when ego involvement is present. A purchaser of clothing may prefer designer labels and may pay more simply because the label designates styling considerations. An air traveller, placing a premium on comfort or possibly status, may select to fly first-class instead of economy, even though he or she does not arrive at his or her destination any sooner. An investor in diamonds, a rare art piece, or valuable stamps does not value the object in question in terms of its cost of extraction or production, but rather in terms of its value to him. The features/benefits provided by a product are the market determinant of its worth. Consumers are not aware, nor do they express concern about, manufacturing costs for most of the products they purchase.

Incorrect or Distorted Cost Information

It is obvious that using incorrect or distorted cost information can seriously erode both competitiveness and profitability. A major problem is costing a single product in a multiproduct firm. Conventional accounting systems employing such bases as benefit, cause, fairness, and ability to bear are practically useless in today's businesses.

There are also differences of opinion on the treatment of fixed and variable costs in arriving at total costs. A period of a year fits standard accounting procedures, but pay-off periods that extend over several years such as product life would seem more appropriate. There is also a certain amount of haziness in defining fixed and variable costs, particularly within the context of a year. Finally, the whole notion of total costs is being challenged as inappropriate in selling a lower limit on prices. Many would argue that including the write-off of an investment is unrealistic in that it pushes total costs to uncompetitive levels. In those instances where fixed costs are sunk costs in that they are not retrievable, allocation is not attempted in arriving at total cost. For example, the allocation of the investment in construction of a resort golf course would push green fees (prices) to uncompetitive levels, which would severely limit the size of the market and make it difficult to develop competitive golf vacation packages.

The Circular Reasoning Phenomenon

Cost-oriented methods of pricing involve circular reasoning. The price arrived at based on a calculation of all costs involved will affect the volume sold of a product. A low price may enhance sales, while conversely a high price may hinder sales. The volume produced, on the other hand, affects the per-unit cost calculation. A high volume will mean lower costs per unit, whereas a low volume pushes costs to a higher per unit level. Thus, volume determines cost that sets price that in turn affects volume and so on. This phenomenon is particularly true in high-overhead industries, where the allocated share of such costs varies significantly, depending on the volume produced. Figure 5.1 illustrates this circular relationship.

Figure 5.1   Cost–price–volume relationship

As a hypothetical example, assume a new compact car model will be introduced next year as part of the product line. Suppose the investment, allocated overheads, and direct costs are as shown in Table 5.1. Suppose still further that sales for the first year are projected to range from 60,000 units to 20,000 units. Obviously the price will vary with the sales forecast. In the hypothetical example, the retail price almost doubles for the pessimistic forecast. Obviously the price based on the pessimistic forecast is too high. Just as obvious, the lower price requires a substantial volume of sales that might require added marketing support and reductions in price to attain.

Unless the product is well established and fairly accurate forecasts of demand can be made, the cost-oriented approach may lead to an unrealistic price that negatively affects sales. Only where the market has no option to buy from another seller can a firm successfully set prices based on a targeted rate of return over and above costs at a given production volume; a good example is a utility. For other firms, however, cost-plus pricing virtually guarantees trouble. If costs are higher than the competition's, you price yourself out of the marketplace. If your costs are lower then you leave money on the table, as was the case with a windshield washer fluid marketed by a major oil company: its original price reflecting low production costs has been raised several times without materially affecting demand.[1]

Table 5.1 Hypothetical example of costs and prices of a new compact car model using optimistic and pessimistic estimates

Cost elements		Optimistic estimate, 60,000 units	Pessimistic estimate, 20,000 units
Overheads			
Fixed costs	$140 million		
R&D, special tooling	100 million	$4,000	$12,000
	$240 million		
Assembly plant			
Body	$1,000	$500	
Engine	700	350	
Transmission	250	100	
Chassis	1,000	500	
Assembly of vehicle	1,100	4,000 550	4,000
Total of overhead and assembly costs		8,000	16,000
Profit target @ 10% on investment		400	600
Manufacturer @ selling price		8,400	16,600
Average @ transportation cost		550	550
Dealer markup @ 14% of selling price		1,367	
Retail price		$10,317	$19,582

Another disadvantage of basing price on cost–volume relationships is the possibility of having to raise prices when sales volume falls below expectations. This is the antithesis of what may be needed, namely a price cut. Even with a high degree of accuracy in sales prediction, and a competitive cost position, use of a cost plus approach is basing everything on the effects of volume on costs and the market's reaction to price as the sole determinant of sales. Price is an outgrowth of volume, which in turn is based on price. When the firm should be lowering price to stimulate sales it must raise price to cover costs. Following the same logic, when sales exceed expectations then the price should be reduced.

The Volume Fulfillment Assumption

Calculation of unit costs under a cost-oriented approach requires an estimate of sales volume. The underlying assumption here is that estimated sales volume will actually materialize at the price level that results from this cost-plus approach. The question that arises is: how does management know that the estimated volume will be attained at the cost-plus price? Whether or not the estimated sales would materialize is a function of the dynamics of market demand, which is not considered with the cost-oriented method.

Failure to Recognize Competitive Forces

A price arrived at through the cost-oriented approach reflects what is seen as desirable for the company to charge, considering only its particular cost structure and profit objectives. No consideration is given to either the competitive forces at play in the marketplace or the behavioural characteristics of consumer demand. The price level for similar products offered by competitors will undoubtedly affect the company's performance. If the calculated price happens to be much higher than the competitor's prices, then a negative impact on sales may ensue, unless the company has established a sustainable competitive differential. As an example, Hewlett-Packard has remained competitive at a high price by a programme of technological advances in terms of features and new products. On the other hand, if the price is set much lower than competitors, the company may jeopardize customers' perception of its products' quality and face retaliation from competitors. It will also incur an opportunity loss by pricing below what could be attained in light of the marketing environment. In either case, the company stands to lose as a result of ignoring the realities of the marketplace.

Overlooking Price as a Strategic Option

Price, in many cases, is used as an instrument to attain certain strategic objectives for the firm. In such cases, price may not cover full cost, but attains other important goals necessary for the survival and growth of the firm. Examples of using price as a strategic tactic include the following:

1. *Pricing complementary products* (that is, products that are used in conjunction with one another)   Cameras and film, staplers and staples, copying machines and copying paper, washers and dryers, computer hardware and software, razors and razor blades, shampoo and conditioning rinse are all products that jointly share manufacturing, distribution channels, markets, types of customer, or similar aspects of the production, distribution, or consumer-use process. In such cases, the price of one of the jointly used products is set low to enhance sales of the other. The price of a camera may be lowered to enhance the sale of associated film and processing. The profitability is usually higher on the film, which is more frequently purchased, processed, and printed than on the less frequently purchased cameras.

2. *Pricing end-products*   Pricing strategy necessitates, in many cases, placing a lower price on the product situated at the low-quality end of a product line. The products at the low-quality end of the line are traffic builders, they are more noticeable, and are better remembered than other prices in the line. They have a considerable effect on marginal buyers. As such, pricing these products, regardless of cost, can serve strategic purposes of building traffic, serving a segment which may trade up, encouraging trial, attracting attention in promotional appeals, and enhancing sales of the entire line.

3.   *Presence of excess capacity*   Manufacturers sometime face the problem of excess capacity, in either the short or the long run. In either case, the idle capacity is translated into a loss in proportion of idle capacity to total capacity. To avoid or reduce such losses, a manufacturer may seek to supply products to buyers at a price similar or identical to those he produces that falls short of covering total costs. Fixed cost losses are minimized as long as the bid price covers variable costs. To illustrate, let us assume that the Michelin Tyre Company has the capacity sufficient to produce three million tyres per year. However, sales under its own name will not top two million, giving Michelin excess capacity of one million tyres. The total cost of producing a tyre at capacity is $17 (divided as $10 variable and $7 fixed cost). At a production level of two million tyres fixed costs per tyre jump to $10.50. If Sears were to make an offer to purchase one million tyres per year to be made under their label at a price of $15 per tyre (which is less than Michelin's total cost per tyre), Michelin may accept such an offer, as the price is capable of covering all variable costs, in addition to a $5 contribution to overhead. In addition, the total cost per tyre for the entire volume of tyres drops $3.50 ($10.50 – $7.00).

4.   *Protection of market position*   The competitive forces in the marketplace may force the manufacturer to reduce the price of one or more products in his product line below their respective total costs. This is not necessarily a product at the low-quality end of the product line, but rather a product whose quality matches that of products which other competitors are offering to the market. Strategy considerations require such action to protect or enhance market position.

WHY ARE COST-ORIENTED APPROACHES USED?

Considering the foregoing criticisms of the cost-oriented method, the question is: why is this approach to pricing used? There may be a number of reasons that justify the popularity of this approach.

Cost-oriented Approaches Are Defensible on Ethical Grounds

Historically, manufacturers and merchants have determined their prices based on cost. No one can deny that an honest manufacturer should be rewarded by some profit over his cost. This method has gained respect over the ages, as religious ethics and cultural values supported the view that enterprise is deserving of its worth. Many businessmen still believe that society will have more confidence and respect for a company that determines its prices based on cost, rather than relying on less-understood and much-suspected techniques such as competitive or demand-oriented approaches.

Cost-oriented Approaches Use Readily Available Data

The process of calculating price using the cost-oriented approach requires no external data. The necessary accounting and financial data are found in the records available within the firm. Management will not have to step beyond the physical boundaries of the firm to be able to set prices. A proper cost-calculating technique and a decision concerning the profit margin required over and above costs are all that is necessary to set prices. It is not surprising, then, that this approach can produce prices so easily, and in such a short time, since no market surveys or demand studies are needed. Then, too, internal data may be the only available information in selling technological innovations to ill-defined markets.

Absence of Knowledge of More Sophisticated Techniques

Pricing today is both an art and a science. Unfortunately, many executives assigned the responsibility for pricing lack the necessary training in and knowledge of more sophisticated pricing techniques. The pricing process, is in many instances perceived as an extension of the accounting and costing process. This is particularly true when management sets profitability levels in terms of a certain return on investment, return on sales, or return on cost. In such cases, those making decisions on prices perceive their role as simply calculating costs and fulfilling the required profitability ratios set by top management.

Industry-wide Accepted Practice

The cost-oriented approach may be the only approach recognized and accepted in certain industries. Contract tendering, construction, public utilities, service industries, retailing and wholesaling, and product customizing are all examples of situations where the cost-oriented method is predominant. It is customary, in the above-mentioned instances, to use cost as the basis for price, either because the buyer is knowledgeable about the costs involved, or because of the abundance of competitive suppliers willing to perform the same function or produce an identical product for a lower price.

HOW IMPORTANT IS COST IN THE PRICING PROCESS?

One cannot question the fact that cost plays an important role in pricing, a fact supported by noting the sheer number of pricing decisions based almost entirely on cost factors. Even though strategic price considerations may require selling a product occasionally at a price below cost, in the long run a producer will not produce a product unless all costs are covered and a margin considered satisfactory is attained. A glance at the market would reveal the multitude of products that are not being offered commercially today, because the market value is lower than the cost of production. Nuclear-powered ships or vehicles and space travel for commercial use are examples of products or services of this type. Undoubtedly cost is an important part of the decision-making process in setting prices. However, it is not the sole consideration. A strict adherence to cost in the pricing process can lead to rigidity of the pricing system and the deterioration of the innovative initiative that characterizes free-enterprise systems. This innovative initiative surfaces mainly in environments where new products or ideas can reward their initiators beyond what is considered to be an average return. In contrast, in many socialist countries the pricing process is controlled by the government, and management has no choice but to calculate production costs and then add to them a predetermined, government-endorsed margin rate to reach the final price. In such situations, it is easy to see that this pricing formula encourages cost exaggeration, overruns, and waste that leads to inefficiencies and produces high prices. It also tends to smother innovative ideas and products.

One important role of cost is a point-indicator, revealing to management the lower economic limits of the price range. Asking prices should fall somewhere in that range, between the highest price point determined by what customers are willing to pay for the product in view of their perception of its value, and the lowest price point determined by what the seller is willing to accept in return, a value that may sometimes be equal to or below its cost. Only in this sense can pricing in view of cost calculations become more dynamic and less rigid, as decision makers consider the other market forces that have an important bearing on the appropriateness of the set price.

Perhaps more important is the flexibility that knowledge of costs for product features gives management in responding to the ever-increasing complexities of the market. Pricing and differentials in product makeup are the most effective ways of responding to competition and changes in customer behaviour. However, without being able to make comparisons of cost and customer evaluation, management efforts may be counter-productive or at best ineffective.

VOLUME ASSUMPTIONS FOR PURPOSES OF COST CALCULATIONS

An important point to bear in mind is that changes in volume will affect per-unit costs. There are four different approaches to the question of volume.

An Assumption of Low Volume

This approach is a conservative one. Management is cautious about the future sales performance of the product and assumes a low volume. This seemingly safe approach, however, may result in high overhead per unit of output, leading to higher prices. This in turn increases the possibility of less sales than would be anticipated with a more market-oriented, possibly lower, price. The ultimate result is a price that works against the sales goals of the company. What starts as a conservative approach proves, at the end, to be radical in nature.

Assuming the Continuation of Current Volume

Here, management assumes that business conditions in the upcoming period will not change, and bases its cost calculations on present volume configurations. This approach can be reasonably sound, particularly for industries which experience little or no cyclical fluctuations in their business, and for markets where demand is relatively stable over time. However, this approach is applicable only to industries with existing operations, and not to new products or firms.

Using the Best Estimate of Future Volume

This approach is based on the company's forecast of sales volume for the next time period. The weakness of this approach is in its dependency on circular reasoning in arriving at a the price. In order to be able to forecast future sales, it is necessary to have a price. However, both price and per-unit costs are absent from the equation needed to solve for price. The per-unit costs are a function of volume, which, at this point, is unknown. Nevertheless, this approach uses yet-to-be-determined costs to reach a price, which, in turn, is the major determinant of volume. The weakness of this approach lies in the artificiality of the volume assumptions that the price setter will have to make in the absence of price, which in turn is used to calculate unit cost.

Using a Standard Volume

Standard volume is a projection of unit volume, taking into consideration the varying conditions over time in the firm as well as the cyclical fluctuations in business conditions, demand, and capacity utilization. It is designed to be a representation of volume that is expected to prevail under 'normal' or 'average' conditions, adjusted periodically to reflect favourable or unfavourable market conditions. While standard volume has many useful managerial functions for budgeting and control, it can also be effectively used in pricing, as it readily provides a base for cost calculations.

BREAK-EVEN ANALYSIS

A management tool commonly associated with pricing is cost–volume analysis, or, as it is commonly called, break-even analysis. This analysis stresses the relationship between the various factors affecting profits. The break-even point is the point where there is no profit or loss, and is a portrayal of how many units of the product are to be sold if the firm is to recover both fixed and variable costs from sales revenue. Every time a firm sells a product, the sales revenue is expected to be in excess of that product's variable costs and to generate a contribution to fixed costs and profit. At the break-even point, the profit is zero, which also means that the contribution margin times the number of units sold is equal to the fixed costs. Profits start to appear as the actual volume of sales exceeds the break-even volume at a rate equal to the contribution per unit. As an example, assume that a manufacturer of digital watches specializes in producing and selling a certain model and that the price and cost structure for the product are as follows:

Digital watch price	$20
Variable cost per watch	10
Unit contribution margin	10
Total fixed costs	$200,000

Based on these figures, each watch sold contributes $10 towards fixed costs and profits, and the manufacturer would have to sell 20,000 watches to break even. This figure is calculated by dividing the total fixed cost by unit contribution margin, as shown below:

$$\text{Break-even point} = \frac{\text{Total fixed costs}}{\text{Unit contribution margin}}$$

$$= \frac{\$200,000}{\$10}$$

$$= 20,000 \text{ watches}$$

If sales were only 20,000 watches then sales revenue would cover variable costs per unit plus total fixed expenses for the period. However, if sales exceed 20,000 then profits would appear and would be equal to the sales in excess of 20,000 units multiplied by the unit contribution margin. Thus contribution turns to profit at the break-even point. Let us assume, for example, that the digital watch manufacturer was able to produce and sell 40,000 units. This would mean that he is operating at 20,000 units above the break-even point. As such, he will not only be able to cover all the fixed costs, but he will also be able to attain a profit of $200,000 (20,000 watches above the break-even point multiplied by $10 unit contribution margin).

If on the other hand, his sales volume falls short of the 20,000 watches needed to break even, and he only sells 15,000 units, losses will be realized in the amount of $50,000, as calculated below:

Sales (15,000 watches commercial at $20)	$300,000
Less variable costs (15,000 watches commercial at $10)	150,000
Contribution	150,000
Less fixed costs	200,000
Losses	<$50,000>

The Break-even Chart

Pricing decisions can be made using the break-even approach in either arithmetical or graphic form. The break-even chart (Figure 5.2) is a graphic representation of the relationships discussed above between costs, volume, and price. Dollars are shown on the vertical scale on the chart, and units produced or sold are shown on the horizontal scale. To arrive at the total cost line, total costs are plotted for the various quantities to be produced or sold. When these points are connected, the total cost line emerges. The total revenue line is similarly arrived at, and it represents the number of units produced or sold, multiplied by the unit selling price.

Figure 5.2   A break-even point chart

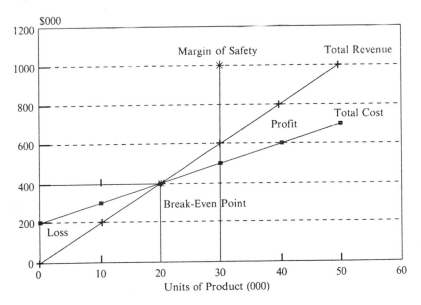

The break-even point is the point at which the total revenue line inter-sects with the total cost line. Profits and losses can be measured directly on the chart for any volume level. Profits are measured to the right of the break-even point and, at any volume, are equal to the dollar difference between the total revenue line and the total cost line. Losses, on the other hand, are measured to the left of the break-even point and, at any volume, are equal to the dollar difference between the total cost line and the total revenue line. Thus, by looking at the chart, management can readily observe how profitable each level of output is, given a price per unit.

For pricing purposes, the person taking the decision can use the break-even chart to make a judgment as to whether or not the quantity that can be produced or sold at the prevailing price is greater or smaller than that required to break even, and, in either case, by how much. The fundamental facts regarding the operation thus become easier to grasp. The difference between the break-even volume and the forecast of unit sales for the same period or time is called the margin of safety. The obvious assumption is that a product will not be produced and sold if forecast volume falls below break-even volume. The greater the gap between the break-even volume and the forecast volume, the greater the safety in producing and distributing a product with the assumptions of price, cost, and volume.

The Profit–Volume Graph

In addition to the break-even point chart, management may find that a profit–volume graph is a useful guide, showing how profits are affected by changes in the volume produced or sold (Figure 5.3). Profits and losses are represented on a vertical scale, while the volume produced or sold is represented on a horizontal one. A horizontal line is drawn on the graph, dividing the vertical scale into two halves, the upper portion representing profits and the lower portion representing losses. This line indicates the sales revenues that can be attained by selling the different quantities of output at the given price. Using the figures from the previous example, the sales revenue line shows a revenue of $200,000, which resulted from selling 10,000 units, and a revenue of $400,000, which resulted from selling 20,000 units.

Figure 5.3   A profit–volume graph

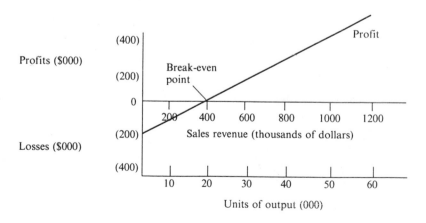

A profit line can now be drawn on the chart by plotting profits and losses at various sales levels, and then connecting these points to obtain the desired line. The break-even point lies at the intersection of the profit line with the horizontal sales revenue line. Management can readily observe from the profit–volume graph the profits and losses at any point of production or sales. Unlike the break-even chart, however, the profit–volume graph does not show the relationship between cost and volume, and, as a result, it is typically used in conjunction with the break-even chart to attain the benefits of each method.

REFERENCE

1.   Charles W. Kyd 'Pricing for Profit', *Inc.*, April 1987, pp. 119–22.

6 Demand and Competition-oriented Pricing

Pricing strategy, if not the most important part of the marketing mix, has become the trickiest. It's hard for outsiders to know why a company initiates a price change, and it's equally difficult to gauge how the new price will be perceived by consumer, retailers and competitors. For instance, last year American Airlines introduced a simplified pricing scheme which reduced ticket prices by 30 per cent to 40 per cent and eliminated many discounts. American said at the time it would initially lose money but in the long run the prices would be the best medicine for American and the rest of the industry, if all the players went along. They didn't, and American finally had to withdraw the new tariffs. Travel agents also were up in arms over American's plan, just as most retailers are hostile to Procter & Gamble's 'value pricing' in which it has cut back on trade allowances and couponing and lowered list prices on about 90 per cent of its items.

(Rance Crain, 'Pricing Mistakes Carry a High Cost',
Advertising Age, 9 August 1933, p. 13)

The above comments from the *Advertising Age* shed some light on the problems attendant on pricing in today's business world. Costs are important, and so too are the consumer and product variables present in a given market.

OVERLOOKING THE LINK BETWEEN COST AND PRICE

Under both demand and competition-oriented approaches to pricing, management is concerned less with the notion that cost is the main basis for price and more with the variables underlying the personality of the purchaser and the character of the product. It is agreed that consumers tend to react in one way more than in others. Some respond to rational claims, others are sensitive to price; still others respond to product images, while an increasing number demand the highest quality and the best customer service combined with low prices.

Under demand-oriented pricing, sellers differentiate their products through the introduction of features or benefits: quality, styling, or image and service as a way of developing a market niche. Even though the products may be physically similar, the differentiation allows the sellers to charge different prices to market segments that perceive certain desirable attributes in the brand. As a result, there may not be much correlation between costs and prices charged for products. For example, one company was successful in expanding its product line by adding a product feature, namely a light on an iron that signalled when it was ready for use, that cost one dollar, but allowed a price $5 higher than the next-highest-priced iron.

A meaningful way of understanding what happens in the marketplace for consumer products is to classify behaviour into two groups. In one group are those that react to features/benefits such as quality, customer service, design, and special features on primarily a rational basis. In the other group are those consumers who think of the meaning of the purchase rather than functioning of the particular product. A member of this group would seek distinctiveness and uniqueness through identification with a product. Obviously, the first-class air traveller will not reach his or her destination any sooner than the coach class traveller, but the former pays considerably more. To one group of customers, it could be the roominess and comfort of the seating plus the enhanced food and beverage service that substantiates the premium price, for others, it could be the prestige and status of travelling in the special section of the same aircraft. This group would be responding to what first-class travel symbolizes.

DEMAND-ORIENTED PRICING

Under this approach to pricing, the price maker looks beyond the mere costs of material, labour, overheads, and other expenses associated with the production or marketing of the product and considers instead the intensity of demand for it. A demand schedule for the product in question is needed for this type of pricing. In other words, the manager needs to have some idea of the quantities of the product that can be sold at different prices. The demand schedule becomes in turn the basis for determining which level of production and sales would be most profitable for the firm. The most profitable level, or the one which attains the firm's desired objective, can be ascertained by interjecting manufacturing and marketing cost projections at various sales levels with the previously determined demand schedule. Interactions between cost projections at various sales levels and anticipated revenues from sales volumes corresponding to given prices result in the determination of the appropriate price.

To illustrate this method, assume that a television manufacturer is capable of producing 50,000 units of a particular model. Marketing analysis shows four possible prices: $290, $260, $230, and $200. The problem facing the firm is knowing which of the four prices to adopt. Cost estimates, including production costs, distribution costs, marketing costs, and after-sale service costs are used to arrive at total cost at various levels of production. With this type of data, the firm can prepare a break-even chart showing the various break-even points as determined by the interaction of the total revenue (TR) line, representing each price, and the total cost (TC) curve, representing cost projections at the different levels of production (Figure 6.1). Four break-even points (A, B, C, D) are computed for the revenue projections using the four break-even points.

Figure 6.1   A revenue possibility chart

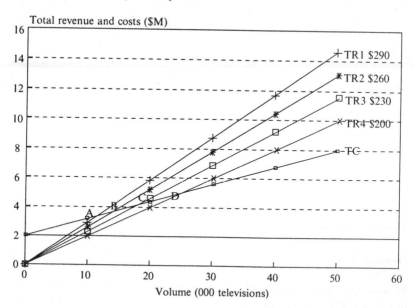

This type of analysis does not help in the effective selection of the best pricing alternative, however one vital piece of information is missing, namely a demand schedule for the company's television set. Management needs to have some idea of the quantities of the set that could be possibly sold under each pricing alternative. The necessary information for making a decision as to the most profitable pricing alternative is contained in Table 6.1.

Table 6.1   Outcomes with different pricing alternatives

Price alternative ($)	Estimated sales volume	Total revenue ($m)	Expected total costs ($m)	Difference ($m)
290	10,000	2.9	3	(0.1)
260	25,000	6.5	5	1.5
230	40,000	9.2	7	2.2
200	50,000	10.0	8	2.0

The $230 price yields the greatest difference between expected total revenue and expected total costs. Any other price would be less desirable. A price of $200, for example, will result in a greater volume of sales, but revenue generated by the increase is less than incremental costs. A higher price of $260 results in lower revenue and even lower profitability. The high price of $290 will result in a loss because the sales volume will not compensated by the higher price. In other words, there are not enough customers at that price to cover costs.

By using sensitivity analysis, it is possible to have different outcomes by shifting the demand curve totally or in part to obtain pessimistic, optimistic, or the most likely demand estimates. A consideration of these different possibilities will help in determining the optimum price and output level. A weak profitability picture caused by a slight variation in these demand estimates should be alarming to a manager and should prompt him or her to reconsider the entire market strategy. On the other hand, if profitability seems strong, even with reasonable variations in demand estimates, the manager is positively assured of the original estimates.

Demand Estimation

To be able to determine the optimal price when a number of price possibilities exist, one must obtain an estimate of the responsiveness of the quantity demanded of the product to price changes. Demand estimation is by no means an easy task, as it requires knowledge of all the forces in the marketplace that may affect the quantity of the product sold at a particular place.

For example, the historical data that a firm might have can be of value in revealing a schedule of the prices and corresponding quantities that occurred in previous years. This data, however, would be relevant only if the assumption is made that all the other factors remain constant – a naive assumption at best in today's business world. But even though difficulty surrounds such a task of demand estimation, an educated guess is better than a random selection of a price from a number of price possibilities.

There are a number of methods of estimating demand. The specific conditions in a particular case may require using a different technique, or may favour one over another. Each one of these methods has its advantages and limitations.

Aggregate Sales Representative Estimates

One of the most frequently used methods of estimating demand, particularly by manufacturers of industrial products, is asking sales representatives to estimate the percentage increase (or decrease) in demand associated with an x-percentage increase (or decrease) in the price of a given product. The fact that sales representatives are aware of competitive offerings and their prices, and are sensitive to market trends and customer needs, places them in a good position to make such estimates.

In utilizing this method of demand estimation, it is usually desirable to provide the sales representative with a forecast on the business outlook for the period in question, and to have the regional manager discuss the demand estimates with each representative.

There are a number of limitations in using this method, however. First, one must ensure that sales representatives will take this job seriously and make a conscientious effort to reach the desired estimates. A second problem results from intended or unintended bias by either optimistically or pessimistically stating the likely estimates occurring under each of the given price possibilities. Sometimes these over- or under-estimates result from the perception of the sales representative that performance and reward systems will somehow be tied to attaining future sales volumes equivalent to these estimates.

Expert Estimates

Experts are individuals who have developed skill and knowledge in a particular field because of their role or position. Experts may include, among others, executives of the company, market researchers, channel members, and consultants. Experts have the skill to make educated estimates of demand as a result of price changes.

Demand estimates obtained from experts can be in one of three forms – a point estimate of sales, an interval estimate of sales, or a probability distribution estimate. A point estimate of sales is an estimate of the most likely quantity of the product that will be sold at the given price. An expert, for example, may state that if the given price for brand X of television set is $230 then the quantity most likely to be sold is 3,000,000 units. Point estimates are the simplest estimates to prepare, since they contain no information on the likelihood of this demand estimate materializing, nor do they provide a probability error to aid in reaching the specific estimate.

An interval estimate of sales is an estimate that sales will fall within a stated range with a given level of confidence. An executive in a car manufacturing facility, for example, may state that if a particular make is sold at $12,000 then he is 90 per cent confident that the sales units will range between 500,000 and 600,000. The probability assigned here is purely subjective.

A probability distribution estimate is an estimate which assigns probabilities to two or more possible sales intervals. An example of this type of estimate is provided by a personal computer executive who states that he feels that if the unit are priced at $1500, probable sales will be as follows:

Possible sales units	*Probability*
50,000–55,000	.30
56,000–60,000	.50
61,000–65,000	.20

In reality, the executive is saying that he believes that there is a greater likelihood that sales will not be less than 50,000 units nor more than 65,000 units. The intervals he listed represent pessimistic, most likely, and optimistic sales levels.

In practice, it is possible to use one estimate provided by a single expert, or better yet, to combine a number of estimates made by a group of experts. In this latter case, a number of methods can be used to obtain a single estimate from those provided by the experts. One method would assign equal weights to each expert's estimate if the degree of expertise for each is perceived to be equal. A second method assigns proportional weights to a subjective assessment of expertise.

Analysis of Historical Data

Estimates of demand at different prices can also be accomplished by analysis of sales histories and time series. A time series is a set of observations on a variable, such as sales volume, in which those observations are arranged in relation to time. Demand estimates using historical data is based on the assumption that relationships between quantity sold and price in past periods can be used to predict sales at given prices in future periods. These causal methods of demand estimation involve either the use of a simple regression model, in which changes in the level of sales are assumed to result from changes in price alone, with price the independent variable and quantity sold the dependent variable, or multiple regression analysis, which requires identification of all causal (predictor) variables that are believed to have influence on sales.

Simple regression can be used to predict the likely demand for any price level using historical data. However, the assumption must be made that only minor variations have occurred in the product itself, competitors, and targeted consumers, and that random and cyclical effects are believed to be negligible.

Use of multiple regression allows the determination of percentage change in quantity demanded corresponding to a 1 per cent variation in any predictor variable, with all other variables held constant. As such, multiple regression allows simulation of market conditions, which would otherwise be difficult to obtain given the realities of the marketplace.

Surveys of Buyers

Demand estimation is essentially the practice of anticipating what actual and potential buyers are likely to do when different prices for the product prevail. This suggests going directly to buyers and asking them the probabilities of purchasing the particular product at various price levels. This method, however, is not without its flaws. Buyer responses, in many instances, do not necessarily reveal their future intentions or reflect what they would do in actual circumstances. Buyers in responding may also attempt to quote artificially lower prices, since many of them may perceive their role as conscientious buyers as that of helping to keep prices down.

The value of a buyer survey in estimating demand at various possible prices rests on two assumptions. One is the assumption that buyers can be identified and persuaded to participate. The second assumption hinges on the veracity of buyer responses. Given several different price levels, the question must be asked: will the expressed opinions translate into actual purchase behaviour?

Worth of Product's Functional Performance

There are many instances where the product for which the demand estimate is sought is an innovation or an improvement of an existing product that can successfully substitute for an existing product with savings in operational costs or time. For example, in pricing a new or improved product, it may be possible to use the potential labour- and time-saving characteristics from use as the basis for pricing. The value (price) of the new product becomes approximately the value of saved labour and time spent previously in the use of the products that the new version will replace. The demand curve for the new product can thus be estimated by considering the costs of alternative approaches to the same function.

This procedure is more applicable to industrial products than to consumer goods. In the case of industrial products, an estimate of the costs of other equipment, labour, procedures, time and expertise that the newly developed product eliminates or replaces is often an important purchasing consideration. The same cannot be said for consumer products, where evaluation of time saved or effort expended are not often considerations in purchasing.

Test Markets

Test marketing involves trying out the desired marketing mix for a limited time in a small number of well-chosen geographic areas by offering the product for sale in an actual sales environment, and observing consumer reaction to the marketing element(s) being tested. Test marketing is a much more common practice for companies producing consumer goods than for those that manufacture industrial goods. In the case of industrial products, demand schedules can be estimated by 'market probing', or gathering potential buyers' reactions concerning the most likely price for the proposed product.

To test and evaluate demand for a product as a result of price changes, for example, the product can be placed in a number of test markets and offered for sale at a different price in each test market. Sales volumes in each test market are observed to determine the relationship between quantity sold and price. Selecting geographic areas for a test market is an important decision. Selection is usually based on the presence of characteristics that typify the market for the product in question. The most desirable test market is one that resembles the target market for the product in question on the key characteristics defining the customer.

The duration of the test is determined by the average repurchase period for the product in question, that is the normal period of time that it takes the purchaser to consume the product before restocking. In the case of soft drinks the average repurchase period may be a matter of days, while in a case of shampoo or toothpaste it may be weeks. The cost of test marketing is also a function of test duration.

Laboratory Experiments

A demand schedule for the product may be obtained by using laboratory experiments in which price is manipulated in an artificial setting to observe the effect on quantity demanded.

One big advantage of laboratory experiments is the attainment of the desirable results quickly and relatively inexpensively. Also, such experiments have the advantage of reducing or eliminating the effect of other factors that may obscure or confound the relationships under study.

Since laboratory experiments are contrived and characterized by artificiality, however, it is questionable whether the results can be readily generalized to other situations. In using simulated shopping trips, for example, the fact that the experimenter calls the subjects' attention to the price may lead to more price consciousness than would otherwise be the case under normal shopping behaviour. Also, subjects under scrutiny may tend to become more rational in their purchase behaviour that might otherwise be the case. Moreover, since the subjects do not take actual possession of the items purchased, this method fails to reflect the 'stocking-up' effect than is characteristic of actual purchase situations and immunizes the purchaser from repurchasing at the same price soon after making the initial purchase.

COMPETITION-ORIENTED PRICING

Under competition-oriented pricing, prices are set on the basis of what the firm's competitors are charging. The firm first determines who the competitors are at the present time. This step is followed by a competitive evaluation of its own product. Taking this knowledge into consideration, the price set for the firm's product can be raised or lowered from the prevailing 'market' price, taking into consideration the unique characteristics of its own brand, the relative strengths or weaknesses of its competitive position, and the reaction of competitors to the set prices.

In following this price approach, the firm will have to be aware of the reaction of competitors to the set price. This is particularly important where there is a small number of firms competing in the particular field. In this case, price changes are likely to lead to immediate price changes by competitors.

The popularity of this approach stems from its simplicity and the number of advantages it offers. These advantages can be summarized as follows:

1. The firm can determine prices for its products relatively easily and quickly, because the need for prior determination of market demand or other difficult-to-obtain market data is eliminated.

2. Because this method uses as its base competitive offerings and prices, it is likely to be more sensitive to competitive leader–follower positions and more attuned to possible reaction to established price.

3. From the angle of consumer perception of the determined price, this pricing approach is the most logical, as it follows the price level that customers expect. Customers judge competitive offerings by a criterion established through the prevailing price levels, differentiating between these offerings partly on the basis of price as an indicator of quality.

4. The cooperation of the distribution channel is important to the survival and success of any product, particularly new offerings. Channel members are usually more willing to carry another brand when it fits within the price range of the product offerings they handle, particularly if this product can maintain their customary markups. There is a better chance that a price determined on the basis of competition would also be more sensitive to dealers' markups than those prices determined via other pricing approaches.

5. This pricing approach offers the firm the choice of a number of pricing strategies to fit its objectives. Since the prevailing price level for a particular class of products in the marketplace is in fact an established yardstick against which customers judge qualities of existing offerings, the manager can manipulate customer impressions of the brand by pricing above, at, or below competitors' prices.

If one were to consider cost-oriented approaches to pricing to be 'forward' in nature, one could consider the competition-oriented method a 'backward' exercise in pricing. Recall that, under the cost-oriented pricing approach, prices were determined on the basis of total cost calculation to which a reasonable profit margin was added. In other words, the pricing process proceeded 'forward' with the calculations of variable and fixed costs, to which a desirable return is added to finally reach a price. Under the competition-oriented approach, price is the starting point in the calculation process. This price is obviously only an indication of the appropriate price to charge in view of the competition in the marketplace, but has no necessary relationship to cost. Therefore, the manager works 'backwards' from this given price to see if the designated price is sufficient to cover costs and desired profitability. When the price does not cover costs plus the firm's profit objectives, management will have to decide whether (1) to bear the losses or reduced returns for a period of time until the product is strong enough to be profitable; (2) to adjust the choice of materials, equipment, and manpower to produce the product at a lower cost sufficient to make it profitable; or (3) as a last resort, to drop the proposed product entirely.

Competition-oriented Pricing: An Illustration

As indicated above, competition-oriented approaches to pricing require the manager to work 'backward' from a given price to determine whether or not the price is sufficient to cover costs and desired profits. In order to clarify this process, assume that a manufacturer of a portable stereo cassette player set determines that, in line with the existing competitive conditions in the market, his product should be sold for $149 at retail. Once the retail price of $149 is set, the next step is to determine whether this is sufficient to cover all costs, and return the desired margin.

For this example, assume further that the normal channel of distribution for this type of stereo equipment includes a distributor whose commission is 10 per cent (10%) of the company's selling price, and a retailer whose markup is 40 per cent (40%) of the retail selling price for the product. The manufacturer further calculates his total fixed cost for the product and finds it to be 2 million dollars. He also estimates his sales volume using the given price of $149 to equal 100,000 units. Marketing costs are estimated to be 25 per cent (25%) of the total variable costs of the stereo set.

Selling price per unit at retail	$149.00
Retail markup (at 40%)	59.60
Price to retailer	89.40
Distributor margin (10%)	8.13
Price to distributor	81.27
Unit direct labor cost (3 hours at $7 per hour)	21.00
Materials and parts	20.00
Variable manufacturing costs (unit)	41.00
Marketing costs (25% of variable cost)	10.25
Total Variable and Marketing Costs	51.25
Contribution	$ 30.02

There are two ways to calculate the feasibility of the given price. One is to calculate the break-even point in order to determine to what extent anticipated sales deviate from this point. The other is to compute the total contribution to profit and subtract the fixed costs. The break-even point is calculated as follows

$$\text{Break-even (in units)} = \frac{\text{Total fixed costs}}{\text{Unit contribution}}$$

$$= \frac{\$2,000,000}{\$30.02}$$

$$= 66,662 \text{ units}$$

The anticipated sales volume was estimated at 100,000 units. Therefore, the anticipated sales exceed the break-even point by 33,378 units (100,000 − 66,622). Since the contribution per unit was previously calculated as $30.02, anticipated profits at this price for an estimated sales volume of 100,000 is $1,002,000.

Using the second approach, total contribution is calculated by multiplying the estimated sales volume by unit contribution.

Total contribution	=	100,000 × $30.02
	=	$3,002,000
Total fixed costs	=	2,000,000
Anticipated profits	=	$1,002,000

It becomes clear that the price selected by the company in this case is sufficient to cover all costs at the anticipated sales level, and that this price would allow an anticipated profit in excess of 1 million dollars.

7 Pricing Decisions by Manufacturers

> Organizations are changing by necessity. Globalization is simply a fact of life. We have slower growth in the developed worlds. This puts more pressure on all of us since we are all after a piece of the pie. Therefore, value is all there is to provide. For example, in the computer business, if you miss a cycle you lose your company. So if you're going to provide the most value, if you're going to have the lowest cost and the highest quality product available, you've got to engage every mind that you have.
>
> Now we are much more globally competitive, and 'value buying' is everywhere. The competitive pressures have dramatically changed, and so has the number of people chasing a particular consumer, be it an industrial or retail consumer.
>
> (Jack Welch, Chairman and CEO of General Electric, in *21st Century Leadership*: *Dialogues with 100 Top Leaders* (New York: Leadership Press, 1993))

THE PRICING ENVIRONMENT

The structure of industry has changed dramatically in the last decade. The major forces of change are the global impact, changing competitive conditions calling for a sharper focus on customers, greater operational effectiveness and flexibility, and critical changes in customers and market structures.

In a free enterprise-system, pricing by manufacturers has a pronounced impact on the society. Its effect is felt by consumers, government, labour, distributors, and financial markets. In the last decade, one can observe, for example, what effect the rise in oil prices has had on world economies. Similarly, pricing policies by major corporations such as Procter & Gamble, DuPont, Unilever, Mitsubishi, and Nestlé can set an atmosphere of certain economic expectations that sends clear signals to the rest of the economy.

Even though the pricing environment varies from one industry to another, there are some basic objectives and strategies that may apply equally to various industries. Pricing decisions and product decisions are obviously related. Companies, now more than ever before, attempt to carve out a niche or a small, viable market segment that can be addressed with a unique marketing strategy. Price in such a strategic context is a positioning dimension for each segment, differing between segments.

While some companies follow a segmentation strategy, others examine the strategic role of the product in relation to other products in the company's product portfolio. Factors such as the product's market share, its growth rate, and the stage of product and/or market evolution are considered.

It should be clear that in pricing a product, the manufacturer is confronted with a number of alternatives. The lower limit of the range is usually determined by product costs, the upper by what the market can bear. Locating the product's actual position on the price range is an administrative decision which should be done individually for each product. Obviously many circumstances will influence the product's location on this price range. Two such important influencing factors can be identified. One is the segment or segments the company chooses to serve, and the second is the position of the product in the company's product portfolio.

Pricing and Segmentation Strategy

Not all customers have the same needs for a product or service, nor are they equipped with an equal willingness and ability to pay. This realization leads automatically to the strategic implication that manufacturers may elect to serve different customer segments. Segmentation is the process of classifying customers, products, or markets into distinct subsets on the basis of their characteristics that cause them to respond differently. The purposes of segmentation are to focus efforts and to develope an advantage that can be sustained.

The characteristics may be unrelated or related to the product in question. Market segmentation involves the use of customer characteristics to divide a market into segments. These will include geographic location, lifestyle, size of firm, and various demographics. A division of the market by type of industry would be an example of this approach to segmentation. Another useful and very popular means of segmentation is to use characteristics related to the product. The benefits sought in a product, the usage of a product type, and how the product is used are examples of product-related characteristics.

The price structure for each defined segment, in combination with other elements of the marketing mix, must reflect the strategic focus and, most importantly, sustain the initial advantages the firm has in serving the segment. This makes it all the more important to know how defined customers value the product in question, as well as the changes in both customers and competitors.

Pricing and the Product Portfolio

Product lines or market segments of any manufacturer may play different roles in achieving overall corporate objectives. Strategic planning today requires management to abandon the idea that each product in the product line or each segment is expected to 'carry its own weight' in terms of contributing to profits and return on investment. Instead, each product or segment must be looked upon as having different needs and objectives. Differences can be expected in terms of the stage of growth in the product – life cycle, market share, and growth potential of the market. As a result, a product or segment may be a source of cash or a user of cash with different growth potential, market share, and return on investment. The term 'portfolio' has been used to describe such a classification structure.

By using the growth-share matrix (Boston Consulting Group), each product is assigned a strategic role on the basis of its market growth rate and market share relative to competition. The individual roles are then integrated into a strategy for the whole line. There are 'cash cows', that is, products that have a dominant share of a slowly growing market; 'stars' that are high-growth, and high-share products; 'problem children' that are products with low share of fast growing markets; and 'dogs' that are products with a low share of a slowly growing market.

Using this basis of classification, different pricing policies could be viewed to reflect each distinctive category. Penetration pricing, for example, may be the strategy to use in the case of 'problem children' in order to enhance market share, while 'milking' may be an appropriate strategy in the case of 'dogs'. Texas Instruments Inc., for example, uses a pricing system based on high sales volume for a limited product line. This system is called 'design-to-cost' planning which relies on the concept of economies from learning.

In the 1970s, flexible pricing schemes began to replace the traditional target return pricing. Setting prices that met the profit targets of the company over the long run was suited to the growth climate that prevailed during the twenty-five years following World War II. However, as competition intensified, accompanied by low levels of capacity utilization and the unpredictability of future courses of costs and product demand, companies had no choice but to turn to a flexible pricing strategy. This strategy meant juggling prices of their different products by raising some and lowering others in order to attain the maximum mix of sales and profits.

Pricing Objectives

Even though the most logical starting point for pricing would be the company's objectives, it appears that a number of firms have no formal objectives. Many firms have unstated, or intuitive objectives that have never been articulated or analysed. If pressured, executives of such firms may state some form of profit objective. Further investigation, however, may reveal the existence of different implicit objectives such as maintenance of market share or production output. It is also possible that companies with profit maximization as their goal are in actuality profit satisfiers and not maximizers.

Overall company objectives can function as a guide to pricing policy. A landmark study of twenty large-scale U.S. corporations reveal the following major goals of pricing:[1]

1. Achieve a specific target return on investment or on net sales.
2. Maintain or enhance a market share.
3. Meet or prevent competition.
4. Maximize profits.
5. Stabilize prices.

Target Return on Investment

Many large as well as small firms seek to achieve a certain percentage return on investment or on net sales. Target return pricing is concerned with determining the necessary markup per unit sold, which will permit achieving the overall target profit goal. The executive attempts to estimate the needed margin that he feels is just, reasonable, or customary, so that this margin can be added to each product's cost. Using this pricing method, both cost and profit goals are based on standard volume. The word 'investment' is defined as net worth plus long-term corporate debt. Though it is popular, target return pricing is effective as an overall performance measure of the entire product line, but not of the individual products in the line. For individual items in the line certain strategic pricing considerations may require raising or lowering the price, causing either higher or lower target rates to be achieved in each case. A high price, for example, may be adopted for a product or a model in the line to lend prestige or a quality image to the entire line. A low price on another item may be used to generate traffic.

The question of how the executive allocates the ROI among the various products in the line still exists. Using the target rate of return can create a number of problems. One difficulty lies in correctly valuing capital assets. The question is: should the executive use the book value or present value of assets in calculating the desired ratio? Another problem lies in deciding what percentage of the target return should be derived from the different items in the line. Products in the line vary in terms of their capital investment, market share, established image, stage in the product life cycle, and competitive pressures. It would be strategically erroneous to expect to receive the same rate of return on investment from each product in the line, or to achieve this rate of return equally every year.

Market Share

Another pricing goal is the achievement or maintenance of a certain share of the market. Market share is sought as a goal, because companies with a large share of their respective markets are generally more profitable than their smaller-share counterparts.

Building share strategies can be either offensive or defensive strategies. An *offensive* strategy is intended to increase profitability. Henry Ford used this strategy in pricing his popular Model T, which eventually commanded half of the market share. Even though his engineers were in absolute disagreement with him regarding the lower prices, his plan led to lower costs as a result of scale and experience which made the lower price profitable. Black & Decker successfully used this strategy in the hand-held electric tool market. Prices were reduced as costs fell with experience. The lower prices helped enhance share and at the same time increased the primary demand for the company's products. By a *defensive* strategy, a firm whose market share is much smaller than the leader's attempts to reach a minimum relative share to be able to survive against competitive pressures.

Reducing market share may also be a viable strategy in the case of products with poor positions in declining markets, that is, products which may be labelled 'dogs'. The company in this case may purposely allow the share of the product to decline and harvest the market by maximizing short-term earnings.

Meeting Competition

With this pricing goal, the firm simply prices its products at about the level of the average price in the industry. Prices, of course, are adjusted to take advantage of any unique features of the product, company, or middlemen involved. A firm that follows the price lead of others does not, in reality, have a price policy. Price is a given, and the firm will have to work backwards, tailoring costs to fit the price. Cost considerations may in turn dictate the choice of materials, product features, and marketing methods. Firms that are likely to follow this pricing practice are usually either smaller firms, which would rather follow a price leader, or large firms where the product in question is a fairly standardized product or commodity lacking the advantages of differentiation.

Maximize Profits

Economic theory makes the assumption that the purpose of the business organization is the maximization of profit. Even though not publicly admitted, firms may still adhere to such a profit goal. Business executives of firms seeking this goal when pressured, usually state other goals because of the negative connotations the term profit maximization gives to the public.

Economic theory makes the assumption that in 'competitive industries', a normal goal for the firm is to seek profit maximization. Theoretically, if high profits prevail, the field becomes attractive to possible competition and the additional suppliers will keep prices at a reasonable level. Profit maximization in this sense becomes a desirable objective, since it results in a better allocation of society's resources.

In recent years, some economists started to question the validity of the notion of profit maximization, and argue instead that the objective of business today is 'satisficing behaviour'. Cyert and March, for example, have given an explicit description of satisficing behaviour, where firms have been setting a less demanding objective than maximizing profit.[2]

Profit maximization as a goal is usually a non-operational objective in real-world situations, even though firms may state such an objective as a primary goal. The highly complex structure of organizations and the diversity of competitive offerings would make it difficult for executives to know which alternative courses of action to choose in order to maximize profit. For example, it would be difficult for a multi-product firm to know exactly what effect a change in output and sales will have on the costs of any particular product in the line.

Stabilize Prices

Price stabilization is a policy that attempts to keep prices stable in the long-run despite minor fluctuations in raw material, labour, or other costs. Companies maintain what they consider to be socially fair and just prices, without any attempt to take advantage of market conditions by charging what the market can bear. The price level, under this pricing goal, is not subjected to sharp fluctuations. Price changes can take place, however, but occur very infrequently and rarely at an unreasonable rate.

Stable prices serve well the purposes of the known, publicly visible large corporations. This policy builds public's trust and earns the firm goodwill and popularity. It portrays the corporation's objective as that of concern for the public.

PRICING STRATEGIES

An important decision that the manufacturer must make relates to the price strategy the firm is to follow, that is, the firm's price position in relation to competition. A manufacturer may choose a high-price policy for his products in relation to prices of competitive brands, in order to differentiate them from those of competitors and to build a quality image for them. Alternatively, another firm may choose to follow a low-price strategy for its products, aiming at carving out a larger market share for itself. Whichever price strategy is followed by the firm, it will directly affect the other marketing-mix factors such as product features, distribution methods, and advertising and promotional strategies.

The price strategy selected by a firm is naturally dependent on the objectives the firm has chosen to pursue. Profit maximization may call for higher prices through charging what the market can bear. Enhancing market share, on the other hand, may require a low-price policy designed to penetrate new or existing markets.

Skimming

Skimming involves charging the highest possible price in the short run. A product priced as such is usually one that is an innovation or a desirable variation from what exists in the market. As such, the product enjoys a relative monopolistic advantage, where the demand for it, at least at the initial stage, is relatively inelastic. The short run condition associated with skimming is due to the realization that sooner or later competitors will enter the market with similar or identical products, which would then eliminate the monopolistic advantage gained through primacy and the price premium that can be affixed to the product.

Skimming is an effective pricing strategy for innovative, unusual, or highly improved products. In the case of such products, the research and development cost is usually high, and so are the promotional outlays needed to bring the product to the attention of the potential market. High prices and margins are needed to cover these costs, as well as to recover the high costs associated with the smaller production run at this initial stage.

In addition to allowing the firm to recover its investment in a hurry, skimming can also be instrumental in building a higher-quality image for the product through its initial high price. Moreover, it is always easier to lower prices than to raise them. Charging high initial prices allows the firm the leisure of lowering them when the threat of competition arrives, but a lower initial price would be difficult to raise without losing volume.

Skimming can also be an effective strategy in segmenting the market. A firm can divide the market into a number of segments, and can tap each segment individually through successive price reductions where the price level for each segment is lowered enough to win its business. Since skimming also means a high price, this policy is to the liking of dealers, since the high price is translated into high markup for them.

Skimming is particularly successful in the case of products that are conspicuous. When digital watches were first introduced, for example, their price was set at a high level because of the realization by their manufacturers that the buyer at that initial point is more prestige conscious than price sensitive. Also, if the quality differences between competing brands are perceived to be large, or if differences are not easily judged by customers, the skimming strategy would work well. Many manufacturers of 'designer-label' clothing and fashions have been effective users of the skimming strategy.

Prestige Pricing

Unlike skimming, the premium or prestige price is designed to be maintained throughout the life cycle of the product in order to lend prestige and quality connotations to the item. The high price in itself is an important motivation for purchasing the product. Buyers of luxury brands of cars, cameras, perfumes, and liquor, for example, acquire much of the satisfaction from the prestige gained through use and possession of these highly priced items. Business history abounds with many cases in which price reduction for some prestigious products resulted in declining sales. In such cases, the gains in volume as a result of the lower price do not usually match the loss in sales to customers in the upper economic and social groups. The lower price for such groups would have the same effect as removing the prestige image that is instrumental in securing the purchase of the specific brand. Lower prices may actually discourage sales, rather than increase them.

The rapid rise in personal income and the quest for quality in the last two decades seems to have dulled the price sensitivity of many consumers. Quality in the broadest sense and prestige have become two of the primary buying motives in recent history. A glance at most advertising and promotional themes used today confirms their importance.

While prestige is sought and will continue to be sought through purchasing, the term 'prestige pricing' might give way to such a term as 'quality pricing'. This term has positive as opposed to negative overtones and more importantly links customer satisfaction to the product and the accompanying pricing structure. Stated another way, 'quality pricing' focuses the customer's attention on how the product can satisfy expectations.

Penetration Pricing

Penetration is a low-price strategy designed to infiltrate markets and achieve a large market share for the firm. This strategy is workable only if the price elasticity of demand for the product in question is high enough, so that the lower price will result in a large increase in sales volume. Henry Ford, in pricing his popular Model T, was convinced that the low price would result in a mass market, which in turn would cause per-unit cost to fall drastically.

As mentioned earlier in this chapter, high sales volumes and large market shares lead to lower costs. The effects of economies of both scale and experience cause per-unit cost to decrease. In industries where a significant portion of total cost can be reduced owing to scale economies and experience, important cost savings justify using penetration price strategy to gain market share. This is particularly true when the market rewards low prices, and when the firm has the resources to implement them. In regard to the latter, a firm has to have the production and distribution capabilities to meet the anticipated high demand when a penetration price strategy is successfully implemented.

The dangers inherent in penetration pricing lie in the probability of retaliation by competitors, and in the possibility of endangering the product's image as a result of the low price. Competitors may match the price set by the low-price initiator, thus nullifying the relative advantage unless the product in question is sufficiently differentiated from competing brands. A low price can endanger a product's image, particularly when there is an almost knee-jerk perceptual association between price and quality.

Expansionistic Pricing

The expansionistic pricing strategy is a more exaggerated form of penetration pricing. It is a very low price policy aimed at establishing mass markets, sometimes at the expense of other competitors. Under this strategy, the product enjoys a high price elasticity of demand, so that the adoption of a low price leads to a significant increase in volume.

In international markets, for example, many countries attempting to open new markets for their products, or expand existing markets, use expansionistic pricing. Toyota and Honda used a version of expansionistic pricing to gain market acceptance of their products in the US market. Standardized, low-cost versions of the Toyota Corolla and the Honda Civic were introduced to gain market acceptance for each company. Once this was obtained, more expensive versions and models were introduced.

Such practices have always been under tight scrutiny by the government in order to prevent any attempt to use dumping. Dumping is a negative domination strategy involving selling a product abroad below its manufacturing costs. If carried to its extreme, dumping can force the host country's manufacturers out of business. As such, dumping is an extreme case of expansionistic pricing. Anti-dumping laws have been enacted in many countries to prevent such extreme pricing practices being used.

Expansionistic pricing has been effectively utilized by publishers of magazines and newspapers in the USA. Circulation has been expanded dramatically through low annual subscription rates for many well-known magazines and newspapers. Benefits to such publishers result from the higher advertising rates they charge to advertisers. Such charges are tied to the publication's circulation rate. In a similar manner, book, record and tape 'clubs' use expansionistic pricing to expand club membership.

Preemptive Pricing

A pre-emptive or stay-out price strategy is a low-price policy designed to deter or discourage possible competition from entering the market. As a result, the prevailing price in the market is unattractive to possible competitors. This strategy is particularly well suited to situations where the firm does not hold a protective patent or have a differential advantage over other firms, and where entry into the market is relatively easy. Delaying competitors' entry gives the firm the chance to gain share, reduce cost through scale and experience effects, and acquire name recognition as the original entrant. RCA Corporation, for example, selected pre-emptive pricing in 1955 when it first introduced colour television to the market. The low price was intended to give RCA time to improve the colour-tube technology before competition rushed into the field, reduce attendant costs, and establish a strong market position for itself in colour TV technology.

Extinction Pricing

The price under the extinction strategy is set low, to eliminate competition. Usually the price is below what the firm can justify on the basis of its cost of production. The intention is to financially harm the competition even if the firm incurs a financial loss. Once the competition is eliminated, prices can be raised to profitable levels.

Standard Oil, for example, used extinction pricing at the end of the nineteenth century to get rid of competition. By reducing prices in local areas to half the costs, competitors were eliminated and then bought out at nominal prices by Standard Oil. The company made up the losses in non-competitive areas by charging higher-than-normal prices.

The term 'cut-throat predation' has been used to describe such pricing practices. To be able to practice predation, a firm must be dominant in the industry, with strong financial standing to be able to take the monetary losses resulting from this policy. In the nineteenth century, predation was a widespread practice in the oil, concrete, sugar, and tobacco industries. Such practices, however, have come under severe attacks, because they are considered as a form of illegal price discrimination if they substantially lessen competition or tend to create a monopoly. However, for alleged predation to be established, evidence has to be presented that the price in question is below the defendant's average cost.

Some firms today use a mild form of price predation involving selective price cuts on certain items within the product line. For example, a camera manufacturer may establish a an unprofitable price for a camera at the low end of its product line in order to enhance the sales of the total line. It is anticipated that losses sustained with the lower price will be offset by increased sales of the more profitable items in the line.

DISCOUNTS AND ALLOWANCES

It is critical for any manufacturer to maintain good working relationships with members of the distribution network. A manufacturer will find it necessary to negotiate prices with his distributors as they typically attempt to receive the most favourable price and discount terms. In order to compensate distributors for their services and to maintain their cooperation, most manufacturers offer a variety of discounts from their list price. These discounts can include: (1) quantity discounts, (2) trade or functional discounts, (3) seasonal discounts, (4) promotional discounts, and (5) cash discounts. Even though each type of discount is granted by the manufacturer for a specific purpose, the buyer may obtain all of these discounts in a single transaction if the requirements for granting them are met by the buyer.

Quantity Discounts

A quantity discount is a reduction from the list or suggested price that is granted to encourage volume purchases. These discounts may be based either on the number of units purchased by the dealer or on the dollar value of the purchase. Discounts can be stated as a percentage discount figure, as a number of extra units without charge, or as a monetary value expressed in dollars or cents.

There are several reasons for granting quantity discounts. From the manufacturer's point of view, selling in larger quantities can translate into savings in shipping, order filling and billing. Moreover, enhancing volume would mean making more effective use of production capabilities, less capital tied in inventories, less insurance cost, and less administrative expenses. From the buyer's point of view, the discount is welcomed because it means lower per-unit prices.

Noncumulative Quantity Discounts

With a non-cumulative quantity discount the purpose is to encourage placement of larger orders. Savings to the manufacturer in the form of selling, storage, order possessing, and delivery cost can result. Such practice, in addition to being valuable in building goodwill with the channel members, is often necessary as a competitive policy, and practically necessary to satisfy the wishes of large buyers.

Table 7.1   Example of quantity discount schedule

Tons purchased on single order	Percentage discount from list price
1–5	0.0
6–10	2.0
11–20	3.0
21–30	4.0
over 30	5.0

A manufacturer may set up a quantity discount schedule such as that shown in Table 7.1, which is used by a manufacturer of linoleum. The determination of the minimum quantity which must be purchased to obtain a quantity discount would normally be the quantity where savings from selling in quantity offset the amount of discount that compensates the buyer for stocking the additional number of units. In the example, shown in Table 7.1, the buyer receives a 2 per cent discount for buying at least 6 tons.

Next, the seller needs to set up a schedule of the discounts for increasing purchase quantities. One feature of discount schedules that is often questioned from a legal point of view is the number of, as well as the gap between, the discount breaks. Discount breaks are questionable when they are skewed to benefit a few large buyers.

The selection of the size of discount, the number of breaks to which they apply, as well as the applicable minimum and maximum quantities, should be based on careful analysis of cost and benefits. These may include savings and other possible benefits for the seller, as well as the costs associated with the potential change in buyers' inventory costs as a result of changing the size of their orders.

Cumulative Quantity Discounts

This type of discount is applied to the total amount purchased within a stated period of time. The purpose is to encourage patronage and to hold customers over a period of time. The buyer is rewarded for continuing to patronize the same supplier. The amount of discount increases proportionately with the increase in the year's total business.

Cumulative quantity discounts are more suitable for certain products than for others. In the case of products whose style or model may change fast, where technological innovations can depreciate the value of existing models, where perishability is high, or where distributors' inventory costs are sizable, cumulative discounts are more effective than non-cumulative types. In such cases, a certain amount of resistance to purchasing large quantities of the product at one time is understandable. The manufacturer, as a result, focuses not on the quantity per order, but rather on the distributer's total yearly volume.

Unlike the case of administered pricing, where the manufacturer is unilaterally free to set the price level for his product, the firm's quantity discount schedule can be subject to legal scrutiny even when such discounts are offered on an equal basis to all comparable buyers. The manufacturer is not free to offer whatever amount of quantity discount he may simply feel necessary to encourage volume, because such discounts are subject to the rules of the Robinson-Patman Act.

It is clear from the rules of the Robinson-Patman Act that quantity discounts are legal only to the extent that they can be justified on a cost-savings basis. Manufacturers who may be questioned by the Federal Trade Commission regarding their quantity discounts have to be able to cite primarily savings in cost of selling and physical distribution. Even though, theoretically, cost savings in terms of manufacturing are also included in the Robinson-Patman Act, as a practical matter they have been difficult to defend. In the many cases where firms attempt to defend their discount schedules on the basis of savings in manufacturing costs, courts have insisted that arbitrary cost allocation is not acceptable, and that the uniform allocation of overhead cost is a necessity. The manufacturer, in other words, cannot arbitrarily allocate all overhead costs to the first batch of his product, and claim only variable costs for any additional units. Each product in the line has to carry its fair share of the fixed costs.

As a result of the scrutiny exercised by the Federal Trade Commission over quantity discount users, firms that maintain such schedules attempt to base them on evidence of savings in logistic costs. In cases of questionable legality the lower per-unit costs of shipping larger quantities combine with detailed documentation typical of shipping to provide the necessary evidence. The second justification for price discrimination under the Robinson-Patman Act is the good-faith defence; here a manufacturer will maintain that it is necessary to lower his price to meet the equally low price of a competitor. In practice, however, this defence has rarely been effective in justifying a manufacturer's discount system. Its intent, as revealed in many court cases, focuses only on individual and isolated cases where the price is lowered by a manufacturer for the benefit of a specific buyer in order to meet, in good faith, an equally low price offered this buyer by a competing seller. As such, the good-faith clause cannot be used to defend a whole quantity discount system.

The status of cumulative quantity discounts is even more in jeopardy: they are more difficult to justify on a cost-savings basis than are non-cumulative discounts. The frequency of purchasing smaller volumes makes it difficult to claim direct measurable cost savings; cost savings are practically non-existent when the firm is filling and shipping a multitude of orders. Most true economies, rather, are associated with the larger shipments of the individual order type. If the number of orders purchased per year is the basis for the discount schedule, it is harder to justify on a cost than if the schedule is based on volume purchased per order.

Many firms, as a result of these possible legal questions, are being exceptionally cautious in using a liberal policy of quantity discounts, particularly when the company is considering a cumulative quantity discount policy.

It should be pointed out, however, that price discrimination through quantity discounts is not illegal *per se*. The defendant has to prove that the discount schedule of the firm in question has resulted in a lessening of competition or in injury to other suppliers.

Trade Discounts

Trade discounts are reductions from the list price given to the various classes of reseller commensurate with their position in the distributive sequence. They represent payments for the performance of marketing functions at each level of distribution.

Discounts offered to successive distributors are usually stated as a chain of discounts. For example, a manufacturer of calculators with a suggested retail price of $10 may offer trade discounts of 40 and 20 per cent to retailers and wholesalers, respectively. In this case, the manufacturer would receive $4.80 for each calculator sold. The amount of $4.80 is the price the wholesaler is billed for the calculator. The wholesaler, in turn, resells the calculator to a retailer at a price of $6.00 with a markup of $1.20, or 20 per cent. If the retailer in turn sells the calculator for $10, then the markup is $4.00, or 40 per cent.

Traditionally, trade discounts were granted to buyers on the basis of trade classification, that is, their trade status as broker, wholesaler or retailer. A problem that has arisen is that it is becoming more and more difficult to define the various members of a marketing channel. Large retailers buy direct from manufacturers or perhaps through brokers, but do their own warehousing. In fact, Wal-Mart has an arrangement with Procter & Gamble whereby the latter manages the inventory of its respective products. Distributors, on the other hand, may integrate forward through ownership or franchising of retail outlets.

Because of these and other changes in the distribution networks of manufacturers, the usefulness of setting up a trade discount structure can be seriously questioned. Instead, many manufacturers are using such terms as stocking allowance and slotting allowance.

Seasonal Discounts

Seasonal discounts are reductions from the list price to encourage buyers to order early in the season or in the off-season. In the case of certain merchandise, such as toys, air conditioners, snow tyres, and lawn mowers, there are off-seasons or slack periods of the year when sales virtually stop. Since manufacturers of these products do not find it feasible to close down their manufacturing facilities during the slow sales periods, a viable alternative is to offer seasonal discounts to their resellers. By doing so, the manufacturer, in effect, shifts the responsibility and all the attendant expenses for carrying the inventories to resellers.

Seasonal discounts amounting to a significant percentage are not uncommon. The seasonal discount has to be large enough to compensate the dealer for storing the goods for several months, and to cover the opportunity loss on the investment in additional inventory. From the point of view of the manufacturer, offering seasonal discount is an alternative to closing down the production facilities and enduring the cost disadvantages which this alternative entails. For the reseller, seasonal discounts are an opportunity to buy merchandise at a reduced cost.

Since seasonal discount schemes partition the market on a time basis by offering different prices for products in different times of the year, it would seem logical that the longer is the time span between the transaction and the beginning of the selling season, the larger will be the seasonal discount. Conversely, the closer the transaction is to the beginning of the selling season, the lower will be the seasonal discount. Following this logic, a manufacturer using a seasonal discount policy would be expected to scale the trade discounts to coincide with the time frame of the transaction. A higher trade discount is offered to buyers who buy early in the season, with a progressive reduction for transaction at later dates.

The Robinson-Patman Act allows the vendor to use seasonal discounts as long as the same discount is given equally to comparable buyers, and as long as the discounts granted do not exceed cost savings of the seller. Comparability is interpreted in court rulings to mean buyers who purchase in the same time frame.

Promotional Discounts

A promotional discount is granted by the vendor to his dealers as a form of compensation for the sales promotion efforts undertaken by them in promoting his product. National advertising campaigns undertaken by large manufacturers are usually insufficient to promote a manufacturer's product effectively because of their failure to mention the local sources where customers can purchase the product. In addition to national promotion, most vendors prefer to advertise their products in local markets by associating them with the names and locations of local dealers. This policy usually results in increased sales, and allows the vendor to take advantage of the lower rates for local advertising and promotion.

Promotional discounts may take the form of a percentage reduction, for example 2 per cent, below the list price of a product, or they may be stated on a monetary or merchandise basis: so many dollars per case, off the normal price or so many extra units per case.

Promotional discounts can be the implicit or the explicit. An implicit discount is the reduction in cost of the merchandise or the additional merchandise which in effect lowers the cost of the merchandise ordered by the reseller. The explicit type, on the other hand, involves reimbursing the reseller for part or all the actual advertising or promotional expenses incurred in promoting the manufacturer's product. As such, the explicit type is not in effect a pricing matter. It is merely an allowance, which is only given if, and when, the dealer chooses to advertise or promote the manufacturer's product. Cooperative advertising policies, adopted by some manufacturers for example, typify this explicit type of promotional allowances. In such cases, the manufacturer usually requires proof of promotional expenditures before reimbursement is granted.

Viewed as such, the two types of promotional discounts and allowances are subject to different rules. The implicit advertising discounts affect the price paid by a buyer, and consequently are subject to the provisions of the Robinson-Patman Act. Allowances, on the other hand, do not directly affect price but represent 'acts or practices in commerce', making them subject to the rules of the Federal Trade Commission Act.

The Robinson-Patman Act limits the legality of promotional discounts to situations where the vendor offers them on 'proportionately equal terms'. The Act, however, did not explain the intended meaning of the word 'proportionately'. Court decisions, however, had made it clear that proportionality means that discounts must correspond in amount to the volume of business purchased by various dealers receiving the discount. The discount, thus, may be proportionately tied to units purchased, or to dollars of volume, provided that this system is used uniformly among all competing buyers.

Cash Discounts

A cash discount is a reduction from the list price granted by the vendor to encourage dealers from promptly payment of invoices. Although the cash discount is normally offered as a reward for the prompt payment, it can be used as a means to extend an additional discount to resellers. Some disagreement exists as to whether cash discounts taken are a reduction in the cost of merchandise or other income.

A cash discount term involves three elements: (1) a permissible discount rate, (2) a specific period of time during which the permissible discount rate is effective, and (3) a time limit for the payment of the entire bill if cash discount is not taken. The familiar terms '2/10, n/30' mean a 2 per cent cash discount is granted if payment is received in 10 days, with a limit of 30 days to pay the full bill.

The amount of cash discount granted is usually a function of the prevailing industry practice as well as of the competitive position of the particular vendor. Where the industry practice is to offer cash discounts, a nonconforming manufacturer may seriously hurt his business by not offering them. A glance at one of the most common cash discount terms offered by manufacturers, namely '2/10, n/30', reveals an effective annual rate of interest of 36 per cent. This high rate of discount is justified because of its positive effect on the manufacturer's resources. Early payments by buyers speed up the manufacturer's cash flow, because accounts receivable are more quickly converted into cash. Also, credit risks and the costs of collecting overdue accounts are reduced. With resources in accounts receivable minimized, and allocated to more effective uses, it is not surprising that manufacturers reward early payments with cash discount rates.

REFERENCES

1. Robert F. Lanzillotti 'Pricing Objectives in Large Companies', in D. F. Mulvihill and S. Paranka, eds, *Price Policies and Practices* (New York: John Wiley 1967) pp. 63–83.
2. Richard M. Cyert and James G. March *A Behavioral Theory of the Firm* (Englewood Cliffs, NJ: Prentice-Hall 1963).

8 Product Line Pricing

In 1921, an executive committee at General Motors Corporation headed by Alfred Sloan made three decisions that would affect the firm's product policy to this day. The first was to enter the low-priced mass market and compete directly with Ford, the industry leader. The second was to limit the number of product categories, while the third was the avoidance of price overlap between designated product lines.

While there has been a change in brand name (Oakland to Pontiac) and prices now overlap between categories, the essence of the differentiation of product lines by price remains intact to this day. The original price categories were as follows:

Chevrolet below	$ 600
Oakland	$ 600–900
Buick (4-cylinder)	$ 900–1,200
Buick (6-cylinder)	$1,200–1,700
Oldsmobile	$1,700–2,500
Cadillac	$2,500–3,500

(See Alfred P. Sloan, *My Years with General Motors*, reprint edition (New York: Anchor, 1972))

Companies rarely produce and market just one product for which a single price and a specific marketing strategy is developed. Rather, they produce a line or several lines of products with a multiplicity of options that are marketed to defined customer segments. No longer is it possible or for that matter plausible to make pricing decisions with respect to a single product in isolation.

A product line is defined as a grouping of products that are closely related in use, in method of distribution, in price range, or in attracting similar customers. The depth of a product line is measured in terms of the number of items in the line. The greater the number of items in the product line, the deeper the product line. For example, General Electric with seven models of dishwashers would have a deeper product line than a competitor with only three models of dishwashers.

A product line can be enlarged by stretching or filling. Honda, Nissan, and Toyota have stretched their product line upward to the luxury class with the Acura, Infiniti, and Lexus models. Chrysler, on the other hand, has stretched its product line downward with the Neon. By filling, a company adds products within its present range. Frequently, a company in the higher and lower ends of a market might fill through adding a middle-range product or products.

Product mix is defined as the total number of product lines offered by a company. The width of the product mix is measured in terms of the number of product lines, regardless of how closely related they may be. Procter & Gamble, for example, whose products include such items as toothpaste, disposable diapers, cake mixes, and deodorants has a product mix that is both extensive and diverse. Other well-known firms with both extensive and diverse product mixes are General Electric, Mitsubishi, Black & Decker, Beatrice Foods, RJR Nabisco, and Panasonic.

PRICING RELATED PRODUCTS

Multiple products for most companies have come about from the exploitation of opportunities as they have presented themselves over the course of time. Products are added in some cases because marketing management feels, rightly or wrongly, that the more products a company has the greater the market strength of the parent firm. It is also contended that the greater the number of products, the better the chances of appealing to a broader cross-section of consumers. Conversely, a firm with one or a very limited number of products is much more vulnerable to changes in the marketplace. IBM and Apple Computer are not one-computer companies, and Coca-Cola and Pepsi are not one-soft-drink firms. Many of their respective successes have resulted from having multiple products.

Another reason for adding items to a product line or a product mix is a more efficient utilization of selling efforts or distribution facilities, particularly if the products are directed toward the same customer targets. Giving a salesperson more products to sell allows he or she to make more efficient utilization of time with the customer, and spreads the cost of selling over more products. The Sherwin-Williams Company, for example, has added numerous product lines such as floor coverings, draperies, and shades to broaden the drawing appeal of its branch outlets and to gain more sales from a given investment in distribution. The products added in such circumstances are typically complementary in nature.

Still another reason for adding products is to provide a means of gaining entry to markets where existing products can also be sold. These products are competitively priced and often loss leaders. Reactions to competitors can also lead to more and more items being added. For example, it may be decided to add a product simply to match competitors' efforts, to exploit a weakness of competition, or to fill a gap in the marketplace. Finally, added products may be 'specials' developed for major clients'marketing promotions or specific circumstances. For example, one company added a line of beverage glassware that was originally developed for a promotional campaign for an oil company.

Products are frequently added to utilize idle productive capacity, to balance seasonal ups and downs, or to make more efficient use of by-products. As an example, a commercial decorator of chinaware developed a new line of souvenir plates for area high schools in an effort to reduce an inventory buildup of ceramic blanks.

Segmentation Strategies

Multiple products can, and often do, result from segmentation strategies developed to deal with heterogeneous markets. Because customers may differ greatly, a seller may divide up the total market into homogeneous sub-markets, each with a different marketing mix, because one sub-market will respond differently from others to competitive strategies. Often this means a different product and price for each segment. Segmentation may be based either on variables that are unrelated to the product, such as demographics, or on those that are related to it , such as usage situation or benefit sought from it. As an example of benefit segmentation, Nabisco, using what they call franchise extensions, goes after additional sales by matching products with eating situations. As an illustration, the original Oreo is positioned as an eat-at-home biscuit, while Big Stuff, an oversized version of the Oreo, is positioned as a snack to be munched on the go, while fudge-covered Oreos are designed as a rich treat for adults.[1]

Other product-related variables include price and application. By using price, a product line is broken down into pricing points or distinct price levels. Hartmann luggage, for example, has four distinct pricing points. There are three distinct price lines under the Hugo Boss umbrella. The Hugo line is priced 10 per cent less than the Boss line, which in turn is 30 per cent less than the top-of-the-line.[2] Application segmentation differs from usage, in that the product remains basically the same, but it is applied in different ways by different customers. This leads to multiple products only in the sense that the total package sold to a customer will differ because of the extras that are necessary to facilitate a particular application. A bank, a retail clothing store, and a research lab will all purchase the same PC. The differences in total package will arise from the different software included to facilitate the application.

Demand and Cost Interrelationships

With multiple products, the demand may be interrelated, the cost structure may be interrelated, or both demand and cost structures may be interrelated. When demand is interrelated, the demand for one product in a line will affect and in turn be affected by the demand for other products. If the effect is direct, an increase (decrease) in demand for a core product increases (decreases) the demand for the other products, or what are called complementary products. For example, sales of timbers, a core product, increases sales of nails, and the construction of new residences, as core products, increases the demand for household appliances. Other forms of complementary product are options that can be added to the core product, such as automotive accessories, and expendables, such as razor blades, camera film, and staples, that are combined with a core product that is a using device.

When there is an inverse effect, an increase in demand for one product decreases the demand for another. The products are viewed as substitutes for each other, with a decision to purchase one eliminating the need to purchase the other. The competitive battle between plastics and steel is a good example. Increasing use of plastic in cars automatically translates into a decrease in the demand for steel, and vice versa.

End-items in a product line, the lowest-priced and the highest-priced, play important roles in the demand for the entire line. The lowest-priced item attracts potential purchasers for the entire line and acts as a 'volume generator'. Thus it is important in expanding the customer base for a product line. The danger is that the lowest-priced item will take sales away from the rest of the line, that is, 'cannibalize' the line, and hence lower profits. The highest-priced item, on the other hand, while less visible than the lowest-priced item, is viewed as the highest quality or best available item in the line.

A major problem for a manufacturer who offers several versions of product of a closely-related product mix is the difficulty in allocating common costs to a specific item. It is also bothersome to trace costs to a single product when it and other products are joint products of the same production process. In this situation, increasing the output of one will lead automatically to an increase in volume for another. This is the case with by-products, or in the processing of agricultural products where only a certain portion of the basic raw material can be used for the core product because of quality or size restrictions. Common costs also arise with alternative products where an increase in the output of one brings about a corresponding decrease in another. Producing more cheese, for example, reduces the possible output of fluid milk.

Profit Contribution

Because of the difficulties in sorting out common costs that arise from production of multiple products, it is often useful to think in terms of profit
contribution. Using only variable or direct costs as deductions from selling
price, profit contribution presents a picture of the relative worth of a single
product. Profit contribution, defined as net sales less direct costs incurred in
making and marketing the specific product being considered, is different
from gross profit in that all direct costs are considered rather than just those
related to manufacturing the specific product. If a specific product has a
contribution of 35 per cent, this means that for every dollar of selling price,
35 cents goes to pay off common costs and contribute to profit. In over-
simplified terms the formula for determining contribution is

$$PC = SP - DC$$

where PC represents profit contribution, SP represents selling price, and
DC represents direct costs.

Knowing profit contributions, a marketing manager is in a much better
position to set prices or to revise them for a line of products. The starting
point is the determination of contribution for all the products in the line.
Suppose a company with four products in its line reports sales and cost data
for the year as shown in Table 8.1. The overall totals do not provide any
useful information on any of the four products in the line, except a bench-
mark of 40 per cent for contribution. Let us suppose sales and direct costs
for each of the four products can be broken out as in Table 8.2.

Table 8.1   Sales and cost data

	$m	%
Net sales	60	100
Direct costs	36	60
Contribution	24	40
Common costs	12	20
Taxable income	12	20

In this hypothetical example, suppose the product line in question is
lawnmowers. Model Z has the highest price, Model Y the next highest price
and so on. Models Z and Y are self-propelled, while models W and X are
push mowers. The most obvious question is in regard to the differential

Table 8.2   Sales and direct costs

Product	$m		
	Sales	Direct costs	Contribution (%)
W $200*	30	17	13 (32.5)
X $300	12	9	3 (25.0)
Y $400	10	4	6 (60.0)
Z $500	8	6	2 (25.0)
Totals	60	36	24 (40.0)

*Price to dealer.

between pricing points for models *X* and *Z* and similarly equipped lower-priced versions. Seemingly, the higher-priced versions of the push and self-propelled mowers cost much more to make and market than the respective lower-priced versions. The fall-off in sales with an increase in price signifies that customers don't recognize or don't feel the added differences are worth the extra money, and buy the lower-priced version of either self-propelled or push. Certainly, questions should be asked about redefining models *X* and *Z* or dropping them from the line. Looking at the relative high contribution for model *Y*, marketing management might want to lower the price to attract more sales.

COMPLEMENTARY PRODUCTS

Demand for complementary products originates from several sources. The most obvious is when the complementary product is used with a principal product which can be called the using device. This is the case with film and cameras, blades and razors, staples and staplers, and more recently software and computers. You might even consider furnaces and heat pumps as using devices for gas and electricity, respectively. A more tenuous relationship exists between cars and products that repair, maintain, care, or beautify them.

Complementary demand also arises from products that enhance or add value to principal products. This would include the whole diverse range of accessories for a car or truck, as well as attachments for a vacuum cleaner. In such instances the sales of the principal product do not necessarily ensure sales of the complementary product, because the owner of the principal product does not need the complementary product to use the principal product. The attractiveness of complementary products, even when there is no using device involved, comes about in several ways. Salespeople have more to sell when making sales calls, and complementary products also provide completeness to the offerings of outlets. Complementary products may also allow the seller to take advantage of competitive gaps in the marketplace and to gain an edge over competitors.

Considerations in Pricing Complementary Products

The key to pricing complementary products is to treat the principal or core product and the complementary product as a unit, and use either the principal or complementary product to subsidize the sale of the other. In this way, profits can be maximized for the total line rather than for any one individual product within the line.

The first question that must be asked concerns the relationship between the principal product and the complementary product or products. The nature of the combination, and in turn the pricing situation, will differ, for example, between a using device and an expendable product as opposed to a principal product and an accessory. With the former, demand for the expendable is assured because it is essential to the operation of the using device. In the latter case, on the other hand, there is a lot less certainty of demand for the complementary product being triggered by the sale of the principal product. When demand for the complementary product is assured, the principal product is priced lower than would be the case if there was no complementary product. Thus, for a comparable camera Kodak's price will be lower than that of a competitor who does not produce film. When demand is not assured, such as in the case of car accessories, complementary products may be priced lower to add to the attractiveness of the car.

The second question concerns the match between principal and complementary products. Although this is a particularly important consideration for expendables and accessories, it can also be obtained for other forms of complementary products. A good example is the harmonization of colours and patterns for paint, wallpaper, and furnishing materials. Toys, clothing, and cosmetics are other examples of lines where there may be a match between principal product and complementary products. If the design of the principal product is such that only the firm's complementary products can be used in conjunction, direct competition can be avoided, at least initially, and the complementary products are called captive products. However, it may be difficult to protect the uniqueness of the fit between principal and complementary products. For this reason, it does not make much sense for marketers, other than those with large market shares, to attempt such an approach.

The third and final question concerns the sales balance between the principal product and the complementary products. Stated in simple terms, the question is: what number of complementary products will be sold as a result of selling a principle product? If the complementary product is an expendable, then the important information is how many units will accompany the initial purchase, as well as how many units are likely to be used in the first three months of operation, the first six months and so on. If the complementary product is an accessory, then the marketer will want to know the proportion of principal units that will include the accessory. For example, marketers of such products as anti-lock braking systems and air bags will base their sales forecasts on car manufacturers' plans to include either or both in their vehicles.

These sales ratios are important not only to pricing decisions, but also to questions of availability. Enough of the complementary product must be available in relation to the principal product or it loses much of its value in the marketplace. Kodak, for example, stopped selling a new camera and withdrew it from the market when it was discovered that the unusually high and unexpected demand for the new camera (principal product) created a demand for film (complementary product) that could not be supplied. The camera was later reintroduced when the supplies of film reached acceptable levels. This action, although drastic, prevented a buildup of consumer dissatisfaction at not being able to use the new product upon purchasing it.

Pricing the Using Device and Expendable Combination

The sales ratio of expendable to using device, and the limitation on competition as a result of the match between the two, are the two critical considerations in pricing both products. Basically, there are two types of expendable. One is a unique expendable that is not exposed to competition. The other is a standard expendable that will face competition.

Using a camera–film combination as a hypothetical example, suppose it is determined when buying a new camera that a customer will also purchase two rolls of film one of which is loaded in the camera at the place of purchase. Suppose further that during the first six months of ownership it is estimated that the customer will buy another four rolls of film, followed by another three rolls during the second six months, making a total of nine rolls for the first year of usage. In the next two years, sales are estimated to be six rolls per year. Competition, if the film is standard, will reduce volume by approximately 30 per cent (see Table 8.3).

Table 8.3   Hypothetical example of balance between sales of camera (using device) and film (expendable)

	Unique match		*Standard match*	
Initial market	Camera plus two rolls of film		Camera plus two rolls of film	
Aftermath market	First year	7 rolls	First year	5 rolls
	Next two years	12 rolls	Next two years	8 rolls
(three years)	Total	19 rolls	Total	13 rolls

Because the using device, in this case a camera, triggers the sales of film, the price elasticity of the camera is important because its volume of sales maximizes the number of expendable units sold, regardless of the degree of uniqueness. Suppose two pricing scenarios are being considered for the new product–skimming and penetration. The estimated demand for retail price of $100 ($70 to the retailer) is 3,000 units per month, while demand is projected to be 5,000 units/month with a $80 retail price ($56 to the retailer). It is fairly obvious that total profit contribution from the two products is maximized when the sales of the expendable subsidize the using device (Table 8.4). There is also a possibility that an even lower price for the using device may lead to significant profit increases. If the marketer is also involved in film processing, as is Kodak in supplying paper, then the profit possibilities of lowering the price of the using device to expand sales take on greater significance. Any loss on the camera is more than offset by the potentialities of increased sales of film and paper.

When the expendable is not unique, competition will reduce sales. The extent to which competition can make inroads into the expendable market depends upon the competitive status of the expendable and the carry-over effect from the using device. There is also a fairly good chance that, in order to meet competition, the price of the expendable will have to be reduced, thus reducing contribution unless there is a trade-off in terms of economies of scale with a larger volume. A recalculation of total contribution with a standard expendable is shown in Table 8.5.

The increased profitability shown with the higher, or skimming price, might be somewhat down played, because in future years having more

Table 8.4   Hypothetical example of two pricing scenarios with unique expendable

Skimming price		Penetration price	
Suggested retail	$100	Suggested retail	$80
Discount (30%)	30	Discount (30%)	24
Price to reseller	70	Price to reseller	56
Direct costs	50	Direct costs	50
Contribution	20	Contribution	6

Estimated demand: 3,000 units per month		Estimated demand: 5,000 units per month	
Contribution of film: $1 per roll		Contribution of film: $1 per roll	
Contribution		Contribution	
cameras (one month)	$60,000	cameras (one month)	$30,000
film	63,000	film	105,000
Total	$123,000	Total	$135,000

Table 8.5   Hypothetical example of two pricing scenarios with standard expendable

Skimming price		Penetration price	
Suggested retail	$100	Suggested retail	$80
Contribution	20	Contribution	6
Estimated demand: 3,000 units per month		Estimated demand: 5,000 units per month	
Contribution of film: $1 per roll		Contribution of film: $1 per roll	
cameras (one month)	$60,000	cameras (one month)	$30,000
film	45,000	film	75,000
Total	$105,000	Total	$105,000

units out will be more profitable. For example, if in the fourth year purchasers of the camera buy just three rolls of film then total profitability is greater for penetration price ($114,000 to $120,000). In addition, the fact that, with the penetration price, there are more units being used, increases the odds of gaining more from sales of the complementary product with a multiple of 5,000 as opposed to 3,000. Thus it is obvious that in pricing the using device the emphasis is on creating greater sales opportunity for the expendable. The larger the ratio between expendable and using device, or the greater the units sold of expendable to that of a using device, the greater the opportunity to increase total contribution through lowering the price of the using device to increase the potential for sales of the expendable.

Realization of this marketing relationship has prompted the idea of giving away the using device to get expendable sales. One sales executive for a maker of staplers and staples for industrial uses pictured the relationship as one where his firm could give away the stapler even though it was a fairly expensive item of equipment if they were assured in turn of that particular customer's staple business. A disadvantage, however, of giving away or providing free of charge the using device, whether it is a paper cup dispenser, a razor, or a complex piece of machinery such as a stapler is the illegality of a tying contract that forces the buyer to use one particular brand of expendable. Another disadvantage is that the customer places no value on the using device. The latter is seen as particularly disadvantageous by producers of consumer products such as razors. Ideally, the using device should be priced low enough to maximize market expansion. It is also strategically important to make continuous programmed innovations in the using device that may or may not mean changes in the expendable.

Package Pricing

When products are complementary, but the relationship between the principal product and complementary product is less definitive, and the complementary product is not strictly necessary, the marketer may want to engage in some form of package pricing to promote combination sales. To illustrate, suppose a company wants to sell both a rock crusher and a heavy-duty conveyor system. During the last year, 27 rock crushers were sold, and 7 conveyor systems, 2 of which were sold in combination with a rock crusher. Marketing management feels the problem is that the crusher is competitively priced, whereas the conveyor appears to be overpriced. Cost and price data on the two products are as follows:

	Price	Contribution	Range of market prices
Rock crusher	$48,000	$9,600	$48,000–$54,000
Conveyor system	18,000	6,000	15,000–18,000

Total contribution from sales of both products last year equalled $301,200, of which 86 per cent ($259,200) could be attributed to the rock crusher. If the rock crusher is treated as the principal product and the conveyor system as the complementary product then several pricing schemes can evolve. One could be a package price of $60,000 for the two, which in essence eliminates the contribution of the conveyer system, with separate prices of $54,000 for the rock crusher and $15,000 for the conveyor system. Assuming the same number of rock crushers are sold as last year, but that 20 are sold in combination with the conveyor, then the total contribution would be $192,000 for the package sales, and an additional $124,200 for single sales of 7 rock crushers and 5 conveyor systems for a total of $316,200. Thus, by eliminating the contribution of the complementary product in pricing the package, total contribution is increased by almost 5 per cent.

Value pricing and piggyback pricing are two variations employed with packages of principal and complementary products. In the former, a lower price is set on a principal product that is packaged with attractive options; such schemes are fast gaining favour as a powerful marketing tactic, particularly in the car industry. In the case of the Chevrolet Cavalier, for example, a lower price combined with attractive options has resulted in a 25.9 per cent sales increase for the 11-year old model, making it the seventh-best selling vehicle in the USA. Manufacturers can still make money with value pricing because of the efficiencies of producing a large volume of cars with the same equipment.[3]

The objective of piggyback pricing is to expand the sales of complementary products by packaging them with a more widely accepted principal product. The price of the package is only slightly higher than the price of the principal product when purchased separately. As an example, one company included bath gel and body lotion with their popular cologne.

SUBSTITUTE PRODUCTS

Unlike complementary products, where the sale of one boosts the sale of another, the sale of a substitute product reduces the sale of an other, because a consumer will substitute one for the other under certain conditions. The risk for a marketer in adding a substitute brand to the product line is that sales will shift from the older brand to the newer one. Thus, Miller Lite has been a very successful line extension of a successful brand – Miller High Life; but here a see-saw relationship has developed where Miller Lite's market share has increased at the same time as Miller High Life's has gone down.[4]

Marketers, usually those with large shares of the market, extend their product lines to further increase their market share by attracting non-customers for their products and by strengthening their market positions by having more than one product for customers to choose from when making a purchase decision. Line extensions piggyback on the reputation of existing brands and tend to be less costly than separate brands to introduce. Examples of line extensions can be found with soups, soft drinks, cars, detergents, breads and bakery products, wine coolers, and textbooks.

The risk for marketers is the see-saw relationship where no new customers, or only a scattering of them are attracted to the product line and demand shifts from the existing product to the extension. The marketer is left with a more costly product because economical production volumes are not attainable with any product version in the line and greater inventory costs are usually incurred. As an example, suppose a peach-flavoured wine cooler is introduced to the market. The purpose of the new flavour is to attract new customers to the line of wine coolers, the assumption being that the existing flavours did not attract these customers. There is also the possibility that certain individuals may not want to buy a product that everyone else buys.[4]

In pricing the line extension, a marketer must take into account the interlinkage between substitute products. Obviously, the differences in price of substitute products in a company's line strongly influence the proportions in which they are sold. If there are no discernible differences then the higher-priced item will lose sales to the lower-priced one. Cross-price elasticity (CPE) of demand measures the competition between two specific items by comparing the percentage change in the sales of one item with the percentage change in the price of the second item:

$$\text{CPE} = \frac{X_1/X_1}{P_2/P_2}$$

where: X_1/X_1 is the percentage change in sales of product 1 and P_2/P_2 is the percentage change in price of product 2.

If cross-price elasticity is positive then the products are substitutes. Complementary products, on the other hand, produce negative elasticity. The higher the proportion, the greater the intensity of competition between the two selected items. Suppose, for purposes of illustration, a line extension priced 10 per cent below the existing product produces a 15 per cent reduction in sales of the latter. Cross-price elasticity is calculated to be 1.5 and the two products can be considered to be substitutes.

Since price is not the only variable in the marketing mix, the other interdependencies, namely advertising or promotional effort and distribution, need to be considered. For advertising the formula for computing cross elasticity is as follows:

$$CAE = \frac{X_1/X_2}{A_2/A_2}$$

where: X_1/X_2 is the percentage change in sales of product 1 and A_2/A_2 is the percentage change in advertising of product 2.

Unlike the case of price, when cross advertising is positive then the product in question is complementary, and when it is negative then product 2 is a substitute for the product 1. The same implications hold true for distribution. Therefore, if cross elasticity is positive for all of a substitute product's three elements (price, advertising, and distribution), then the product does affect the sales of another product in the line, just because it is a substitute. Conversely, if cross elasticity is negative for price and positive for advertising and distribution then the product is considered complemetary.

The objective in setting prices for the entire product line is to maximize profit contribution. This makes it extremely important for the marketing manager to be fully conscious of the potential adverse effects of substitute products. Marketing management must know the degree of potential risk in adding a substitute product to the line. The substitute product will cause some customers to switch from the existing product because of lower price, but it will also increase the customer base with sales to new customers. If switch sales are greater than incremental sales, the substitute product will subtract from profitability. If, on the other hand, incremental sales are greater than switch sales then the substitute product will add to profitability.

In setting up the different pricing levels for a product line composed of substitutes, the marketing manager should get the answers to several relevant questions:

1. What is achieved by adding a substitute product or in developing an entire line of substitute products?
2. What is the actual and/or potential demand for each of the substitute product levels?
3. What is the interlinkage between the substitute products in terms of shifts in demand?
4. What are the common costs and incremental costs for each of the substitute product levels?
5. What is the price-feature differentiation between products?

END-ITEMS AND IN-BETWEEN ITEMS

In setting the pricing points for a line of substitute products, the marketing manager must (1) establish price differences that make sense to the

Pricing: Policies and Procedures

potential customer and (2) contribute to the interests of the selling company, particularly in terms of profit gain and market position. It is obvious
that optimizing individual prices for items in a product line does not get the
job done. The best approach is to consider individual prices simultaneously. It is also obvious that to make sense to the potential customer
there must be some relationship between the features and/or benefits of
each individual item and that item's price relative to the other items in the
line. In other words, the answer to a potential customer's questions concerning the differences must be more than price. Ideally the features/
benefits dimension should be structured in terms of primary buying criteria.

The first step in analysing prices or proposed prices for a product line is
to relate the prices or proposed prices of individual items to a dimensioning
of features/benefits. To illustrate, suppose six minicomputer models are
arrayed in terms of a defined measure of performance such as speed,
memory or capacity, compatibility, and upgradability (see Figure 8.1).

Figure 8.1   Hypothetical example of price versus performance for a line of minicomputers

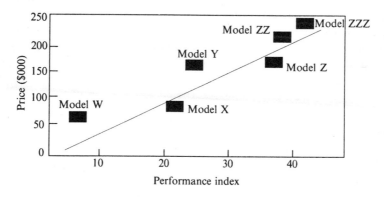

A plotting of the six minicomputer models in terms of price and performance shows that four are overpriced in relation to performance and particularly vulnerable to substitution by the two underpriced models. The most
vulnerable is probably model W. Positioned as it is, it will certainly lose
sales to a higher-priced in-between item that delivers more performance
value per dollar. Thus it does not fulfil its intended role as an end-item.

The second step is to estimate the total profit contribution if model X is
substituted for model W or Y, and model Z is substituted for model ZZ or
ZZZ. Assuming the profit contribution is 10 per cent of the selling price for

the three low-priced models, and 25 per cent of the selling price for the three higher-priced models, the substitution trade-offs are as follows:

Model X ($90,000) for model Y ($160,000)
$9,000 for $16,000 = $7,000 *loss*
Model X ($90,000) for model W ($50,000)
$9,000 for $5,000 = $4,000 *gain*
Model Z ($175,000) for model ZZ ($225,000)
$43,750 for $56,250 = $12,500 *loss*
Model Z ($175,000) for model ZZZ ($240,000)
$43,750 for $60,000 = $16,250 *loss*

With a highly sophisticated, well-informed customer, it is apparent is that the pricing scheme for the line will have disastrous results. A better alignment would be to raise the prices for models X and Z, and drop model ZZ from the product line. The relationship of model W to model X is out of line, even though the potential substitution is positive, because model W is not performing its role as an end-product. It must be remembered that the lowest-priced item is the most visible price in the marketplace and a way of attracting customers to the line who may possibly upgrade later. In this particular situation, the price of model W should be lowered if that product faces competition. If there is little or no competition for model W, then the price of model X should be raised. It might also be wise from a marketing standpoint to raise the price of model ZZZ because potential customers will assume more quality with the highest-priced items, even though this may not be true. Thus, instead of pricing along a proportionate line as *ab*, the marketing manager may want to raise the price of both end-items, such as is shown by line a_ib_i in Figure 8.2.

After setting the prices for the end-items, the next step is to price the inbetween items or to set the differentials between adjacent items. Usually

Figure 8.2 Two different approaches to pricing a line of products in relation to benefits/use

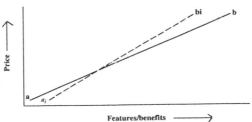

prices are justified as shown in Figures 8.1 and 8.2 by a measure of a discernible step-up in features/benefits. Features/benefits should relate directly to primary buying criteria. What contributes to inbetween prices being both equitable and reasonable is some relationship between increasing features/benefits and cost. However, the price differentials should not be too small or too large. Small price differentials do not pose clear and distinct alternatives, while large price gaps provide an opportunity for competition. It is also important to monitor sales continually to determine if and where sales concentrate.

REFERENCES

1.   Bill Saparito 'The Tough Cookie at RJR Nabisco', *Fortune*, vol. **118** (18 July 1988) pp. 32–46.
2.   Raymond Serafin 'U.S. Cars Build Share with Value Pricing', *Advertising Age* (12 July 1993) p. 41.
3.   An interview with Al Ries reported in 'The Mind is the Ultimate Battlefield', *Journal of Business Strategy*, vol. 9 (July/August 1988) pp. 4–7.
4.   Ibid.

9 Pricing over the Product Life Cycle

> Experience has taught us it is not enough to invent a new product. The real payoff is to manage that brand with such loving care that it continues to thrive year after year in a changing marketplace. We don't believe in the 'life cycle' of products because if a brand dies, we have failed to do our job.
>
> The Tide product we are selling today is vastly different from the Tide product we introduced in 1947. It is different in its cleaning performance, sudsing characteristics, aesthetics, physical properties, and packaging. In total, there have been 55 significant modifications in this one brand during the first 30 years.
>
> (Edward G. Harness, Chairman of the Board, Procter & Gamble, in a speech to the annual marketing meeting, Conference Board, New York, 1977)

To keep an established brand healthy and growing over the long term, the successful marketer must continually improve the product and develop marketing plans to capitalize on these changes. In any business it is necessary to study the ever-changing consumer and to try to identify new trends in tastes, needs, environment, and living habits.

Based on a sound rationale and keeping things fairly simplistic, the product life cycle concept has influenced management thought and actions for almost thirty years. While there is debate over the stages of the life cycle and the nature of progression through the stages, almost everyone agrees on the basic premise of the life cycle, namely that products emerge, exist, and falter in terms of some time period. It is not uncommon today to hear the life cycle of a product is getting shorter.

CONCEPT OF THE PRODUCT LIFE CYCLE

The basic premise of the product life cycle is that a product, or in some cases a brand, passes through a number of identifiable stages after its introduction (Figure 9.1). Following introduction, growth is characterized by

Figure 9.1   Typical product life cycle

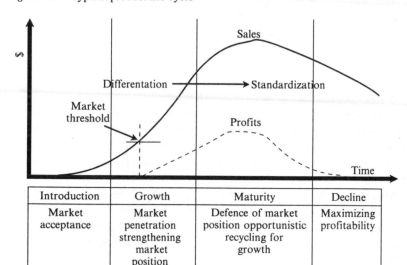

Introduction	Growth	Maturity	Decline
Market acceptance	Market penetration strengthening market position	Defence of market position opportunistic recycling for growth	Maximizing profitability

rapidly accelerating sales, the introduction of product variations, and product improvements and the emergence of profit. Maturity is character- ized as intensely competitive, with customers knowledgeable about the product which is often labeled a shelf item. The growth in sales slows and levels out. Maturity is followed by decline where sales have started to diminish, because the product has been displaced by newer introductions and/or changing market requirements.

As a product moves through the life cycle, the basis of competition shifts from performance that provides product differentiation to product stand- ardization and customer service. Product standardization, plus long pro- duction runs and experience in manufacturing, will usually result in lower manufacturing costs. However, in turn, greater competition will place downward pressures on price and increase the expenditure of funds for marketing and related services.

Managerial Implications

There are several reasons for the widespread acceptance of the product life cycle concept:

1. Management of a product over its life cycle increases the chances of maximizing profit from that product.

2. The life cycle provides a pattern of development to follow in developing new products.
3. The life cycle allows comparison of the profits possible through sustained product life (longer maturity) to the marketing impact from the introduction of a new product.

While the product life cycle will not fit all products, it does provide a basic conceptualization of product evolution, from entrance into the market, to possible product withdrawal. As such, it can be an effective management tool and of value to decision makers in regard to pricing decisions. First of all, use of the product life cycle gives marketers the opportunity to assess current market position, while at the same time keeping an eye open to what is necessary to ensure continued growth and success. Maturity, the most profitable stage of the product life cycle, is also the beginning of decreasing profitability as the typical responses to increased competition, price cuts, and larger expenditures for promotional spending erode profits. This dispels the common assumption that simply selling more will automatically lead to more profits.

Secondly, the life cycle concept provides a clear picture of the need for new products if profitability is to be maintained. Excess profits generated during the early stages of maturity should be invested in new or growing products. New products can be defined either as recycled products or as innovations in the maturity, or possibly the decline stages.

A third benefit from the use of the life cycle concept is unifying direction over the management of a product from when it is first introduced, through each successive stage. Competitive moves are made in relation to the patterns of sales and profits rather than to a set time frame. Instead of planning that is based on a span of elapsed time, timing is cued to the changes brought about by moving through the stages of improving the chances of extending a product's life to its economic maximum. For example, promotional pricing is best used in maturity to gain or keep market share.

Practical Limitations

While the patterns of product and human existence are remarkably similar, there is nothing predetermined about a product's life like there is about human life. Humans will die but products may not. Proof of this is the market tenure of Tide, with numerous modifications spread out over a life of nearly 50 years that have kept it a leading brand. What is predictable about a product is that it will age and enter the decline stage if management does nothing. The goals of marketing management are to move a product from introduction to growth to maturity, but not to decline. The transition to decline results from management inattention or ineffectiveness in extending maturity or rejuvenating growth.

Also, it is not necessarily true that the product life cycle is irreversible. All too often, marketing managers make decisions that hurry a product toward maturity and eventual decline. One of these is running out of technological innovations, and de-emphasis on technology as a way to rejuvenate growth. Additionally, it does not necessarily follow that products or brands will follow a clear and predictable sequence of life stages. A product may skip one or even two stages. One frequently encountered case is when a new product does not gain market acceptance and goes from introduction to decline. It is also possible that a new product will exhibit rapid growth immediately upon introduction and skip the growth stage. Then, too, recycling has been successfully done for both motorcycles and bicycles as late as the decline stage, contradicting the idea that the product life cycle is irreversible.

STAGES OF THE PRODUCT LIFE CYCLE

Introduction

Introduction, the first of the recognizable stages, can be characterized as a period of slow sales growth as the new product is introduced to the targeted market, and acceptance by a critical mass of consumers is sought. Because many new products fail, this stage can be considered critical. Because sales revenue is not adequate to cover developmental and introductory marketing costs, profits are not evident in introduction.

The strategic focus is on gaining market acceptance, principally through market awareness and product trial. There are two variations to the expected slow sales buildup (Figure 9.2). One is a very rapid sales growth once the product is introduced, which virtually eliminates the introduction stage as it is normally conceived. The market can be described as ready-made. Members of the targeted market made aware of the product through pre-introduction publicity place advance orders and eagerly buy up the product once it becomes available in the marketplace. Common examples are books by prominent authors, record albums and tapes by popular performers, and vaccines to prevent the spread of prevalent diseases. The other variation from a normal pattern of sales growth is new product failure, with sales starting to decline shortly after market entry.

Figure 9.2   Patterns of sales development upon market entry

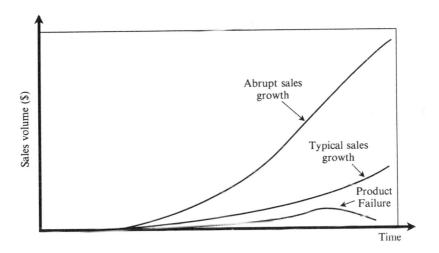

The price of a new product is set before it is introduced. Assuming a typical slow buildup of sales as portions of the targeted market are made aware of the new product, there are four important considerations in making the initial pricing decision. The first pertains to the question of distinctiveness. The distinctiveness gives the supplier a monopoly position as the sole supplier of a product, and, with no comparable alternatives, a premium price can be placed on the new product. However, distinctiveness disrupts consumer behaviour necessitating new learning requirements and value perceptions.

Consumers must perceive the benefits emanating from the features of the new product as having value. They must also perceive the supplier as a qualified source for a product of this type. Otherwise, the monopoly position of the supplier can not be exploited, and a lower price will have to be charged to overcome consumer resistance to change and to promote the perception of greater value from the new product.

A second consideration in developing an initial pricing strategy concerns whether market entry is to be full-scale, where the entire targeted market is exposed to the new product at the same time, or phased in on some basis such as geographical region. The latter permits greater flexibility, in that price changes can be made in accordance with consumer reactions in a particular area. The pricing process with a phased entry resembles a learning process in that market reaction to price is observed in a customer segment or geographical area, and changes are made, if necessary, prior to consumer introduction in the next designated phase. This process can be repeated over and over again as the total market is penetrated one step at a time.

A third consideration influencing the pricing strategy adopted for a new product is the cost and investment structure of the new product. The policy of the supplier on the length of the pay back period for investment in product development is a crucial determinant of the price that is set for a new product. If top management wishes to recover developmental costs quickly then the price will necessarily be higher because of the shorter pay-back period. High developmental and introduction costs may also lead to high prices, because top management will want to shorten the payback period to reduce risk.

Product cost structures will vary as the product moves through its life cycle. In the introduction stage production costs are unrealistic, with short production runs and numerous changes. As production volume increases, paralleling sales increases, unit costs recede as the result of economies of scale and experience. This reduction is partially offset by steady increases in marketing costs, particularly the need to maintain inventories. As a consequence, the threshold market share or the minimum level of market penetration that must be reached to obtain profitability with a product is of primary importance in setting initial prices.

A fourth consideration in developing a pricing strategy for new products is the goal orientation of its firm – cash flow (short-term) or market share (long-term). Prices of new products will necessarily be higher with a cash flow orientation, and the accompanying pressure for generation of funds, than when market share is the dominant influence.

Growth

In the growth stage, sales climb abruptly as acceptance is followed by purchase of the product by substantial numbers of the targeted market. Once a threshold market share (emergence of profitability) is attained, marketing management can turn its attention away from market penetration to strengthening its market position and building market share. This change is predicated on the expectation of increased competitive entries once the threshold has been attained.

In the early part of the growth stage, the demand generated through successful attainment of product acceptance must be matched with product availability. After the threshold market share is reached , the emphasis on distribution shifts to ways of counteracting the entry of competitors. This, typically, is accomplished by expanding the customer base – adding new customers, selling more to existing customers, and/or finding new uses for the product. The latter can bring in new customers, but, more importantly, it increases the value of the product for present customers, which can lead to increased sales.

Typically, new versions and features are added to appeal to new market segments. For example, a maker of microwave ovens who started with just one model progressed to eight with different combinations of twenty-one features including solid state controls, automatic memory levels, and an automatic temperature probe. Hartmann, who started out with one line of luggage, now has four lines at different pricing points.

The addition of new features provides the potential customer with an incremental product. An incremental product gives the customer the opportunity to add features, and in essence, create his or her own product. The range is from a low-end, low-priced version with no added features to a premium version with all the possible added features.

Limitations on the variety of options offered are the additional costs of manufacturing and warehousing, plus greater risk because of the difficulties in forecasting demand. One compromise is to group features into packages. Another is to package features in terms of product versions at different price levels.

Prices have to be set for the versions and features that can be selected. Pricing can also be utilized in strengthening market position for the product during the growth stage. These include, in addition to the customary trade discount structure, quantity discounts for both resellers and consumers, aggressive promotional pricing programmes, and what can be called loyalty discounts.

Most importantly quantity discounts encourage buying large quantities at the reseller level and passing on at least a portion of the savings to their customers. Aggressive promotional pricing can ward off competitors as they enter the market, and, in doing so, build a dominant competitive position. Loyalty discounts are ways of rewarding customers for repeat purchasing of the product. One example would be a price reduction coupon in each package that reduces the price of the next purchase.

Maturity

The maturity stage begins as sales growth slows perceptively. There are three recognizable phases in maturity.[1] In the first phase, growth maturity, sales growth slows as market expansion possibilities are exhausted. Distribution pipelines are saturated, and there are no new possibilities. Growth maturity is followed by stable maturity, where replacement sales constitute all or most of the market. Decaying maturity occurs when sales begin to decline as product obsolescence begins and portions of the market shift to newer products. The third phase marks the beginning of a decrease in profits for the product. Nowhere in the product life cycle is competition as intense as it is in maturity, particularly the first two phases where possibilities of market expansion are relatively small or non-existent.

Competition takes two forms in maturity.[2] It is most intense between products that are perceived as similar by the marketplace. A product of this type is usually termed a commodity; examples of include many agricultural products, paper products, plastics, and metals. A second form of competition occurs when products have differential advantages that match differences in the competitive environment. These differential advantages give products relative value within segments of the marketplace. Examples of such products include appliances, cars, and furniture.

When products are similar, the pressure is on pricing to create differences. As a general rule, the greater the degree of similarity between products, the greater the emphasis on pricing. Thus a lowest-price strategy is often followed with commodities to ease the price pressures, every effort is made to differentiate between sellers in terms of responsiveness to customers and flexibility of operation. When competing products have differential advantages, each product will compete in a segment of the total market. Pricing in this situation is an integral part of the marketing efforts to monopolize the distinct advantage within each competitive segment. Flexibility in pricing, as well as other marketing efforts, is essential to adapt to changes in the competitive segment.

Unlike other stages of the product life cycle, the length of time a product stays in maturity is substantially a result of marketing management efforts. The strategic focus in maturity is twofold. First, the position or market niche of the product must be defended against competing brands. This may involve product improvements as well as new approaches to customer service, promotion, and pricing. Second, marketing management must be alert to opportunities to recycle the product into a second growth stage. Usually recycling growth is in response to significant changes in technology or market structure and will involve substantially more investment and accompanying increased costs than simply product improvements to extend maturity.

Strategies for mature products may entail changes in the product itself, the market, and/or the marketing mix. It is useful to classify strategies for mature products in terms of change in the products themselves and the markets they compete in, as shown in Figure 9.3.

Figure 9.3   Possible strategies for mature products

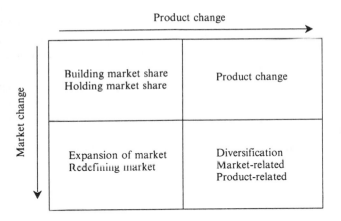

The least risk is encountered where there is no change involved with either product or market. Building strategies are aimed at increasing market share at the expense of competitors, or in other words taking business away from competitors. There are two occasions when marketing management will want to consider a building strategy. One is when market share is below the minimum necessary for viability. The other is when market share is above the minimum, but still less than the level necessary to yield satisfactory profitability. Examples of building strategies are market segmentation, repositioning, and redefining distribution.

Holding strategies, on the other hand, are designed to maximize the profits from maintaining present market share. Typically, holding strategies for companies with large market shares will be the direct opposites of those of their counterparts with small market shares. Finding new applications for a product, minor product adjustments, increased customer service, and premium pricing are holding strategies that have proven advantageous to companies with large market shares. Conversely, companies with small market shares rely primarily on pricing below the market. A holding strategy for both large and small market shareholders is seeking a mandatory consumption situation where purchase of the product is shifted from a voluntary to an involuntary status. Examples include seat belts, lead-free petrol, and smoke detectors.

A value-added strategy, whereby added services are bundled together with the principal product, could be considered a building or holding strategy. Value-added marketing for IBM means bundling IBM hardware together with software, service, and installation into a package that in all probability will be offered by an outside consulting or services firm. For Techimetrics, it means bundling free consultations and other services such as books and research reports into a complete service at a premium price.

When there is a change in the market but not in the product, the strategies are: market expansion, notably in geographical terms, redefining the market, and changing the focus from the product to the consumption system, of which the product is part. Some years ago Sherwin Williams redefined the market for paint and associate products as do-it-yourself. More recently, they have shifted to painting professionals. Makers of the so-called 'imitation' cheeses have redefined their market as institutions such as schools, fast-food chains, as well as the military establishment. Examples of the change from product to consumption system include lube stops and climate control systems.

Restyling and product improvement strategies are categorized as product change with no change in its market. Both of these present opportunities to increase prices. Diversification strategies that can be either manufacturing- or marketing-related bring about changes in both product and market. Diversification strategies are also the riskiest, because marketing management is dealing with change in both product and market. An example of a manufacturing-related diversification strategy is the development of a thermostatic control component for appliances by an electronics division of a car manufacturer. Disney's diversification into theme parks, all forms of related merchandise, and resorts is an example of marketing-related diversification.

Decline

In the decline stage, sales shrink steadily as the market is affected by product obsolescence, inability to continually meet customer expectations, shifting of demand to newer and better products, and changes in buyers' needs or desires. The extent to which reduced sales erode profitability depends upon (1) how readily competitors pull out of the market and (2) how fiercely the competitors who remain try to contain their shrinking sales.[3] The strategic focus in decline is on obtaining the highest possible profit.

The strategic options available to marketing management are deletion, divestment, harvesting, market leadership, and niche development. Pricing decisions play a formidable role in the latter three strategies. In adopting a harvesting strategy, the intention of marketing management is to maximize the remaining profits from a product that is irreversibly in decline. This can be accomplished by simultaneously raising prices and cutting marketing-related costs. The assumptions are that demand is inelastic and that related marketing efforts will not expand demand.

Pursuing a leadership strategy, marketing management attempts to establish the product as one of the few remaining of this type in the decline stage.[4] A firm seeking to establish a dominant position for its product usually adopt aggressive pricing tactics. Somewhat similar to the leadership strategy, a niche strategy identifies a segment of the market for a declining product that displays more stability or is declining at a slower rate than the overall market. Pricing with a niche strategy is at the point that maximizes the volume of sales.

PRICING STRATEGIES FOR PRODUCT LIFE CYCLE STAGES

Management of a product through its life cycle assumes distinctive strategies for each of the four stages. At the same time, consumers are changing as they gain familiarity with the product. Thus, as the product moves through introduction, growth, and maturity, the consumer gains familiarity through increasing amounts of exposure and experience. This in turn produces pricing discretion and the need for marketing support given to new products. Purchasing decisions become more price sensitive, and there is less reliance on marketing support programmes.

The marketing manager, in making pricing decisions, must take into account not only product evolution as patterned by the product life cycle, but also consumer evolution through experience that may or may not parallel product evolution. Customer relationships, once defined, can not be expected to last indefinitely, because the consumer is continually undergoing change through gaining experience.

At the same time as a product is moving from introduction through growth to maturity, the consumer is going through four possible stages of accumulated experience. This is shown in Figure 9.4.

Obviously, when the product is first introduced, the consumer has little experience with it. The greater the degree of innovativeness or differentiation from presently available products, the greater the latitude in pricing. This translates into premium prices for products given adequate marketing support. For consumer products, marketing support can include customer education regarding the differentiated features, service backup, and warranties. For industrial products the support tends to be technical assistance and applications. For both types of products, customer satisfaction is becoming the key element in the marketing of the product.

Figure 9.4   Product familiarity cycle

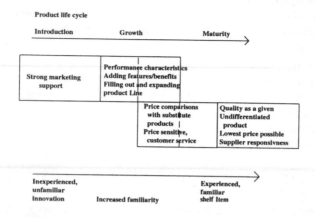

As the consumer gains experience and familiarity with the product, it is purchased primarily on the basis of its performance characteristics. Value is built into the product with the introduction of new versions, new features, and/or new applications. It should be noted that the experienced buyers control the market in terms of sales volume, even though many buyers of the product may be inexperienced. This stage of consumer evolution corresponds to the part of the growth stage before the entry of substantial numbers of competitors.

The availability of substitute products, coupled with increasing consumer familiarity, pushes prices downward. Marketing support is also subject to price comparisons. This stage of consumer evolution overlaps the latter part of a product's growth stage and the early part of its maturity. With the push towards standardization to provide more flexibility in pricing, the market assumes the profile of an experienced consumer buying an undifferentiated product or commodity. Consumers will unbundle the product feature/benefit package and delete the features not related to their dominant buying needs. For both consumer and industrial products, adequate quality replaces superlative quality and the lowest possible prices are sought. For industrial products, on the other hand, consumers will also seek quality assurance and supplier responsiveness to production schedules.

Introductory Pricing

A major shortcoming of conventional price theory is the focus on the short term, and the generation of instantaneous profit flow. Nowhere is this more apparent than in the introduction stage. Pricing should be based on profit attainment throughout some planning period such as the product life cycle, at least to late maturity. Looking ahead, even the most innovative product will eventually be matched against competition. Ideally, then, the price set for a new product is based on an analysis of market conditions and associated costs, both production and marketing, over the product's projected life cycle and not just at market entry.

At the onset, the market situation resembles a monopoly. As the sole supplier of the product, a premium pricing strategy can be adopted. However, as growth is sought and market share stabilizes, the price premium declines with the entry of competition. Initially, competitors will tend to price at about the same premium level. Subsequent competitors, however, will tend to enter at a lower price with variations in quality. Examples of the latter are the clones of the IBM PC and the PING golf club. Production costs will decline as experience is gained and it becomes possible to take advantage of the economies associated with increasing volume of output.

New product pricing strategies can be characterized as skimming or premium price and penetration or low price. If we go one step further, both strategies can be classified in terms of rapid and slow.[4] A rapid-skimming strategy features a premium price and a high level of promotional effort to accelerate market awareness and penetration. A slow-skimming strategy features a high price and a low level of promotional effort to keep introductory costs down. Likewise, it's possible to have a rapid-penetration strategy and a slow-penetration strategy.

Several considerations enter into the decision to select a skimming or penetration strategy. These include the following:

1. How innovative is the new product?
2. What is the price elasticity for the product?
3. What is the threshold market level?
4. What are the organizational constraints in terms of payback policy?

It is obvious that the level of innovativeness in a new product determines the amount of discretion the supplier has in pricing. As a general rule, the more innovative the product, the more the pricing situation resembles that of a monopoly. However, the more innovative a new product is, the greater is the necessity for increased promotional expenditures to convince consumers that the new distinctive product benefits have value. Thus, the premium price and the need for increased promotional effort offset each other. The additional revenue from the higher or premium price will have to be used to pay off the increased promotional spending.

Not all new products will be highly innovative, however. Most new products are developed as solutions to perceived market needs, because there is less risk in regard to the question of whether the new product can be successfully sold. These products can be classified as subject to market pull, while those involving the performance of a new function or the substitution of a new technology in an existing product (for example changing from electromechanical to solid state electronics) are classified as subject to technology push.[6]

The most innovative products are those for which there is no market in the strict sense of the term.[6] A good example is the overnight parcel delivery service developed in the USA by Federal Express. Examples of new products offered to established markets are paper diapers, plastics of various forms, optic fibres, and solid-state electronics. Somewhat less innovative are new products for currently served markets. Cordless power tools and compact discs are examples of this level of innovation.

Less innovative, and presenting far less pricing discretion, are product line extensions, product improvements and modifications, and restyling. The tendency is to use penetration pricing for these new products simply because value perceptions for the general type of product are well established. Therefore, a 'big-screen' television set, a lawn-mower with guaranteed starting, and a restyled car are likely to be priced lower just because they represent less innovation. Use of a skimming price is risky because the degree of innovation may not match up with existing value perceptions. In other words, the market may perceive the change as an inducement to buy but not worth an added increase in price.

The optimal pricing strategy for a particular stage of the product life cycle depends upon the relative magnitude of the demand and cost factors from introduction, through growth, and into maturity. Nowhere is this more apparent than in making the initial pricing decision. There are two diametrically opposing views on price sensitivity over the product life cycle. The more traditional view sees price elasticity increasing through maturity. In other words, buyers of new products are less sensitive to price than are later buyers of the product in question. Undoubtedly the innovativeness of the new product overcomes price considerations and a skimming price policy can be adopted.

The opposite view sees price sensitivity decreasing from a high on introduction through growth, to a minimum in maturity. Accordingly, the chances of gaining or losing a customer are much greater when it is first introduced. Because the product represents less of an innovative change and substitutes already exist. In the marketplace both Toyota and Honda used a penetration price with a standard, no-frills car to gain market acceptance for their respective brand names in the US market. Once market acceptance was obtained, prices were raised for an expanded and enhanced product line.

With every new product there is a minimum or threshold share of the market that must be earned for it to be profitable. For example, Lockheed originally estimated sales of 300 L-1011s to reach the threshold share. Inflation was to push this to 500 planes, but actual sales were to be significantly lower, resulting in the company losing $2.5 billion.

The threshold market share can be viewed as a breakeven point and as such is cost driven. The breakeven point (BEP) by definition is equal to fixed costs (FC) divided by contribution (C): BEP = FC/C. Contribution is equal to the price/unit (*P*) less the variable cost/unit (VC): C = P − VC. Thus BEP is a function of the chosen price and the related costs of the product. Knowing the fixed costs and the variable costs per unit, the marketing manager can insert various price levels into the equation. Suppose fixed costs are $10,000 and variable costs are $20/unit, the BEP for a price of $40 would be 500 units. If the price is $30, the necessary number of units to breakeven would be $1,000.

The next step is to take this information and combine it with other data such as sales estimates, predictions on price elasticity, and company policy on paybacks on investments. Continuing on with the example, suppose the sales estimate for the first year is 1,200 units, there is a probability that price sensitivity will be high (with comparable products already on the market priced in the high $20 range), and a company policy exists that calls for no more than a period of one and a half years to recover investment. Without going into a detailed solution, it is obvious that a price of $30 or more fits company policy on recovery of new-product investment, provides a margin of safety in regard to estimated sales, and allows for price reductions to increase volume.

Another way to compute the price of a product is to let the sales estimate (S) or some adjustment of the sales estimate equal BEP. The price equation will read

$$P = \frac{FC}{S} + VC.$$

Using the sales estimate from the above example, the price at BEP is

$$P = \frac{\$10,000}{1,200} + \$20$$

$$= \$ 8.34 + \$20$$

$$= \$28.34$$

If a safety margin of 25 per cent is used, sales are reduced to 900 units and the price is

$$P = \frac{\$10,000}{900} + \$20$$

$$= 11.11 + \$20$$

$$= \$31.11$$

Company policies will set parameters for the marketing manager in setting an introductory price on the new product. Obviously, the most important is the policy on recovery of costs associated with the new product. The more conservative is management, the shorter is the recovery period, and necessarily the higher is the introductory price. Also inflating the initial price is the existence of company policy, explicit or implied, on minimum gross margins. Finally, there may be a policy, usually implied, on the approach to pricing. Some companies will want to start high and institute a series of discounts. Others will want to start low and make increases later.

Growth Pricing

One of the important aspects of pricing in the subsequent stages of the product life cycle, and in particular the growth stage, is to take full advantage of the differences in profitability and opportunity at different stages of market development. Early growth is characterized by building upon market acceptance gained in introduction. Sales increase abruptly as distribution pipelines are filled to meet demand. The overriding concern is to match demand with supply. Usually there is no incentive to cut prices, but once the threshold market share has been obtained, rapidly increasing profitability and continued rapid growth attract competitors. By not cutting price and failing to take advantage of the cost economies of production volume and cumulative experience, an umbrella is created under which competitors can enter the market and still be profitable with smaller market shares. These competitors, with necessarily lower margins, will be strongly motivated to gain market share at the expense of the firm that entered the market with the new product. Thus, the decision to not cut prices can be seen as trading current profits for long-run market share.

With a durable product, as adoption increases, the size of the untapped market decreases, unless the customer base is expanded. With a non-durable product, the market is divided up into triers and non-triers. Conversion of nontriers into triers decreases the number of non-triers, but increases the potential for repeat purchases.

From the perspective of sustaining growth, an initial skimming price strategy should be followed by price reductions in the growth stage if demand is stable and production costs decrease with volume. Insufficient price reductions in relation to decreases in production cost during growth create an umbrella for entry of competitors. Competition can help develop the market, but too much often leads to steep, unadvisable price cuts in early maturity as an industry shake-out begins.

Low initial prices are optimal in growth if there is a relatively high repeat purchase rate for non-durables, or if the demand for a durable follows a diffusion process. In both cases low price serves as a promotional device. For durable products, a low price can promote more rapid diffusion of the product. A low price for non-durables increases the rate of repeat purchase by triers. When there is an insignificant repeat purchase market, low introductory prices are less frequently employed.

Maturity Pricing

Pricing strategy in maturity can be characterized as competitively oriented as firms battle over market share. The number of competitors attracted by growth opportunities and the high margins possible under the pricing umbrella can be sizeable. In the housewares industry, it is not uncommon to find 20 to 40 hopefuls entering during growth. Twenty years ago, IBM had 20 competitors: now it faces more than 5,000. The markets cannot support all these firms, so what follows in maturity is a shake-out period with extensive price cutting not only by the firm that pioneered the new product as its technology advantage erodes, but also by late entrants who buy into the market by cutting prices on compatible products.

As a product matures, its competitive differential erodes as competitors bring out compatible and innovative products. For example, Toshiba which at one time virtually owned the market for high-performance laptops, has seen its market share drop as competitors have introduced considerably less expensive and less well-engineered products. At the same, time the effect of experience and scale economies on unit costs and prices becomes less evident. With market saturation come reduced levels of capacity utilization and higher production costs.

Making the market more intensely competitive, customers are more familiar with the product and have become better judges of differentiations between brands. The resulting blurring of differentiations other than price places enormous pressures on price as a competitive effort.

While maturity is usually the longest stage of the product life cycle,it is important in pricing strategy to underestimate its duration rather than try to extend it. By considering a shorter period, productive capacity can be held to the level of replacement and working capital commitments can be limited to the reduced levels. This in turn helps to eliminate the over-capacity that precipitates price cuts and eventually price wars.

What a firm wants to avoid a position where the only option is to slash prices to obtain sales. This in turn necessitates cuts in costs; Apple's gross margin, for example, has declined from 53 per cent in 1990 to 38 per cent in 1993.

The role of price as an integral part of the marketing mix, along with product, promotion, and distribution, is nowhere as important as it is in the maturity stage. Not only must price be consistent with the other elements as part of an integral marketing programme directed toward maintaining or improving marketing share; its relative leverage must be compared with other elements to determine how it can be used to the best advantage in support of the total mix. Knowing the sales response to units of input of the various elements of the marketing mix, the marketing manager can deter-mine whether it is best to invest additional money in advertising, product performance or quality, or to cut prices. For example, it might be found that a product would benefit more from increased spending on advertising and product improvement from than further price cuts.

Firms compete with each other by emphasizing different elements of the marketing mix in seeking an advantage. One basic kind of competi-tive advantage is cost leadership, where a firm such as Anheuser-Busch sets out to be the low-cost producer in its industry. With a low-cost position, such a firm has both more flexibility in pricing and more funds available to spend on other elements of the marketing mix. With differ-entiation, a firm seeks a unique product along dimensions that are widely valued by buyers. If differentiation is an added cost then dif-ferentiation as a strategy is a high-cost position. On the other hand, if differentiation allows the setting of premium prices this will increase revenues, and/or if differentiation increases market share this will push down production costs.

An example of successful implementation of charging premium prices for a differentiated product is Callaway Golf. Today, Callaway Golf paced by Big Bertha Drivers is the leader in sales in the USA

While a low-pricing policy is typically followed by cost leaders, and premium pricing is usually associated with differentiation, a policy of reasonable pricing results from simultaneously following both. Whirlpool, whose appliances are superior in quality and yet priced below the market, is a good example of this hybrid strategy.

Decline Pricing

Unless a product can be revitalized, either by recycling or by extending maturity, decline is inevitable. The best product strategy for many firms is to invest in the early stages of development, attain a dominant position in the marketplace, and hold on long enough in maturity to disinvest before the product reaches decline. Unfortunately this means using production costs as the sole basis of pricing.

The use of cost-based pricing ignores the fact that premium prices can often be used to increase profitability in decline, even though there are fewer customers to serve and smaller quantities to produce. Factors that favour a premium price policy include:

1. segments of loyal customers,
2. highly valued brand name,
3. significant market share, and
4. substantial distribution network.

When premium pricing is not feasible, then a policy of stable prices is the most appropriate to take advantage of cost-cutting opportunities such as efficient operation of a plant at less than capacity. Above all, a marketing manager will want to avoid competitive price-cutting that tends to accelerate decline and rapidly erode profits. In markets where firms are dropping out and thus decreasing competition, it may be profitable to decrease prices minimally to attract customers stranded by the reduction in competition.

REFERENCES

1.   Philip Kotler *Marketing Management*, 7th ed (Englewood Cliffs, NJ: Prentice-Hall, 1991).

2.	Bruce D. Henderson 'The Anatomy of Competition', *Journal of Marketing*, vol. **47** (Spring 1983) pp. 7–11.
3.	Rudie Kathryn Harrigan and Michael Porter 'End-Game Strategies For Declining Industries', *Harvard Business Review*, vol. **61** (July–August 1983) pp. 111–120.
4.	F. Stewart DeBruicker and Georgory L. Summe 'Make Sure Your Customers Keep Coming Back', *Harvard Business Review*, vol. **63** (January–February 1985) pp. 92–98.
5.	Eugene F. Finkin 'Developing and Managing New Products', *Journal of Business Strategy*, vol. **3** (Spring 1983) pp. 39–46.
6.	Donald F. Heany 'Degree of Product Innovation', *Journal of Business Strategy*, vol. **3** (Spring 1983) pp. 3–14.

10 Geographic Pricing Practices

> Shippers, in the last four years, have been able to cut more than $25 billion from the annual freight costs. In 1984, these costs accounted for 6.8 per cent of the gross national product, a figure lower than the 8 per cent which prevailed in 1981. Part of the reduction is due to changes taking place in the nation's industrial profile, but many of the gains are resulting from increased efficiency in transportation. How much of the money saved on freight actually benefits consumers, is not certain. It is estimated, however, that perhaps $10 billion of the freight savings are reflected in lower retail prices.
>
> (Daniel Machalaba, 'More Companies Push Freight Haulers to Get Better Rates, Service', *Wall Street Journal*, 12 December 1985, p. 1 courtesy of Dow Jones & Company Inc.)

Transportation costs are an important consideration in the pricing of most products. The basic question is whether to absorb the costs of getting the product to the customer or to pass the cost along to the customer as a noted extra to the price of the product. Transportation costs and how they are treated relative to pricing also affect the extent of the geographical market served by the seller, the ability to compete beyond the local market on a price basis, as well as the ability to adopt and promote a specific resale price. Thus the policy a manufacturer adopts is an important one. Pricing practices regarding the aspects of transportation can be categorized as geographical or delivered.

GEOGRAPHICAL PRICING SYSTEMS

One of the simplest methods of handling transportation charges is to pass them on to the buyer. An 'FOB (free on board) factory', 'FOB origin', 'FOB mill', and 'FOB name of city' are all terms that denote that the legal title to the merchandise passes on to the buyer at the point of origin. This means that the buyer is responsible for the following:

Cost of freight The buyer bears the freight cost from the point of origin, be it the manufacturer's loading dock or the carrier's shipping dock. The buyer also selects the mode of transportation, and chooses the specific carrier. He may also use his own private transportation equipment to carry the merchandise to its destination.

Risk The buyer is responsible for the merchandise. If loss, damage, theft, or fire should arise during shipment, the buyer is responsible for filing transportation damage claims with the shipper.

Thus, the FOB term designates the point at which title to a shipment passes from the seller to a buyer. Along with the title, other responsibilities including freight and cost are also passed on to the buyer. Under this shipping term, the manufacturer realizes a number of advantages, which may include the following:

1. Realizing the same net return on all sales, regardless of where the buyer is located geographically.
2. Relief from the responsibility of handling the transportation function, including selection of the transportation mode, choosing the specific carrier, handling any damage claims that may arise during shipments, and paying the freight bills associated with the shipment.
3. Predicting future revenues, because pricing is the same for all *sales* of products sold under the same circumstances.

From the point of view of fairness, it could be argued that FOB factory is the best method for allocating freight charges. Every buyer pays exactly the actual costs from the factory to his warehouse. No buyer is discriminated against, and none subsidized regarding the freight charges they pay. The problem with FOB factory pricing, however, is that when it is practiced the manufacturer runs the risk of limiting his geographic market. Customers who are located closer to competitors will be lost; this is particularly true when the products are highly standardized. Producers of bulky, low-value commodities face this type of geographic limitation.

Even where product differential does exist, the use of the FOB factory term will create the problems attendant on one customer paying more than another for a product. This in turn limits the area in which a firm can be competitive, and in effect closes the door on national distribution. Only when transportation costs are a small portion of the product's value, as it is with high-value electronic products, is FOB factory used to a great extent.

Because of geographic market limitations inherent in using FOB factory, that is, where distant markets remain closed to a manufacturer since they are protected by high freight costs, the need for other geographic pricing systems becomes evident. Their main purpose is to reduce the geographic market limitation drawback of FOB factory, and allow the manufacturer to compete in a distant market.

FOB Factory, Freight Prepaid

This is the simplest and most direct way of attaining the objective of pricing equality between customers regardless of their geographic location. Under this arrangement the manufacturer quotes a uniform price to all dealers regardless of location, and prepays all freight charges. The dealer receives the merchandise without having to pay the shipper. However, since this term is still FOB factory in principle, the title to the merchandise technically transfers to the buyer at the point of origin. The manufacturer, however, may perform the services of selecting the mode of transportation, choosing the carrier, filing transportation damage claims for customers, and undertaking other types of services, thus exceeding his legal responsibility.

All the buyers who purchase the same product under the same circumstances are charged the same price. The seller, as a result, receives a different net return from each sale because of the different amounts of freight costs involved in shipping the products to buyers located in different geographic areas of the market. The differences in serving customers in different geographical locations can be accounted for in two ways.

Freight charges to all the marketing locations served by the seller are averaged. To illustrate, assume a manufacturer of appliances is selling refrigerators in an extensive geographical area. The base price for the refrigerator is set at $300. The average freight cost for shipping a refrigerator to each of the 150 local markets, in this case $30, is added to the base price. The resulting price of $330 becomes the uniform price quoted by the manufacturer to buyers in any part of the market.

When a weighted-average method is used, each location in the market is weighted by its respective volume of sales importance. To illustrate, suppose a manufacturer sells his refrigerator in only three markets: distant, intermediate, and local. If the cost of shipping a refrigerator to each market is $50, $30, and $10, respectively, and if the distant market accounts for 20 per cent of sales, the intermediate market for 30 per cent of sales, and the local market for 50 per cent of sales, the calculation would be as indicated in Table 10.1. Normally, an error or contingency factor is added to the calculations to cover unexpected circumstances that result in higher transportation costs.

Balancing out freight to all locations, the manufacturer absorbs freight cost on sales to distant buyers, and at the same time overcharges freight to nearby customers, realizing what is known as 'phantom freight'. Distant

Table 10.1   FOB factory freight prepaid calculation of price using a
weighted-average method

	Distant market	Intermediate market	Local market
Actual freight cost	$50	$30	$10
Percentage of sales of total sales	20	30	50
Average freight	$10	+ $9	+ $5 = $24

buyers pay less than their share of the actual cost of delivery, while closely
located customers pay more than their share – a fact that may prompt some
to assume that this pricing method discriminates between buyers.

FOB Factory, Freight Allowed

The similarity between this approach and than of FOB freight prepaid is
obvious. Like the latter, the seller's responsibility ends at the point of
origin, even though he/she bears the freight costs. Unlike the latter, the
buyer is allowed to deduct actual freight costs from the invoice. The principle with both is the absorption of freight costs on deliveries to distant markets and the overcharging of freight costs on deliveries to more closely
located customers.

Assume the manufacturer of refrigerators also produces automatic washers. He would like to charge a base price of $200 for each. If he were to use
an FOB factory freight allowed term, he would have to calculate the average freight allowed for all the transactions in the markets where he is
involved. If we assume for purposes of simplicity that he is selling his
washers in three markets: distant, intermediate, and local, and that the
freight costs are $30, $20, and $10, respectively. Using a simple average
the stipulated uniform price is $220 (Table 10.2).

Suppose that a buyer in the distant market orders a washer. When he
receives it he pays the shipper $30 in transportation charges. When the
manufacturer's invoice for $220 is received, the buyer deducts the $30
freight from the amount of the invoice and remits the balance of $190. The
manufacturer absorbs the $10 difference. On the other hand, if a buyer in
the local market orders a washer, he will pay the shipper a freight charge of
$10. When he receives the invoice of $220, he deducts the $10 freight
charge paid earlier, and submits to the manufacturer the balance of $210. A
phantom freight charge of $10 is realized by the manufacturer in this case.

Table 10.2   FOB factory freight allowed calculation of price using a simple-average method

	Distant market	Intermediate market	Local market
Actual freight cost	$30	$20	$10
Average freight factor	$\dfrac{\$30 + \$20 + \$10}{3} = \$20$		
Uniform price for washer = $200 + $20 = $200			

It is hoped that when this system is used, the phantom freight is enough to equalize the losses in freight due to selling at loss to distant buyers.

FOB/Factory, Freight Equalized

At the outer limits of the market, a seller will experience severe competition from suppliers located nearer the buyer. To combat this competitive situation, the seller may use a form of freight absorption to reduce the transportation differential by agreeing to share the freight cost. The proportion of transportation the seller agrees to absorb is dependent upon negotiations between the buyer and the seller. The posture of the seller remains the same as with other factory terms; that is, the buyer assumes the responsibility once the merchandise has left the factory. The seller, however, attempts to maintain equality between buyers in terms of a uniform delivered price regardless of buyer location.

To illustrate, assume that a manufacturer of furniture is selling dining-room furniture nationally. He decides on a base price of $900 for each set of dining-room furniture. If he uses an FOB factory freight equalized term, he must consider all his markets, the freight cost to each, and the proportion he is willing to absorb of these costs (Table 10.3). The seller's portion of actual freight charges amounts to $50, $10, and $0 dollars, respectively. This means that he has to charge an extra $20 on each sale to cover the absorbed freight factor. The uniform price therefore would be $920. Table 10.4 shows how much buyers in each market end up paying for each dining-room set, if there is an equal number of buyers in each market area.

Advantages of factory pricing systems include the ability to extend the geographic boundaries of an individual seller's market to a national scale. Also, because these systems are quoted as FOB factory, they technically relieve the manufacturer of the burden of handling the transportation

Table 10.3   FOB factory freight equalized calculation of price using a simple-average method

	Distant market	Intermediate market	Local market
Actual freight cost	$100	$50	$40
Proportion the seller agrees to absorb	50%	20%	0%
Seller's portion of freight cost	$50	$10	$0

$$\text{Freight factor} = \frac{\$50 + \$10 + \$0}{3} = \$20$$

Table 10.4   FOB factory freight equalized landed cost for each buyer

	Distant market	Intermediate market	Local market
Uniform price	$920	$920	$920
Actual freight	100	50	40
Total	1,020	970	960
Seller's subsidy	−50	−10	−0
Landed cost	$970	$960	$960

problem, and any other complications that may arise during the transportation process. Furthermore, the stipulated uniform price allows the seller to feature the uniform price in a nation-wide advertising campaign, because landed costs to dealers are virtually the same. The simplicity of this system of pricing is also an advantage.

A major limitation of geographic factory pricing terms relates to possible negative effects on a manufacturer's competitive position in the local or nearby markets. Since these customers will in effect subsidize the shipments to more distant buyers, they will have to pay more for freight than is actually the case. The local customers, realizing this, may opt for their own transportation to pick up the products at the factory. This, in turn, will upset the cost calculations. Another disadvantage is the difficulty of forecasting sales by area to arrive at the necessary data for calculating delivered prices.

DELIVERED PRICING SYSTEMS

Unlike FOB origin, delivered pricing means that the manufacturer is responsible for the merchandise until it reaches the buyer. As such, the manufacturer must choose the mode of transportation, select the carrier, handle any damage claims, and pay the freight bills.

Delivered Pricing – Zone Systems

Single-zone

Under the single-zone or 'postage stamp' pricing system, a uniform delivered price is applied to the whole market regardless of where the buyer is located geographically. With this system, the actual freight cost on individual transactions is completely disregarded and an average freight factor is added to the price of a product. The manufacturer absorbs freight costs on shipments to distant buyers and overcharges freight to closely located buyers.

Multiple-zone

The market is divided up into zones, each with a uniform price. To determine the delivered price for a zone the seller takes into account shipping charges to that zone as well as such variables as competitive position in that particular submarket. Generally large, highly competitive markets will be subsidized by the seller absorbing a portion of the actual freight costs. Some offset will be attained by charging more in smaller, less competitive areas.

Assume a papermill in the US charges $500 for a truckload of certain paper products. The company located on the East Coast maintains three zones: East Coast, Midwest, and West Coast. To determine the price for each zone, the mill averages the freight to various buyers in each zone, and within each zone. For purposes of illustration, assume only one freight charge for each zone. If actual freight rates in the example are $100, $150, and $230 respectively for the East Coast zone, the Midwest zone, and the West Coast zone, the papermill is at a disadvantage in competing outside the East Coast. Further aggravating the problem, 50 per cent of sales emanate from the Midwest zone, 30 per cent from the West Coast zone, and the remainder or 20 per cent from the East Coast.

Using a weighted average ($164) would only worsen the papermill's competitive position in the largest part of its market. Therefore, management sets a freight charge of $120 for the Midwest zone and $150 for the

West Coast zone. The freight rate is kept at $100 or actual rate for the East coast. The uniform prices in each of the zones would be $600, $620, and $650

While the setting of uniform prices in this fashion is arbitrary to some extent, it does have a number of advantages. The most important is the expansion of the seller's market. It forces the seller to recognize the changes that must be met if he or she hopes to be competitive. This is especially true when transportation costs are relatively significant for the products in question. A second advantage is simplicity. Salespeople can quote prices to a customer without resorting to the tedious process of checking transportation modes and rates. In turn the buyer knows exactly what the landed cost will be for the products ordered.

Another advantage is the possibility of featuring a suggested resale price in regional and/or national advertising. Finally, arbitrary allocation of freight charges permits the seller to capitalize on his strengths and combat competition.

Offsetting these advantages, the seller must continually monitor each of his or her markets. Another disadvantage may be a reduction in gross margin as the seller absorbs freight costs to expand geographically. Another problem that can have serious connotations is the possible discrimination between buyers located near the boundary lines of zones. One buyer may get a lower price than another closely located buyer simply because they are in different zones.

Delivered Pricing – Basing-point Systems

Basing point systems unlike other systems of delivered pricing rely upon common agreement of the members of an industry. The objective of basing-point systems is to ensure that customers in any geographical locality pay the same freight costs regardless of who the supplier is and where the products originate. Under a single-point or multiple-basing-point system there is no relationship between actual freight costs incurred and freight charges paid by the buyer. Some buyers will pay more than the actual freight charges, while others will pay less. Freight charges in excess of actual costs incurred are called phantom freight. Phantom freight has been declared illegal.

Under this system there is no relationship between actual freight costs incurred and freight charges paid by the buyer, that is, the invoiced freight is not a reflection of the actual charges. Some buyers pay over and above the actual freight incurred. This excess is called phantom freight. Other buyers pay less than actual charges with the difference absorbed by the seller. Since the manufacturer has no control over where the orders come from, it is hoped that the system will yield enough phantom freight to counterbalance losses resulting from so-called freight absorption.

Basing point pricing has been used where products are homogeneous and transportation costs are a substantial part of total costs of acquiring the product. Examples would include iron and steel, sugar and corn products, lumber products, and cement. In the scattered instances where basing-point systems are used today, multiple basing points are used rather than a single point.

11 Retail Pricing

> One of the myths of retailing is that a customer's major reason for buying is price. Each retailer has a 'selling proposition'. That's the sum of all the parts that lead to the ultimate sale, for example, pre-sale advertising, the customer visiting the store, and after-sale service. These add up to value perceived – the richness of the shopping experience. Price is part of the equation, but not the total factor.
>
> (Clark A. Johnson, in Arthur Anderson, *Retailing Issues Letter*, vol. 6 (September 1993) p. 3)

The topic of retail prices and price policies followed by retailers is important for two reasons: first, retail prices are important to the consumer since these prices affect what the buyer can purchase with his dollars; second, retailing historically has been a barometer of economic health.

The pricing practices followed by retailers vary depending on their type, the market segment they serve, the amount of services they provide, their size, and their pricing philosophies.

The initial appeal to consumers of many retail firms has been the low price. It seems that most forms of American institutions, such as the department store, the chain store, the mail-order house, the supermarket, and the discount house, started with the appeal of low prices. However, as predicted in the 'wheel of retailing', the trading up in assortment, quality, and service has led many of these institutions to require higher prices as time passes.

Almost invariably, retail firms sell a wide variety of related or unrelated products. In such cases, the pricing process of individual lines is interrelated, the main objective being the profitability of the whole product offering and not necessarily that of individual lines.

ONE PRICE VERSUS VARIABLE PRICES

A one-price policy means offering the product at the same price regardless of status of the buyer. The connotation is a 'take-it-or-leave-it' price, with no bargaining or haggling over price permitted. Today, most retailers in the

USA follow a one-price policy. This is in contrast to many other parts of the world, where variable pricing is still common. Under a variable-price policy, prices are adjusted as necessary to close a sale with each customer. The prices paid by different customers may then be different, depending on the ability of each to bargain in the price negotiations. A variable-price policy is customary in some forms of retailing such as in the car or appliances business. In these cases, the stated price is perceived by the buyer as merely a starting point from which to negotiate to reach a final price. Variable pricing is particularly evident in cases where a trade-in value is involved.

There are basic advantages and limitations in each pricing practice. A drawback of variable-pricing is the need to delegate part of the pricing authority to sales personnel, thereby losing at least some control over the pricing function. The time-consuming factor associated with price negotiations is added cost. In addition, there is the potential of ill-will resulting from a realization by some customers that others paid less for an identical purchase than they did. Also, when this policy is used, price reductions by sales personnel may be misused to enhance the sales of an individual salesperson, particularly if commission is tied to unit sales volume. Nevertheless, retailers use variable pricing because of its flexibility in allowing price adjustments to close a sale that might not otherwise be accomplished.

A one price policy, on the other hand, enhances customers' confidence in the retail store because it assures uniform treatment of all shoppers. From an administrative point of view, the one-price policy is easier to administer. It also simplifies the selling job, allowing sales personnel to focus on the important elements of the product. It is doubtful if large-scale retailing, so common today, could survive without a one-price policy. Certainly it would be difficult to have any form of self-service operation.

The choice between either of these two price policies is basically a function of the types of products being handled by the retailer and of the price philosophy of management. Variable pricing is more likely to be used in the case of durable goods and big ticket items. Even here, however, one-price practices are gaining in popularity. Also favouring a one-price policy is the use of rebates and advertised prices by manufacturers.

PRICE LINING

Consumers apply the principle of simplicity in perception of stimuli, that is when the consumer is faced with a large number of stimuli, he or she attempts to categorize the stimuli into a small number of meaningful classes, thereby facilitating understanding and recall. Psychologists have termed this tendency 'categorization'. Using categorization, many retailers confine their pricing effort to a limited number of price categories or classes for each kind of merchandise they carry, then offer their stock at these limited price categories, where each is assumed to reflect varying merchandise quality. In doing so they are practicing price lining. Neckties, for example, may be offered at $15.00, $27.00, and $35.00, and men's shirts at $25.00, $45.00, and $65.00. These reflect the familiar 'good, better, best' market segmentation philosophy, which recognizes the need for a lower price aimed at the price-sensitive segment, a medium price aimed at shoppers comparing price with quality, and a higher price aimed at the service-conscious segment.

The question arises concerning the number of price zones that are appropriate. Edward Filene, of Filene's department store, stated over half a century ago that three price zones are a sufficient number for a category of merchandise. Retailers today find that three or four price categories serve their purposes well. However, in order for a retailer to select the appropriate number of price zones, sales records should be checked for the specific zones that are popular with shoppers. An analysis should also be made of competitors' practices.

Price lining is advantageous for retailers who carry a wide assortment of merchandise that could be defined as shopping goods. The shopper in this type of store wants to compare the merchandise in terms of price, quality, style, prestige, or like variables. Price lining offers a number of advantages to both the retailer and the consumer. For the retailer, price lining simplifies the inventory control problems, and the retail manager's pricing and buying tasks. Price lining also reduces the need for the sales-training process, as sales personnel have to contend with only a small number of price classes. The advertising and promotional function is also simplified.

As for the shopper, price lining simplifies the customer's buying decision by eliminating the confusion that can arise from the customer being confronted with a multitude of price alternatives. It allows segmentation of the market by providing each segment with the appropriate price zone, thereby creating more customer satisfaction. Self-selection is also facilitated, leading to savings in time for both the customer and the store.

Price lining, however, is not without some drawbacks. The management's pricing problem is solved before the merchandise is even purchased. This translates into a problem for the store buyer, who is entrusted with obtaining an assortment of merchandise that allows a sufficient markup when sold as a part of a specific price line. Consequently, the wider is the assortment required for the store, the more difficult it is for the buyer to choose the optimal selection. In addition, price lining introduces inflexibility into the pricing process and in doing so reduces the effectiveness of price as a merchandizing tool.

Price lines need to be far enough apart, so that the customer perceives distinct differences in quality between the offerings. If prices are close, confusion may arise regarding the quality connotation of each line, Conversely, differences between price lines should not be too wide. Wide variations create consumer dissatisfaction, as the consumer feels the need for some intermediate prices.

One of the difficulties facing retail firms using price lining is what to do about the prices of lines during inflationary periods when costs are rapidly rising and the firm wants to maintain an adequate gross margin. To solve this problem, the retailer can reduce the overall quality of the product line, raise the price of the product line to maintain quality, or reduce the size of product while maintaining the same price. The choice of alternatives depends on whether or not the consumer can easily detect a change in quality or quantity of the product. For example, the Hershey Chocolate Company found that slightly reducing the size of chocolate bars during periods of rising costs is a more effective way of maintaining profitability than raising the prices of their lines. Over the past twenty-five years the company has reduced the weight of the chocolate bars fifteen times, but raised prices only four times. Changing the quality of the line, if it is easily detected by the consumer, can be a dangerous policy, because it may destroy the quality image of the retail firm.

MARKDOWNS AND DISCOUNTS

One of the common practices followed by retailers is price markdowns or discounts. All retailers, regardless of their type or size, have reasons to use price markdowns. There are several reasons for discounts:

Seasonal merchandise The retailer may approach the end of the season with large inventories of unsold seasonal merchandise. For example, winter merchandise may have to be marked down in January or February in order to encourage sales and make room for Spring merchandise.

Buying mistakes The retailer may have failed to match his product offering with demand. Such buying mistakes may include bad timing of purchase, wrong assortment in terms of style, sizes, colours, and purchasing too many items. In such cases markdowns are designed to clear merchandise of such types.

Planned store policy The retail store's policy may be to provide a broad and deep assortment of merchandise to its customers with high initial markups placed on such items. The assumption behind this philosophy is that the wide assortment of each product offering is necessary to satisfy customers and to build the quality image the store desires. This type of policy is followed by discounters and off-price retailers.

'Odds and ends' Over time the retailer accumulates some merchandise which falls into this category. Obsolete stock, odd sizes and colours, scratched or damaged merchandise, and returned merchandise can be moved only by large markdowns.

Discounting represents the most frequently used method of moving merchandise in retailing. Not only are markdowns inevitable, but they are also a largely effective tool of retail merchandising to clear merchandise difficult to sell at its present selling price. There are two important questions with markdowns. One is the size of the markdown, while the other is the timing of the markdowns.

Size of Markdowns

One of the major decisions which have to be made when discounting merchandise is the amount of markdown stated in relative terms. The marked-down price for merchandise is typically established on the basis of a specific percentage of the retail price. For example, an item that is regularly featured at $20, would, under a 20 per cent markdown policy, be priced at $16.

The size of a markdown should be limited to the minimum dollar amount necessary to stimulate consumers to purchase the offering. Ideally a markdown should equal but not exceed the amount necessary to create the just noticeable difference (JND). The amount of markdown over the JND represents a loss of possible income. Some retailers feel that a fairly large markdown made at one time is much more effective than a series of relatively small markdowns taken periodically. They feel that the impact of a one-time large markdown is much more dramatic. Others, on the other hand, prefer slight automatic markdowns in price, in which case the price is cut after specified periods of time.

The size of the markdown, for all practical purposes, should be a function of both the product and the circumstances surrounding the sale of that product. For luxury or durable goods, consumers in most cases do not expect any sizable markdowns and may even begin to suspect the quality of the product, if the price were drastically reduced. Markdowns of more than 25 per cent may be subject to suspicion by consumers. On the other hand, in fashion merchandise, it is customary to take large discounts close to 50 per cent. Off-price retailers, for example, have been successful in deep discounting popular brands of men's and women's clothing. There is no rule of thumb regarding the size of markdowns. In practice, considerable variation in markdown percentages exists.

The issue of cost of the merchandise is also related to the size of the markdown. The question is: to what extent should the cost of an article be considered in determining the markdown? The guide in this case is the purpose of the markdown. Less consideration is given to cost when the intention is to quickly clear merchandise, to combat competition, to create a spectacular selling atmosphere, or to quickly provide needed cash. While end-of-season discounts on fashion merchandise are still prevalent, retailers now have the option of selling the merchandise to discounters and off-price retailers.

Timing of Markdowns

Another decision related to discounting is the timing of markdowns. In this respect, there are two policies followed by retailers:

1. Delaying marking prices down as long as possible.
2. Reducing prices on merchandise as soon as the peak of the selling cycle has been reached, and following with a pattern of periodic markdowns until products are sold.

In the first case, there are a number of advantages resulting from delaying the markdown. Merchandise is given more time to be sold at the more profitable regular price. Infrequent clearances will discourage bargain hunters as they are less likely to wait for annual sales. This policy also avoids creating ill-will among customers who pay regular prices only to find out shortly after that prices have been dropped again. Delaying markdowns also allows the retail firm to have a well-promoted sale event that will attract large crowds looking for bargains. Stores such as Saks Fifth Avenue, and Nieman Marcus as well as other similar exclusive stores use this tactic to clear out large quantities of merchandise at seasons' end.

The second policy of taking markdowns early, that is, shortly after sales begin to lag, implies smaller markdowns aimed at achieving satisfactory sales activity. This policy implies further markdowns if the initial markdown is unsuccessful in moving the merchandise.

Markdowns – of either type (early or late) – are a necessity, because it is unlikely that a retailer would want to hold seasonal goods until the following season. The turnover of inventory and the dangers of style changes necessitate discounting by retailers, both large and small.

It is unlikely that stores would follow only one or the other of these two markdown policies. Stores usually follow a mixed policy of both by taking early markdowns on fashion merchandise, for example, and late markdowns on durable goods. Whichever policy of markdown is followed by the store, it is advisable to limit the frequency of markdowns to a minimum. The public can expect to purchase the merchandise on sale if the store holds clearance events frequently. The public will take the markdown policy for granted refusing to purchase unless the merchandise they desire is offered on sale.

Computers have been used in many retail firms in recent times to indicate which product lines or items are slow movers and thus a target for markdowns. In addition, computers have useful in pointing out to buyers the popular styles or models so that buying plans can be adjusted accordingly.

LEADER MERCHANDISING

A common practice for retailers is temporarily marking down prices on selected products or services in a store. A leader, or 'special', is an article or service that is temporarily sold below its customary price level. The retailer usually offers just a few specials at a time. A supermarket, for example, may offer eight or ten weekend specials. The term 'loss leader' denotes an extreme form of this selective price-cutting where a product is sold below its wholesale price or landed cost.

The primary purposes in using loss leaders include:

1. *Attracting customers to the outlet.* This is done so that they may purchase other profitable offerings available at the same store. Customers who are lured into the retail store by the attractiveness of a bargain are likely to buy other items sold to them at normal or even above normal prices. A supermarket, for example, may attract shoppers to the store by using milk, eggs, cake mixes, and toilet tissue as weekend leaders. The shopper will most likely purchase other food items at the same time.

2. *Increasing net profitability.* Large sales volume of the leader item can increase net profitability, even though the profit margin made on selling the leader is usually modest.

3. *Keeping up with competition.* Leader pricing is a merchandising necessity, because most retail firms use it. In order to meet competition, the retailer finds it unavoidable to either match some or all of the selective price cuts of his or her competitors.

4. *Enhancing overall sales.* A leader can be planned to be a complementary item. A price cut in such an item will lead to enhanced sale of the other item or items it complements. This policy usually results in a higher overall net return, because the increased volume in sales of complementary items will more than offset the low margin on the line that has been cut in price.

One of the issues related to leader pricing is understanding what types of items are natural choices for price leaders. In other words, are there any special characteristics that could help in the choice of products to use as leaders?

Some characteristics seem desirable in a product for it to be considered a leader. They may include the following:

1. wide appeal;
2. frequently purchased;
3. consumers most familiar with its price;
4. relatively small price;
5. high price elasticity;
6. well-known brand;
7. comparison easy with similar items in other stores.

In selecting leader merchandise, care should be taken not to use items in the store that compete closely with other product offerings. Using a competitive product as a leader will increase its own demand at the expense of the demand for its substitutes.

The practice of leader merchandising can be effective in a variety of ways. Two different formats in which leader merchandising may be used are as follows:

1. A few items in the department or store are selected as price leaders. Many grocery stores, for example, use this format to generate shopper traffic for the whole store.

2. A whole department within a large store may be used as a leader. For example, a supermarket may use the meat department as a leader. Research indicates that one of the most important features attracting shoppers to a food store is the quality of its meats. If low prices are charged for quality meats, the meat leader department can be instrumental in attracting large traffic to the whole store and enhancing sales of the many other food and non-food items.

One of the problems with leader merchandising is that bargains may give the false impression to the consumer that the store follows an across-the-board low price policy. Another problem is that leader pricing may also trigger retaliation from competitive stores. In addition, consumers may limit their purchases to the item or items on special, thus defeating the purpose intended for the leader pricing. Even though some manufacturers support and encourage retailers to use their brands as leaders, others frown upon such attempts, because they feel that the practice may hurt the image or quality perceptions of their brands.

ODD PRICES

A look at retail prices today suggests that odd prices so popular just a few years ago have been replaced in many instances by even prices. The use of odd or, for that matter, even prices is due to a desired psychological effect. Odd prices are used to create the idea of a bargain, while even prices are affixed to effect the idea of status or prestige. As might be expected, discounters and food chains prefer odd prices, while up-scale stores in fashion merchandising regularly use even prices.

Questions that deal with the issue of odd–even pricing relate to whether or not consumers prefer odd prices over even ones, and, if preference is indicated, then what causes this reaction? Other related questions focus on the illusions or perceptions associated with odd pricing and the sales effects of such practice, that is, does using odd prices over even ones increase sales volume?

Many explanations have been offered to justify the presence and widespread use of odd pricing. There are those, for example, who claim that odd prices were developed to reduce the opportunity of sales personnel to pocket the proceeds of a sale by forcing them to use the cash register to ring up every sale. Another explanation for their use is the retailers' desire to create convenience for the customer in paying for the product. The cost of the product plus sales tax is an even amount. Still others argue that odd pricing often suggests that the price has been established at the lowest possible level, that is, the retailer has calculated his cost and markup down to the last penny.

From a psychological point of view, it is believed that perception of a price is a function of the way the price is expressed. Since perception functions with a principle of simplicity, the not-so-easy part of the price to remember (the odd) is to some extent subliminal – that is, not consciously noticed. For example, a price of $5.79 may be perceived or conveniently remembered, as around $5.00.

Still another explanation is that individuals may set 'critical points' representing what they consider desirable and acceptable prices. For example, these critical points may be $1, $5, and $10. Thus, for the retailer to establish the 'right' price, the price has to be perceived by the customer as being below these points, that is, below the consumer's mental dollar allotment for a particular purchase. To exceed this point, even with the slightest margin, can result in virtually no sales. Odd pricing offers the possibility of price adjustments going unnoticed or at least tolerated by consumers. For example, less customer resistance can be expected when raising the price from $2.49 to $2.99 than from $2.50 to $3.00.

The way consumers react to odd and even prices seems to vary with the pricing structure prevalent in a market and the objectives of the retailer in question. Pricing as part of the marketing mix must be consistent with the elements. Thus an up-scale store will use even prices and a discounter odd prices. The sales effect of either will be tenuous. Whatever the explanation for justifying the usage of odd pricing, it seems that the psychological effect of odd pricing, as well as the long-standing practice of using it, has conditioned consumers to expect this business phenomenon in many areas of retailing.

CUSTOMARY PRICES

Prices on some products may remain the same for so long that they become almost a tradition. A chocolate bar, a packet of cigarettes, and a package of chewing gum, are examples of products that have customary prices. A retailer who deviates from the customary price stands to lose sales because customers are familiar with these prices and expect them when purchasing.

Changing the level of customary prices is not easy for an individual retailer, especially if other retailers do not follow suit.

Customary-priced items are usually categorized as convenience goods, meaning that if the brand frequently purchased by a consumer is not available then, the next competitive brand is selected. If prices vary between competitive brands of customary-priced products then the lower-priced alternative will always be selected.

BUNDLING

Retailers' experience has indicated that sales can be enhanced to a large degree by using bundling, offering two, three, or more units of a particular product or brand for one price. For example, three cans of soup may be offered for $.89, or two boxes of facial tissue may be offered for $1.49.

The savings the customer may realize by purchasing such items may be real, or they may be imaginary. In many instances, such pricing tactics may only lead the customer to think that savings are being realized when, in fact, the price has not been reduced. In some extreme cases, the bundled price per unit is actually a little higher than the regular price. What is important, however, is that the consumer believes that a saving is being realized by purchasing the bundled offerings.

Bundling is aided by the fact that most customers, because of the arithmetic involved, may not bother to figure out the price per unit, and compare it with what they would have had to pay if a larger size of the product, for example, were purchased instead. The assumption is made by the consumer that the price as stated for such offerings must be cheaper, and psychologically, they *feel* that owing to their quantity purchase they are receiving a price reduction in the form of the (assumed) lower bundled price. In actual practice, where the bundled price is merely a multiple of the unit price sales have nevertheless often increased dramatically with the use of bundles.

In determining products that lend themselves to this type of pricing practice, the retailer should select the ones that are frequently purchased by consumers. If the product is not frequently used, bundling will not lead to higher sales, because the consumer hesitates to maintain a large stock of an infrequently used product at home.

UNIT PRICING

To what extent are shoppers able to do the mathematical calculations when shopping in order to make the right choice? The results from the first national assessment of mathematics made by the Education Commission of the United States indicated that many consumers are unable to solve very simple mathematical problems concerning pricing. To facilitate pricing comparisons between sizes and brands, unit pricing has been adopted by many food retailers. Unit pricing shows prospective buyers the price of a given product by the pound, ounce, quart, or any other standard measure. Unit pricing was developed to combat 'fractional pricing' which is mainly designed to confuse consumers by making it difficult for the shopper to calculate price per unit of a product-offering without having a calculator or a pencil and paper. The unit-price label displayed on the shelf edge below the package shows the name of the product, its contents in weight units, the price of the item, and the price per unit. The shopper, by looking at the unit-price label is able to see the price per unit of that particular product or package. This figure becomes the basis for the shopper to compare prices per unit of competing brands, or alternative packages of the same brand.

POSTING PRICES

Marking merchandise is as important to the consumer as it is to the retailer. While the marked price facilitates the selling process, it helps the consumer in evaluation of products.

The marked price should be legible, easily found, and designed so that customers are unable to change it. The marked price should be attached to the product in a manner which will not damage the product when removed. Price markings and their components vary with both the type of merchandise being offered and on the type of store. A supermarket may have a different marking policy than that used by a department store, and both may use systems that vary from that used by a discount house. Some retail stores mark products with selling price only, while others may add cost data, and still others may include information such as the division that sold the merchandise, the vendor from whom the product was acquired, the lot number, the time of year the item was put on stock, and the size.

If the retailer uses a system in which the marking would show the product's cost, this can usually be accomplished by using any ten-letter word to serve as a code. Any such word with no duplicate letters can be selected, each letter in it representing a number from one up to zero. Thus the following word can be chosen and used:

B L U E P O I N T S

1 2 3 4 5 6 7 8 9 0

So if an item costs the store $275 it is coded as LIP and the ticket shows the selling price (say of $549) and cost as follows:

$549.00
LIP

In selecting the appropriate word to use for coding, it is advisable to use words which cannot be easily figured out by the public. Some retailers use foreign words and Latin terms to discourage cryptographically-minded individuals. In the case of many products today, the manufacturer premarks his merchandise. Not only does this practice save valuable time and effort for many retailers, but it also gives an added attraction to retail stores which discount these premarked prices. The lower marked price compared with the premarked price gives the consumer an impression of a bargain. It is customary for large retail stores, which usually have access to computerized scanning machines, to use tags that display more information than just price. Such information may cover data relating to department number, manufacturer number, style number, class, colour and size. Data of such nature is necessary for inventory management, especially in determining order cycles and in finding out the overall efficiency of each department.

12 Pricing and the Legal Issues

> I would be the first to allow there is no such thing as a perfect market. But nobody is claiming that our mixed economy is anywhere near perfection. Nobody is claiming there's no room for government to enhance and sometimes supplement the workings of a free market. I would be the first to point out that government has an important role in our economy. Moreover, it may appropriately serve as a catalyst to promote the overall competitiveness of our basic industries and even help specific industries where clear spillover effects exist.
>
> (James C. Miller III, Chairman, Federal Trade Commission, in a speech to the Section of Anti-Trust Law, American Bar Association, Washington, DC, 22 March 1984)

Businesses worldwide operate within systems of laws in setting prices for products and services. These legal frameworks, made up of laws, court decisions, and administrative regulations, are focused on preserving competition and preventing restraints of trade, as well as regulating competitive actions that may result in unfairness and deception on the part of the seller. In England, for example, the common-law rule is that all interference with individual liberty in trading and all restraints in and of themselves are contrary to public opinion and therefore void unless justified by special circumstances. From the passage of the original statutes such as the Sherman Antitrust Act in the USA a century ago the scope and interpretation of these legal frameworks have been expanded and redefined to include much of what businesses view today as the essence of competition. It should come as no surprise that much of the legal attention has been and continues to be on pricing, the setting of prices, and the uses of prices in competitive actions. For example, the practice of price fixing is prohibited outright by Sweden's Competition Act 1982. In the United Kingdom, the Restrictive Trade Practices Acts 1976 and 1977 make compulsory the registration of agreements between two or more manufacturers or suppliers doing business that impose any restriction on two or more parties to the agreement as to prices.

155

The legal ramifications of any pricing decisions are not limited to government intervention and prosecution. Competitors can take legal action by seeking 'cease and desist' orders to put an end to anti-competitive pricing tactics, and by seeking damages for the 'injuries' (for example, loss of sales) sustained as a result of anything forbidden in the applicable laws. In the USA injured parties can sue for treble damages. Swiss law is fairly specific on the awarding of damages. Although the law of the country of market where direct damage is done applies, no damages will be awarded beyond those under Swiss law. Legal action can also be initiated by resellers of merchandise to prevent manufactures from actions that restrain trade and decrease output.

Today the consequences of legal intervention can conceivably have social significance. The most obvious case is consumer protection against misleading and deceptive conduct in pricing. Another example is the attended effects of public monopolies for such products as tobacco and salt. Less obvious is the balance between lower prices and restricted acts by the seller to obtain these lower prices.

LEGAL ENVIRONMENT

Perhaps the best way to visualize the impact of the legal environment on pricing is to use two dimensions – restraint of trade and public concern to categorize pricing practices (Figure 12.1). Deceptive pricing practices have little or no effect on competition, and are of lessor concern to the general public than other pricing practices. On the other hand, price discrimination and predatory pricing, although dealt with on a case-by-case basis have a major impact on the flow of trade and the lessening of competition. Price discrimination, for example, is illegal if the effect is to substantially lessen competition or create a monopoly. In the USA the Robinson-Patman Act deals specifically with price discrimination whenever the effect of that discrimination may be to injure competition between individual competitors.

Restrictive pricing in such forms as resale price maintenance and anti-dumping measures is of major concern to the general public, as witness the recent GATT agreement on the latter. Indeed, it was observed at the world trade talks that concluded in December 1993 that the EC and other nations are beginning to use antidumping measures nearly as much as the USA. The agreement provides for tougher and quicker GATT actions to resolve disputes over use of antidumping laws invoked by the USA and Europe to impose penalties on foreign producers that sell goods abroad below cost.

Figure 12.1   Classification of pricing practices subject to legal regulation

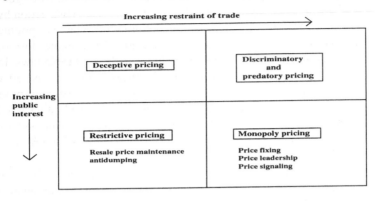

Although potentially troubling in terms of affecting competition, restrictive pricing practices have a lesser affect on competition than discriminatory, predatory, or monopoly pricing.

Monopolistic pricing practices are significant in terms of the general public's concern as translated into public policy and their effect on competition. In England, for example, the Fair Trading Act 1973 empowers the Director General of Fair Trading to control undesirable trade practices. The Monopolies and Mergers Commission is empowered by this Act to investigate and report on the possible existence of monopoly situations. The Belgian Law of 5 August 1991 seeks to preserve a system of vigorous competition. Modeled after the EEC competition law, three types of practices are covered – restrictive practices, abuses of dominant position, and economic concentrations. In Argentina, dominant position refers to situations where two or more entities do not compete between themselves or with a third party.[1]

Act 86 of the Treaty of Rome prohibits 'any abuse by one or more undertakings of a dominant position within the Common Market or in a substantial part of it ... insofar as it may affect trade between member states'. The Court of Justice defined 'dominate position' as a position of economic strength that allows a firm to hinder the maintenance of effective competition.[2] Determination of dominant position requires precise analysis of relevant market data including structure, market behaviour of the firm in question, and the consequences of this behaviour.[3] An abuse of dominant position is any practice that may prejudice consumers directly or indirectly through reducing existing competition.[4] Unfair pricing as an abuse of dominate position was at issue in United Brands Co. Chiquita (1976). The

French Ordinance of 1 December 1986 prohibits (1) agreements, written or tacit, that have as their objective or may result in a restriction of the free play of competition; (2) abuses of dominant position; and (3) abusive supplier enterprises.

In an economy much different from the one that led to its passage a century ago, the Sherman Act, the basic antitrust law in the USA, is viewed as an out-dated reaction that leaves three very important questions unanswered in today's business world. These same questions might now be asked of any statute or legal mechanism dealing with monopolies or, as it is termed in many countries, dominant position. One is: what is the relevancy of antitrust in today's global competition. Another is: do antitrust or monopoly laws present obstacles to the efficiency of business firms.[5] A third question that can be asked is: does the statute protect competition or restrict it, or (as one author terms it) does the law protect the consumer's interest in low prices or the small businessman's interest in high prices?[6]

REGULATORY EFFECTS

Throughout the world from Argentina to Britain, from the USA to France, and from Germany to Australia, nearly every country in the arena of world trade has laws prohibiting agreements and practices of businesses that can and do involve abuses of economic power. Using the price of products to restrain competition is prominent among the stated abuses. More specifically, the pricing practices that will be affected by regulations include horizontal price control (monopolistic pricing), vertical price control (restrictive pricing), price discrimination, predatory pricing, and deceptive pricing.

HORIZONTAL PRICE CONTROL

Horizontal pricing arrangements (price fixing) between competitors are, regardless of their reasonableness, inherently a restraint of trade with adverse effects on competition. The central issue is not concerted action, but the legality of admittedly collective behaviour. Horizontal pricing arrangements are more likely to occur in obligopolistic industries where each firm realizes that the effect of its actions depends on the actions and reactions of its industry counterparts. For example, a price increase by one firm will stick only if other firms follow suit and raise their prices. This conscious commitment to a common scheme, or price leadership as it is sometimes called, is not necessarily illegal collective action, however.[7] It must be shown through direct or circumstantial evidence that firms have acted in concert. In Austria, the law pertaining to the setting of prices by cartels is fairly specific. Under it (Law of 19 October 1988) cartels are defined as agreements, understandings, harmonized conduct, recommendations and announcements between or by economically independent firms for regulation or restriction of competition, particularly in respect to manufacture, distribution, or pricing. Unless the noncommittal nature is specifically referred to, recommendations of price are forbidden. Within the Federal Republic of Germany, cartels may exist, but not for the purposes of price fixing.[8] In Britain a somewhat different approach is taken. The Restrictive Trade Practice Acts 1976 and 1977 require registration of agreements between two or more manufacturers that impose restrictions as to pricing. These agreements can be declared null and void if contrary to public interest. For example, the agreement between Moosehead Breweries Ltd and Whitbread & Company Plc which gave exclusive rights to the latter for brewing and selling Moosehead beer in the UK was granted an exemption because the intense competition in the lager section of the beer market will ensure that the benefits of the agreement are passed on to consumers, and furthermore because the agreement increases rather than restricts competition.

While the term trust, dating back to the Sherman Act, is used to signify an arrangement or combination of independent businesses in the USA, the applicable law in Queensland, Australia, prohibits commercial trusts (any association or combination that has as one of its objectives the control of price). The Treaty of Rome which set up the EEC in 1957 expressly prohibits agreements or concerted practices that restrict or distort competition within the Common Market.

The most common horizontal agreements involve collaborative schemes to raise prices or restrain output where consumers are not likely to benefit. In the USA for example, it was ruled that Toyota distributors cannot utilize discount programmes presented collectively to members of dealers' associations as a means of inducing joint action by members in regard to the actual selling price. The agreement between dealers on the price of new cars facilitated by a discount price on an accessory package was ruled to be illegal price fixing.[9]

Price signalling is a practice whereby one competitor, usually the price leader, announces a price increase to take effect at some later date. Even though no formal agreement exists between competitors, the US courts have tended to view such a pricing practice as collusion to fix prices horizontally. Certain price-signalling practices have been specified as violations by the Federal Trade Commission. They include:[10]

1. Grace periods of more than 30 days between the announcement of a price increase and the time the price takes effect. Long periods of time provide the opportunity for sellers to 'test the waters' in regard to a pricing change and to settle on a uniform price for all to sell at.
2. A promise to each customer that he or she will get the lowest price given to any customer. When all customers have this clause in their respective purchasing contracts then it is impossible to deviate from a uniform price for all customers.
3. A uniform delivered pricing system that eliminates freight cost differences in serving different customers located in different geographical markets.

The Matsushita case presented an international slant on the question of a horizontal conspiracy to fix prices between direct competitors. It was charged that Japanese suppliers of electronics equipment collectively priced below cost in the USA for the purpose of driving American firms from the market to ease later price increases to monopoly levels. The Supreme Court ruled that mistaken inferences of conspiracy could injure consumers by deterring firms from using low prices as a competitive tool and in doing so dismissed conspiracy claims.[11]

VERTICAL PRICE CONTROL

Vertical price control (resale price maintenance) refers to restrictive agreements between manufacturers and intermediaries or resellers of their products to set resale prices. The purposes in controlling the price are threefold:

1. It is an essential ingredient in developing and maintaining a quality image consistent with the character of the product, the promotional effort for the product, and the distribution scheme.
2. The provision of adequate distribution margins allows for the desired promotion and customer service at the point of purchase.
3. The desired market penetration is achieved in the geographical territory served by the reseller.

The major question manufacturers have is: what actions may they take in setting and maintaining prices charged by resellers of their products? Fixing of resale prices is not allowed in Germany. The exceptions are publication materials and tobacco products. Under certain circumstances recommendations of resale prices may be made for brand-name products. However, these may be declared null and void in cases of abuse. In the Netherlands collective resale maintenance is generally prohibited, while individual resale maintenance is prohibited for certain consumer products. In Britain the Restrictive Trade Practices Acts 1976 and 1977 prohibit the collective enforcement of resale price conditions attached to goods. Individual suppliers imposing such conditions can enforce them by legal proceedings if traders acquiring goods are given notice of such conditions.

The worldwide tendency to prohibit collective effort and allow individual effort was reaffirmed in the Monsanto case. In this case, the US Supreme Court distinguished between concerted action that is illegal and independent action that is not illegal in terminating a dealer. Thus, for a termination to be illegal *per se*, it must be pursuant to a price agreement with another dealer, or, in other words, concerted action.[12]

In the Wood Pulp case (*Wood Pulp Cartel et al.* v. *E.C. Commission*) 41 wood pulp producers, one American trade association, and one Finnish trade association were charged with violating Section 85 of the Treaty of Rome by engaging in concerted activities to set prices for resale of pulp products in the EC. Fines were imposed on 36 of the pulp producers, the EC Commission disregarding the claim that the price-setting agreements took place outside the EC, and held that such action had substantial effects within the EC.

Australia's Trade Practices Commission brought an action against Sony's Australian subsidiary, alleging that it used market dominance and the threat to withhold products to prevent dealers from reducing the prices on Sony products below recommendations. The Court found Sony guilty and assessed fines (*Trade Practices Commission* v. *Sony (Australia) Pty Limited*).

The trend in the USA has been toward the use of the rule of reason, with the result that very few reseller terminations for price cutting were found to be antitrust violations. In a study of 203 private resale price maintenance cases between 1976 and 1982, the Federal Trade Commission found that 75 per cent were resolved by rejection of the charges by the courts. Collusion among manufacturers or dealers, an antitrust violation, was found in less than 15 per cent of the cases studied.[13]

Tie-in agreements, where the seller combines the sale of one product (the tying product) with the sale of another product (the tied product) that is distinct from the tying product, are generally viewed as violations in that they may lessen competition. The courts, however, have experienced difficulties in distinguishing between a legal tie-in and an illegal one. A requirement by a car manufacturer that its authorized dealers also purchase replacement parts was ruled legal in the Mercedes-Benz case because it was necessary to the firm's goodwill and reputation.[14]

Act 85.1 of the Treaty of Rome prohibits restrictive agreements that have restriction of competition as a purpose or intent. It doesn't matter whether competition is restricted, as long as it appears from the legal and economic context of the agreement clauses that is restrictive. Included among the restrictive agreements are price fixing, tied-in sales, and discriminatory practices.

PRICE DISCRIMINATION

Price discrimination is defined as the sale of products of like grade and quality to different buyers at different prices, the effect of which might substantially lessen competition or create a monopolistic situation. Price discrimination specifically prohibited by law in the US Robinson-Patman Act may be between a manufacturer and other competing manufacturers, between a buyer and the buyer's competitors, or between customers of the buyer. As such, price discrimination occurs in the marketing channel with the exclusion of sales to final consumers or retail sales.

Price discrimination, defined as a difference in price that can lessen competition, can be direct or indirect. Direct price discrimination occurs when a seller charges different prices to different buyers. Indirect price discrimination occurs when different terms or conditions of sale result in different prices to different buyers of essentially the same product. Generally, it is not illegal to charge different prices in situations where buyers are not in functional competition with each other.

Price discrimination can substantially lessen competition at three levels of competition. At the primary level, competition is between direct selling competitors. Suppose seller *A* cuts prices in one geographical territory. The purpose of the price cut is to drive seller *B* out of business, or at least to reduce seller *B*'s competitive impact (Figure 12.2). This is obviously price discrimination, but the US courts have demonstrated a reluctance to discourage price cutting at the primary level when the purpose is not to lessen competition but some other one such as building market share.

Competition at the secondary, or buyer's, level is between customers of a firm that discriminates in price. In Figure 12.3 an example of price discrimination at the secondary level is shown. Seller A sells to two different buyers, reseller A and reseller B, who in turn are in direct competition with each other. Seller A sells to reseller A at a lower price than to

Figure 12.2   Illustration of price discrimination at primary level

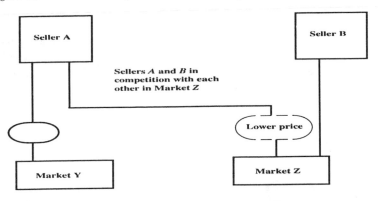

reseller B. When there is a reduction in competition between the resellers or customers of the resellers, there is a self-evident case of price discrimination under the Robinson-Patman Act. Most of the recent cases at this level involve competition between company-controlled outlets or subsidiaries and independents who are competing for the same customers. One of the major considerations is how much control a seller must have over an outlet or subsidiary for it to be considered one firm. While sales to company-controlled sales outlets are not sales under the Robinson-Patman Act, the question of exempting sales to franchisees arose in the Trane case. A stocking wholesaler, who sold portions of the Trane line on a non-exclusive basis, sued Trane and its franchisee on the basis that competitive harm resulted from the franchisee receiving a more favourable pricing arrangement. The court ruled against the stocking wholesaler on the ground that sales through the franchisee could be considered exempt 'intra-company' transfers: Trane and the franchisee constituted a single economic entity.[15]

Much more controversial is the third level of competition. This has resulted in a certain reluctance on the part of the courts to consider the impact of discrimination at this level. There is no primary-level effect and the buyers at the secondary level are not in competition with each other. However, a lower price to one of the buyers at the secondary level could result in a lower price to his or her customers, allowing them to underprice the customers of the other buyer at the secondary level. To prevent competitive injury, the original seller of the product in question needs to control prices at the third level. In doing so, however, the original seller may be in violation of a restrictive trade practice. Thus, the original seller is in the

Figure 12.3   Illustration of price discrimination at secondary level

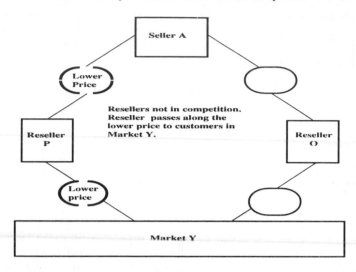

awkward position of having to violate one law to avoid violating another. (See Figure 12.4.)

In the USA, the Supreme Court has ruled that a seller may charge different prices to resellers (primary level) even if the final result is a reduction in competition at lower levels of competition. Falls City, a brewer of beer, charged a higher price for its product in selling to a wholesale distributor located in Evansville, Indiana, than it did in selling to a wholesale distributor just across the state line in Kentucky. There was no discrimination at the primary level, because the two wholesalers did not compete. Indiana law prevents wholesalers from selling beer out-of-state, and retailers from buying beer from out-of-state wholesalers, thus eliminating the secondary level from consideration. The price differential at the third competitive level was a matter of concern because the lower price in Kentucky would be sufficient inducement for Indiana consumers to cross the state line to buy beer.[16] This is a problem that can occur when a metropolitan area comprises portions of two or more states or legal jurisdictions.

Legal Defences

If it is shown that price discrimination exists then the seller has recourse to two legal defences. One of these is cost justification, the other is meeting competition. The courts have allowed that differences in price can be based

Figure 12.4   Illustration of price discrimination at third level

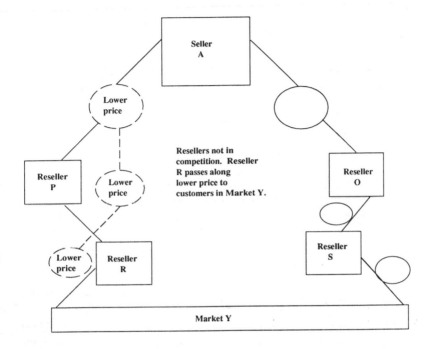

on savings from selling to a particular customer as compared to other customers. However, functional and quantity discounts must reflect actual cost savings and must be available to a large proportion of customer, not just a select few. A seller who lowers his or her price in good faith to meet competition has what is called in legal terms a 'complete defence' against charges of price discrimination, regardless of the effects on competition, and whether it is utilized to retain existing customers or acquire new customers. It is also important to make sure that price reductions apply to specific products that compete directly with products sold at lower prices, and to specific time periods when price reductions are in effect for the competitor.

Merchandising Allowances and Services

The granting of promotional allowances and other forms of merchandising assistance are other ways of discriminating in price between customers. These are generally included under terms and conditions of sale in many countries. Sections 2(d) and 2(e) of the Robinson-Patman Act deal specifically with discrimination in this critical area. In essence, a seller who offers promotional allowances or merchandising assistance must make this offer to all the competing customers on 'proportionately equal terms'. This means that the basis of any offer is a formula that ensures such to all customers who compete with each other. To be proportionately equal, an offer of promotional assistance of a certain amount of money, extra product per case, or unit of product purchased must be communicated to all customers.

On the other hand, if a promotional allowance applies only to large-volume resellers, this promotional allowance will fail the test of availability to all resellers. This is in keeping with the intent of the legal environment to curb the economic power or dominant market position of large sellers and buyers. In addition, the seller must maintain control over promotional allowances and not allow them to become another form of price concession.

PREDATORY PRICING

Predatory pricing, almost indistinguishable from price discrimination, occurs when a firm sets prices so low that an equally efficient competitor having smaller financial resources, or less willingness to incur losses from a price war, is forced out of the market, or discouraged from entering it. In the USA predatory pricing is defined as 'the sequence low-price-now-high-price-later'.[17] Predatory pricing exists only when the price is so low that the costs of making and marketing the product are greater that the revenue received from the product. The courts use three distinct tests to analyze predatory pricing violations. Objective evidence is used in determining a firm's cost–price relation or an industry's market structure. Any price below reasonably anticipated short-run marginal cost is viewed as predatory. Since marginal costs are almost impossible to obtain, average variable costs are usually substituted.[18] A third test allows direct proof of a defendant's subjective intent to harm the competitive process by driving out competition.[19]

The Purposes of Predatory Pricing

Predatory pricing is used to keep smaller competitors in line with the pricing leadership of the dominant firm or firms. The predatory price is, in effect, a warning to the smaller competitors to not use a price discount policy as an economic weapon. Predatory pricing may also be used to eliminate competitors. Large, international air carriers, for example, frequently resort to what smaller regional carriers consider excessively low fares to drive them out of business. In any event, predatory pricing can be construed as price discrimination at the primary level. Predatory pricing may also be used in the decline phase of the product life-cycle to force out weak competitors. However, the firm involved should make sure that the price covers the average total costs or the average variable cost incurred.

Predatory Pricing and Price Discrimination

There are differences between predatory pricing and price discrimination. First there appears to be a difference in intent of the seller. In price discrimination, the seller desires to gain a competitive advantage through the use of price or to react to pressures from buyers, usually those buying in large quantities. Predatory pricing, on the other hand, is used to drive competitors out of the market, thus allowing the raising of prices. Predatory pricing creates a market structure that enables the seller to recoup his or her losses through later price increases in the absence of competition.

Predatory Pricing and Cross-subsidization

Predation and cross-subsidization may be confused with each other. Cross-subsidization refers to the strategy of a multi-product firm, whereby profits earned in other markets and/or by other products are used to subsidize the losses incurred in selling a specified product. One difference is that cross-subsidization is a long-term strategy, whereas predation refers to a short-run strategy of pricing below incremental costs.

What may add confusion is that a multi-product firm may take on the appearance of engaging in cross-subsidization for the purpose of predatory pricing without ever having considered the effects of this strategy on competition. However, it is logical that if a firm can lower its total risk by adding a product line then it will also be willing to accept revenues from the added line that are insufficient to cover its short-run incremental costs.

Shortcomings of Predatory Pricing

The feasibility of using predatory pricing and its importance as an economic problem may be overstated. Indeed, the shortcomings of predatory pricing may be such that its usefulness is severely limited. The most obvious shortcoming is the costs associated with predatory pricing. The losses from increased capital investment, the shifting of cash reserves, and the increased storage costs all impact the financial structure of the firm with carry-over effects long after the period of price cutting.

Another shortcoming is the shift in strategy from growth and development to disciplining and hurting competitors. Business is normally positively oriented, and therefore predatory pricing may be counter-productive as a strategy. Also, competition may not be intimidated, especially if the market is viewed as potentially powerful.

Furthermore, predatory pricing is not effective unless the predator has a sizeable efficiency advantage, in which case non-price competition is usually more effective in gaining market share. Then, too, the current legal system facilitates the complaints of competitors. The ensuing legal procedures add to the costs of predatory pricing and the risks in using this technique.

DECEPTIVE PRICING PRACTICES

Deceptive pricing is defined as misrepresentation of the true nature of a firm's prices. Almost all countries have enacted legislation dealing with misleading and deceptive conduct of sellers in their relationships with persons defined as consumers. In Australia, for example, the Trade Practices Act 1974 specifically prohibits false or misleading representations relating to the value of goods and services. In France, the Arrêtés of 16 September 1971 and 2 September 1977 require professionals to clearly and correctly announce the prices of their respective products and services. The German law against unfair competition (7, June 1909 RGBI) prohibits unfair methods of attracting customers. In all probability the most specific regulations in regard to deceptive pricing are to be found in the USA. There the Federal Trade Commission has published a regulation booklet entitled *Guides Against Deceptive Pricing* that covers five types of deceptive pricing schemes. The general rule is that a pricing tactic must not convey the impression that the price of the product is anything other than what it actually is to the customer at the time of purchase. Under German law it is how the normal, not the particularly careful, consumer would interpret the price attached to the product in question.

Comparison with Former Price

When a seller shows a price to be reduced, the product must have been offered for sale at that original price. The original price is one at which the seller, in good faith, tried to make a sale. For example, suppose a seller

regularly sells an item for $65. Advertising or stipulating the regular price
as $100 and the discounted price as $65 is obviously a false claim.

A fictious former price may also be established by offering a product at a
higher price for a short period of time and then reducing the price to its normal level and promoting the concept of a bargain. Small reductions may
also mislead the consumer when used in conjunction with words or phrases
like 'bargain', or 'prices slashed'.

Comparable-value Comparisons

Another form of deceptive pricing is comparable-value comparison. A
price tag or advertisement stating 'retail value' and 'our price' is an
attempt to keep customers from shopping elsewhere for the product. Such
a representation is deceptive unless a substantial number of retailers do
sell at the stated retail price. As an example, suppose a price tag states 'a
retail or comparable value of $25, our price $16.95'. The truth of the
matter is that only a few stores in the geographic area charge $25. All of
the store's competitors charge about $17 for the item, thus the com-
parison is not false but obviously misleading. One leading off-price
retailer to avoid misrepresentation uses 'compare at prices (lower limit)
and up'.

Suggested Retail Price

Comparisons with suggested retail prices can be deceptive if only a few
sales are made at the suggested retail price. Typically, consumers construe
suggested retail prices to be typical retail prices. If the suggested price is to
be used as a basis for discounting, a substantial number of sales would have
to be made at the suggested price rather than merely being offered at the
suggested price.

Bargain Offers Based on Sales of Other Products

'Buy three tyres and get the fourth tyre free' is not deceptive as long as the
first items, in this case three tires, are sold at the regular price. Obviously,
the customer is not getting anything free in that he or she is required to purchase another item to be eligible to obtain the 'free' or discounted item. If
the price of the required purchase is increased then the customer may be
deceived. It is also deceptive to substitute lower-quality items for the
second items.

Other Deceptive Pricing Tactics

It is deceptive to use the terms 'wholesale' and 'factory' in describing a low retail price that does not really fall under either category. Deception in pricing is also evident in using 'for a limited time only' or 'good until a particular date' if the price is not actually raised to a higher level after this time period.

REFERENCES

1. 'The Uruguay Round's Key Results', *Wall Street Journal*, 15 December 1993, p. A6.
2. *United Brands Co.* v. *E.C. Commission* (1978).
3. *Hoffman-LaRoche & Co. AG* v. *E.C. Commission* (1979).
4. *Europemballage Corp. and Continental Can Co., Inc.* v. *E.C. Commission* (1973).
5. Emil Friberg and Cecil Thomas 'Is Antitrust Obsolete?' *Journal of Economic Issues*, vol. XXV (June 1991) pp. 617–624.
6. Lino A. Graglia 'One Hundred Years of Antitrust', *Public Interest*, Summer 1991, pp. 50–66.
7. William E. Kovacic 'The Identification and Proof of Horizontal Agreements Under Antitrust Laws', *The Antitrust Bulletin*, Spring 1993, Lc. 5–81.
8. Law Against Restraint of Competition (*Gesetz Wettbewerbsbeschrankungen*) 20 February. 1990.
9. Mid-Atlantic Toyota Antitrust Litigation, D.MD. (April 1983).
10. 'Antitrust: The FTC Redefines Price-fixing', *Business Week*, vol. **19** (April 1983) p. 38.
11. *Matsushita Electrical Industrial Co.* v. *Zenith Radio Corp.* 475U.S. 574 (1986).
12. *Monsanto Co.* v. *Spray-Rite Service Corp.*, 104 (S.Ct., March 1984).
13. Resale Price Maintenance: Economic Evidence from Litigation, FTC Bureau of? Economic Report, April 1988.
14. *Metrix Warehouse, Inc.* v. *Daimler-Benz Aktiengesellschaft et al.* (D.C. MD, December 1983).
15. *Eximco, Inc., John D. Spears, Joseph D. Michelli,* and *Rufus I. Davis* v. *The Trane Co. and Shepard Sales and Services, Inc.* (CA-5, July 1984).
16. *Falls City Industries* v. *Vanco Beverages, Inc.*, 103 (S.Ct., February 1983).
17. *A.A. Poultry Farms, Inc.* v. *Rose Acre Farms, Inc.* 881 F. 2d 1396 (7th Cir. 1989), Cert Denied, 110 S. Ct. 1326 (1990).
18. Phillip Areeda and Donald F. Turner 'Predatory Pricing and Related Practices Under Section 2 of the Sherman Act', *Harvard Law Review*, vol. **88** (1975) pp. 711–722.
19. Clarie Taylor-Sherman 'A Unified Approach to Predatory Pricing Analysis Under the Sherman and Robinson-Patman Acts: A.A. Poultry Farms, Inc. v. Rose Acre Farms, Inc., A Case Against the Tide', *Minnesota Law Review*, vol. **76**, pp. 1283–1312.22.

13 Pricing of Services

> The process is the product. We say airline when we mean air transportation. We say movie, but mean entertainment services. We say hotel when we mean lodging rental. The use of nouns obscures the fundamental nature of services, which are processes, not objects.
>
> (Marshall McLuhan, *Understanding Media* (New York: McGraw-Hill, 1964))

Although both are viewed as products, services as intangibles can be distinguished from goods. Intangibility means that services cannot be grasped mentally, cannot be identified physically, but must be experienced for the customer to gain knowledge of with the intent to purchase. Services are not manufactured and shipped to the customer. Rather, services are dominated by experienced qualities and attributes that can be meaningfully evaluated only after purchase and during production–consumption.[1] In combining goods and services into the same product package, goods give tangibility to services (for example, as souvenirs do to entertainment) while services augment goods (as, for instance, customer service does cars).

CHARACTERISTICS OF SERVICES

Although it can be argued that all products whether tangible or intangible create values for customers, there are differences between goods and services that produce special problems that in turn require special marketing efforts. The fundamental and distinctive difference between services and goods can be explained in terms of the degree of intangibility. Other differences include simultaneous production and consumption, customer participation, perishability and heterogeneity, as well as complexity and divergence.

Intangibility

All products are combinations of tangible and intangible elements, with growing emphasis on the latter in the marketplace. What is different about services is the relative dominance of intangible attributes. The inherent benefits from a service are intangible. This can be visualized by comparing an intangible-dominant product such as travel service or investment counselling with a tangible-dominant product like diamonds. While precious stones such as diamonds provide the aura of prestige, their worth is measured in terms of the physical properties of cut, clarity, colour, and caret (size). The customer has no trouble in picturing a precious stone. On the other hand, travel service provides information on the availability, scheduling, and pricing transportation and lodging, and makes arrangements for securing same. The only tangibles are the tickets, reservation forms, and possibly the itinerary.

It is obvious that both goods and services will vary in terms of tangible–intangible dominance (Figure 13.1). Services are activities with an inverse relationship between the attributes of intangibility and associated physical evidence. More intangibility and less physical presence is noted for products that are more intangible-dominant. Thus, travel service is more intangible than interior decorating, which is in turn more intangible than a home security system. Goods, on the other hand, are essentially items where the scale is tipped toward physical presence as opposed to intangibility. A comparison between cosmetics and appliances, for example, demonstrates the dominance of physical presence and a corresponding decrease in intangibility as products become more tangible-dominant.

The latitude in pricing a service is dependent upon the extent of tangibility in the service. For practical purposes, the more intangible a service, the less the opportunity to make competitive comparisons. Conversely, the greater the presence of physical evidence, the greater the opportunity to make competitive comparisons. For instance, a company providing computer-based information services will have more latitude in pricing its financial data base than a company specializing in maintenance services.

Figure 13.1　Degrees of tangibility and intangibility

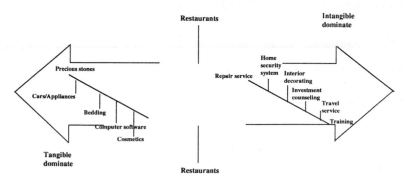

Balanced against this, the dominantly intangible nature of service products may cause more difficult marketing problems (for example: what is being sold?) compared with physical items.

Simultaneous Production and Consumption

For many services, production and consumption occur simultaneously. Usually, this means no inventories. One notable exception is information services. Whereas the sequence for goods is production, sale, and consumption, services are first sold and then produced and consumed simultaneously. The simultaneous nature of production and consumption also means the customer is inseparable from the production process. The delivery system is charged with the task of going to the market or bringing the customer to the service in an in-market location. When a service goes to the customer, fixed costs are normally reflected in a standard service call charge or hookup fee. When the customer goes to the service, fixed costs relating to the location are handled in much the same way as they would be in a plant operation.

Perishability

Services cannot be inventoried, making it difficult to synchronize supply and demand. Unsold seats on an airline flight and vacant motel rooms cannot be stored and held over for peak times. Because there are times when there is too much demand (a convention at a motel, say) and times when there is no or meagre demand (a lawn service in winter, perhaps), strategies have to be designed to cope with these drastic ups and downs of demand. Strategies for peak demand periods include hiring part-time employees, working overtime, taking care of regular customers first and allowing other customers to wait, turning away business, and subcontracting. Strategies for low demand periods include offering price reductions, offering different services to use resources during slow periods, and increasing sales and advertising efforts.[2]

Increased direct costs and lower profit contributions accompany much of what is done to meet the conditions of the highs and lows of demand. Rarely will the extra costs to handle high demand match the extra costs to build up low demand. As a result, the marketer of services must work with two estimates of profit contribution in setting price. If a market-oriented pricing structure is used, the service marketer will want to use the lower of the two profit contributions to arrive at a breakeven point. When cost-plus pricing is used, the higher amount of direct costs is the basis.

Heterogeneity

There is considerable potential for high variability in the performance of services. The quality and essence of a service (health care, a telephone service, the attentions of a beautician) can vary from producer to producer, from customer to customer, and from day to day.[2] As a general rule, the more labour-intensive a service, the more chance there is for inconsistency.

The extent to which a service can be tailored to meet the needs and/or desires of the customer depends upon the amount of judgment that customer-contact personnel are able to exercise in defining the nature of the service, and the nature of the delivery system itself.[3] For example, hair stylists have considerable latitude in fitting their respective services to customers. On the other hand, airlines and spectator sports are quite standardized.

The more customized the service, the less the opportunity to standardize direct costs. One solution is to develop standard costs for a variety of options and price in terms of the package of options utilized. It must be remembered, however, that customer choice criteria will determine the value placed on price–value tradeoffs. It must also be remembered that no two competitive versions of a customized service will look the same to a customer. This is particularly true when service personnel can exercise considerable judgment in defining the nature of the service. As an example, lawn treatment options are fairly standard from one lawn service company to the next. What cannot be standardized is the interface between service personnel and customer. Service personnel can offer advice, take special care in application, make call backs to check on the condition of the lawn, and do little extras, all of which will add value in the customer's mind.

Where the influence of service personnel is low, such as with software, one alternative is to price service options separately, and as part of packages (Table 13.1). The idea, of course, is to sell all of the services so that the price of the various package is well below the total cost if each service were purchased separately.

Complexity and Divergence

Although services can be reduced to steps, options, and sequences, they must be viewed as interdependent, interactive systems as opposed to disconnected pieces or parts. Complexity of a service is the steps, options, and sequences involved in a service. Medical services, for example, are highly complex, while lawn care is fairly simplistic. Divergence of a service

Table 13.1   Example of individual and package pricing (mixed bundling)

Business analysis system	Licence ($)
1. Basic software package for analysis	900
2. Trends module	350
3. Financial ratios	350
4. Industry performance standards module	300
5. Training tape and text	200
6. Annual subscription	200
Total (if purchased separately)	2,300
Total system package (1, 2, 3, 4, 5, 6)	1,820
Credit package (1, 2, 3, 4, 6)	1,670
Accounting package (1, 3, 4, 5, 6)	1,470
Business analysis package (1, 2, 6)	1,300

results from the variability of the steps, options, and sequences as service personnel exercise judgment, use discretion, and make situational adaptions. Pricing considerations are usually thought of in terms of increasing or decreasing complexity, and increasing or decreasing divergence.[4]

Increasing Complexity

This usually results from adding more services, or enhancing current ones, in order to maximize revenue from each customer. Barber's shops and beauty salons are examples of service organizations that have added services for this reason and in doing so become more complex. The price of the added service as part of the service package will necessarily be less than what the customer would have to pay at a specialized competitor.

Decreasing Complexity

This indicates a specialization strategy. A premium price policy is consistent with the image of expertise through specialization.

Increasing Divergence

This leads to greater customization and flexibility in responding to customer desires at a higher price. The question of *how* high a price is usually answered by what the market will bear for customization, as opposed to standardized alternatives.

Decreasing Divergence

Decreasing divergence creates a more uniform service offering, and changes the emphasis to a volume-oriented positioning strategy that will enable economies of scale. This is particularly true when the service involves the use of equipment such as an airline or dry-cleaning establishment. Typically, the price of a uniform service will be lower than its more diverse counterpart, and it will be available on a wider basis.

PRICING DECISIONS

Service marketers, like their counterparts marketing tangible products, must deliver features and/or benefits to the customer at an attractive price. An attractive price can be described as either a lower price than competitors' for equivalencies, or a premium price that is more than offset by added value enhancements. Regardless of the nature of the service, the principal features/benefits are quality (achieving promised or anticipated results), consistency in the product delivered to the customer, and reliability (always delivering what is promised).

Cost Considerations

Traditionally, the pricing of services has been cost-based rather than market-oriented. Because normal accounting procedures do not measure the asset value of people required to provide a service, human resources formulas have been developed for service businesses. One approach, the job-jacket, allocates human resource costs on the basis of actual time spent working on a particular account. Overheads, plus the charges for unused time, are allocated to each account on the basis of actual time spent on that account. As an example, a lawyer spends six hours on an account at a hourly rate determined by dividing yearly salary by total chargeable hours for a year. If, for example, a lawyer is paid $100,000 a year and has 2,000 chargeable hours (50 weeks times 40 hours), his or her hourly rate is $50. If partnership overheads plus unused time costs equal $195,000, and 13,000 hours of actual time have been allocated to accounts by all the lawyers in the firm, then a charge of $15 per hour must be added to each account for overheads and unused time. The resulting cost for this particular account would be $260 (4 hours at $50 per hour) plus (4 hours at $15 per hour).

There are two major difficulties with this approach. The first is the question of whether a time charge based on salary is a good valuation of the individual effort put forth in performing a service. Obviously, individuals performing a service will vary in relation to education and experience. This may result in a more competent person charging less for a service because less time is required than one with less competence who takes more time for same task. Setting up time standards such as in car repair may help solve the problem, but the variability of service tasks works against this.

Another problem is the allocation of fixed costs associated with services and the difficulty of making adjustments to varying volumes of business. To avoid these difficulties, many people-oriented service firms have adopted a multiple of direct time costs to arrive at total costs.

However, in using such a cost basis, the price may not be effective if it is above or below what the customer values the service. In the first case, the service business will lose sales because the price is too high. In the second case, the business will lose profits and perhaps sales because the price is too low in terms of customer expectations. While it is true that allocation of costs, both direct and overhead, is easier in equipment-intensive services than in people-intensive services, there is still the problem of matching of supply to demand. The service business may take on the wrong kind of capacity (as the airlines did in buying jumbo jets), not increase overall capacity, and create an imbalance between primary and support activities (such as at a resort), or undercut its own service by offering lower priced services that closely parallel the value of more highly priced services.[5]

Market Considerations

Because service businesses find it difficult to equate costs with units of service, particularly at varying levels of demand and because price will typically play a decisive role on the frequency with which a service is used, the price of a service is more often based on market perception of value than on cost. One answer that a number of successful service organizations have found is to innovate constantly. By adding new features over time, the service business adds value to its product. The addition of associated goods adds tangibility and identification. A firm that has successfully done both is Walt Disney.

Value pricing is based on estimates of what the market feels the service is worth to them. This means innovations must be matched with the major concerns of the target market. For ServiceMaster Co., a provider of contract housekeeping and maintenance services, this means continuous enhancements to the service for the cost-conscious health care facility customer. This allows cost and price control without sacrificing quality. In the case of Rural/Metro, a fire protection and emergency medical care provider, success is a matter of price and levels of service. Rural/Metro has been able to reduce fire damage and increase customer satisfaction by such innovations as remote-control firefighting equipment, non-union fire-fighters, an emphasis on fire protection, and employee participation.

If at all possible, services should be broken down into their component parts. Analysis of the benefits from each part will determine what parts of the service are essential, what parts can be eliminated, and what additions could enhance the benefits from the service. Holiday Inns, for example, believing the quality level of service is essential, has eliminated the extras that can be found at expensive motels or hotels, and attempted to enhance quality through consistency.

SERVICE PRICING STRATEGIES

Undoubtedly the most troublesome aspect in marketing services is the question of price. As a consequence, service businesses frequently resort to following the lead of their major competitors. Usually this translates into essentially the same price or one slightly below the competitor's. For many service industries such as dining out this will lead to two price tiers – an upscale restaurant and an economy restaurant.

Cost-based Pricing

Cost-plus pricing, which involves charging the customer or client the costs of the service plus a set percentage fee, is common for professional services such as law, consulting, and medicine. In using this pricing strategy, the professional services firm assumes it is delivering a distinctively better-quality service to existing clients than are its competitors. For example, a law firm relies almost exclusively on the expertise of staff and success rate. It also assumes that customers choose the service organization because of these distinctions.

Costs are also relied on more than are market considerations when the service has high material content and when the service is equipment-intensive rather than people-intensive. Material content heightens tangibility for the service and dilutes the portion of total costs billable for performance of the service. Labour-plus-materials is the usual procedure for repair, installation, and maintenance services. Equipment-intensive services lend themselves more to scale economies and capacity considerations than do people-intensive services. Multiple-unit motion picture theatres, jumbo jets, and 24-hour operation of data processing installations are all examples of cost-driven economies affecting the pricing of such services as entertainment, air travel, and information processing.

Where entry barriers exist, such as the amount of capital necessary to purchase the necessary equipment, costs play a bigger role than do market conditions in the determination of prices. For example, the amount of equipment necessary for an excavation service may bar many firms from entering the business. Likewise, the necessity of having a large number of airport locations can serve as a barrier to entry in the car rental business. Technology, another entry barrier, also places more emphasis on costs as opposed to market conditions in making pricing decisions. Consequently, a data processing firm will tend to rely more upon some form of a cost-plus formula than a dry-cleaning service.

Demand Fluctuation Pricing

One of the characteristics of services are the largely uncontrollable ups and downs of demand. A differential pricing scheme, where lower prices are charged for non-peak periods, will stimulate a shift in demand from peak periods to non-peak periods and possibly increase primary demand for the service. Examples are numerous: matinée prices for movies or plays; weekend and evening rates for long-distance calls; weekend rates for hotels and motels; and off-peak pricing of electrical power.

The risk in developing a differential pricing scheme is that the lower price will reduce overall profitability. Creating demand for a service in non-peak periods may mean incremental losses, because the increase in expenses to handle the shift, or the development, in demand is greater than the enhanced revenues. A good example of where this has occurred is in the airlines' offer of lower fares for flying on a Sunday rather than Friday.

What may be called developmental pricing schemes are used in pricing special versions of services for non-peak periods. A special vacation package, for example, might be developed for off-season periods by a resort hotel. Developmental prices are market-oriented rather than cost-oriented, in that their primary purpose is to increase demand. With the basic lodging costs written off largely by the prices set for the peak periods, the price for the resort during non-peak periods can be set much lower to stimulate demand. The only costs that need to be considered are the incremental costs involved in providing the vacation package.

The principal purpose of a developmental price is to increase demand by making patronage of the service (in the example, a resort) more attractive during non-peak times. The added profits (development price less incremental costs plus profits from the extra spending of guests during non-peak periods) can enhance the profitability of the resort, or be used at least partially to lower prices during peak times and allow the resort to become more competitive. The risk in developmental pricing is a flip-flopping of peak and non-peak periods. Suppose, in the case of the resort, that conventions are the main source of business in the peak periods of July and August. Suppose, further, that the development price causes these same conventions to be shifted to non-peak periods. As a consequence, the resort will be doing the same amount of business but at substantially less total revenue.

Capacity Pricing

In equipment-based services, the upswings and downswings of demand cause problems in determining the price of a service. Data processing equipment, for example, might have to handle anywhere from 4,000 to 20,000 transactions in a single 24-hour period. Obviously, the level of demand will significantly affect transaction costs and, in turn, the billable rate per transaction. For example, if the expected return on the data processing equipment is $1,000 per day, 4,000 transactions will result in a cost of 25¢ per transaction, while a volume of 20,000 transactions per day would result in a cost of only 5¢ per transaction. Airlines provide another example where a plane may have only 30 passengers with a capacity of 120 seats.

Using either extreme will result in overpricing or underpricing the service. Therefore, a capacity pricing scheme must be developed that permits the desired return on equipment with a competitive price (see Table 13.2). The first step is to determine the competitive price for equivalent services. This may be stated in terms of a range rather than a single price. The second step is to break down the service into its equipment–return and people–cost components. The purpose here is to determine what costs are essential, what costs could be eliminated, and what costs could be reduced through increased productivity. For example, it might be decided that the minimum return on equipment investment may be used in conjunction with a desired rate of return to constitute a range rather than a single figure.

Table 13.2   Hypothetical example of capacity management

Problem   A Northern Michigan resort has a high demand for golf facilities during the afternoon hours in July and August. Building a new course would be a net loss because the golf season is severely limited by weather conditions.

Desired service level   Each resort guest who wished to play would be given the opportunity to play each day of the visit. At least 75 per cent of the walk-ins would be given an opportunity to play.

Changes in facilities   Opening the course two hours earlier. Leasing of a nearby golf course during the months of July and August. Purchase of a shuttle bus.

Pricing   Discount rate for playing in the morning. Competitive rates for nearby course plus discount coupons for resort course.

Knowing the market and cost structures, the next step is to divide return plus personnel costs by competitive price to find the number of units of service necessary to break-even, given competitive conditions expressed in terms of price. To illustrate, suppose in the data processing example that the desired rate of return is $1,000 per day and the minimum acceptable rate is $900 per day. Personnel-related costs total $200 per day with possible productivity improvements equal to a savings of $20 per day, or 10 per cent. Suppose further that competitive prices for similar processing of transactions range from 7.5¢ per transaction to 9¢ per transaction with the major competitor charging 8.2¢ per transaction.

Table 13.3   Transaction costs

	Per transaction costs		
Alternative	*7.5¢*	*8.2¢*	*9¢*
$1100 ($900 plus $200)	14,667	13,415	12,223
$1080 ($900 plus $180)	14,400	13,171	12,000
$1200 ($1000 plus $200)	16,000	14,634	13,334
$1180 ($1000 plus $180)	15,734	14,391	13,112

From the information in Table 13.3 management knows that the fewest number of transactions needed is 12,000 and the largest number of transactions possible is 16,000. The former supposes a minimum rate of return ($900), productivity improvement, and a market price of 9¢ per transaction. The latter supposes a desired rate of return ($1,000), no productivity improvement, and a market-low price of 7.5¢ per transaction.

Benefit Pricing

The basic assumption in benefit pricing is that the perceived benefits of a service and the price resulting from this customer valuation is unrelated to the cost of performing the service. The benefit price of a service, or what a customer is willing to pay, disconnects price from the cost components of the service. If the benefit price does not provide a desired return on investment or is even below costs then increased features and/or benefits must be added in such a way that overall service performance commands a higher if not a premium price in the marketplace. For example, one financial services company added increased benefits from a financial information service by combining it with free consultations and providing a high level of accuracy (quality) in the provided data.

The first step in benefit pricing is to define the service and the fundamental rationale for the system as a means of satisfying customers. This is followed by a definition of the relationships a customer will have with the performance of a service. These include his or her actions when the service is performed, and his or her interactions with the observable parts of the service. Physical support or environment for the service and personal contact, the two observable parts of a service, are almost wholly responsible for customer perceptions. Even though a service may be a result of what the customer sees and does not see in terms of the internal workings of the service provider, perception of features/benefits leading to value is channelled through physical support, or environmental and personnel contact. This may require shifting some activities from one part to another, depending upon cost and perception trade-offs. Thus, the marketer of a service must ensure that both match the costs of the service. An up-market restaurant, for example, must create an ambiance in décor and service level that matches its pricing level.

Both physical support and environment are defined in terms of how the providers wish customers to perceive them. Physical support such as equipment, instruments, and materials used in performing the service have a direct effect, while décor, layout, and location of the operation have a less direct impact.Contact personnel, because of the humanizing of many services, have a direct effect on perception. It is important to define what each person is to do in performing the service, as well as the relationships between people. The latter are significant because contact may not be with just one person but with several people, all at once or one by one. It is also important to educate customers when equipment replaces contact personnel wholly or partially in the performance of the service. For example, if the conversion to ATMs is to be successful, the customer must be educated as to the advantages over a teller-based system and his or her role in service performance.

Once the relevant value activities have been identified for both environment and contact personnel, competitive comparisons are made wherever possible. The assumption in using competitive comparisons is that in the long run the market will determine the value of a service and thus its price.[6] If it is found that a feature or benefit has a distinct competitive advantage then it is premium-priced, while one with no competitive advantage will be priced at the market price. In the case of a competitive disadvantage, the feature/benefit is priced below the market price.

While it may be difficult and seemingly impossible to determine prices for features/benefits, every effort should be made to do so. For example, where one motel chain may differ from another in that it provides complementary breakfast and a competitor does not then the difference in room charges would be the price of the feature/benefit. From a practical standpoint, it may be necessary to group features/benefits or make estimates based on the normal markup of costs.

Once the prices of features/benefits are found or estimated, they are added to determine the price for the service. If the price calculated by this procedure produces a lower margin than is desired, the service business has two options. One is to increase productivity and/or seek lower cost solutions for features/benefits. The other is to seek increased volume. It should be noted, however, that increased volume may put pressure on scheduling and perhaps increase costs. One way to handle this is to add communications equipment and personalize scheduling so that it becomes a visible feature/benefit that will allow a price increase.

Price Bundling

Bundling of services is the combining of two or more services in a single package at a special price that is less than the total price of the services if purchased separately, for example:

- travel packages that include air travel, lodging at destination, food, special excursions, activities, and car rental;
- banking packages that include a cheque account, free services such as cashier's cheques and traveller's cheques, and traveller's cheques, insurance coverage, loan programmes, and credit cards.
- software packages that include various programs, instruction, installation, and consultation.

● convention packages that include air travel, registration, lodging, food, and special events.

There are two types of bundling. With pure bundling the various services are available only in bundled form. The purpose of pure bundling is to create a differentiated product and enhance the value of a core service. The other type is mixed bundling, where the customer has the option of buying services individually, or as part of a package with a price incentive for buying the package (see Table 13.1). Mixed-leader bundling is pricing one service at the regular price and another at a discount. Mixed-joint bundling is setting a price for two services purchased jointly.[7]

To illustrate the pricing of bundles, suppose two products are combined. If demand for one is independent of the demand for the other, it is hoped that customers who now buy either will buy the package containing both. Another goal is to convert non-customers for either of the two into customers for the bundle. The basic motivation offered customers is price.

A bundling price that provides a discount on the total cost of two services will maximize cross-selling opportunities if the segments buying only one product are about equal. When the two segments are not equal, pricing of the bundle should feature a discount on the service purchased by the largest segment. For example, if a photo-finishing lab has customers who buy only the service of prints from slides and an equal number who buy only the service of enlargements, the best price for a bundle would be one that offers a discount on total cost of the two services. On the other hand, if a greater number buy only prints then it would be better to concentrate on these by providing a discount on prints that are purchased in conjunction with enlargement services.

PRICING TACTICS

Pricing tactics are essentially the same for services and goods. One tactic is differential pricing, where different prices are charged according to a customer's willingness to pay. In the pest control industry, for example, the most common pricing tactic is charging different prices for the same work. Discounts may be used to increase business or develop an image of a low cost structure. Restaurants, for example, may offer a discount on meals purchased before a certain time to allow prospective customers to sample the fare. Hopefully, the positive experience will result in these customers returning and paying full price.

Guaranteed pricing occurs when payment is linked to certain results. Loss leader pricing is the charging of reduced price to get the first order with the hope of further business at the regular price. Offset prices are low prices on core services, and relatively higher prices for necessary extras.

REFERENCES

1. Valarie A. Zeithaml 'How Consumer Evaluation Processes Differ Between Goods and Services', in James H. Donnelly and William R. George, eds, *Marketing of Services* (Chicago: American Marketing Association, 1981) pp. 186–189.
2. Valarie A. Zeithaml, A. Parasuraman and Leonard L. Berry 'Problems and Strategies in Services Marketing', *Journal of Marketing*, vol. **49** (Spring 1985) pp. 33–46.
3. Christopher H. Lovelock 'Classifying Services to Gain Strategic Marketing Insights', *Journal of Marketing*, vol. **47** (Summer 1983) pp. 9–20.
4. G. Lynn Shostack 'Service Positioning Through Structural Change', *Journal of Marketing*, vol. **51** (January 1987) pp. 34–43.
5. Kate Bertrand 'Service Marketers Thrive on Innovation', *Business marketing*, vol. **73** (April 1988) pp. 52–3 and 56.
6. Eugene M. Johnson, Eberhard E. Scheuing and Kathleen A. Gaida *Profitable Service Marketing* (Homewood, Illinois: Dow Jones-Irwin, 1986) p. 287.
7. Joseph P. Guiltinan 'The Price Bundling of Services: A Normative Framework', *Journal of Marketing*, vol. **51** (April 1987) pp. 74–85.

14 Pricing During Inflationary and Shortage Conditions

> What would be the role of marketing management if 'an economy were suddenly plunged into a state of widespread product shortages?... in practice excess demand is as much a marketing problem as excess supply... a company faces a host of difficult customer-mix and marketing-mix decisions.'
>
> (From Philip Kotler and Sidney J. Levy, 'Demarketing, Yes, Demarketing', *Harvard Business Review* (November–December 1971) p. 75)

INFLATIONARY AND SHORTAGE CONDITIONS

Inflationary and scarcity conditions will continue to be an integral part of present-day business environment. The intensity of such conditions may vary from time to time, but the main trend will persist as inflationary pressures strengthen and weaken, and the world's consumption of certain materials outstrips the rate of replacement.

The consensus among business and economic analysts is that the shortage problem is likely to exist for some time because of a continuing worldwide exponential growth in the demand for raw materials, an inflationary spiral in the price of many minerals and industrial commodities, and an increasing dependence by developed countries on undeveloped countries for certain basic raw materials, particularly oil.

The overriding concern in view of these shortages is the upward push on the rate of inflation. This concern is considered to be the key determinant of the pace of advancement in the economic activity of any society.

There are two views concerning the causes of inflation: the cost-push view, and the demand-pull view. The first asserts that the rising costs of capital materials and/or labour push up prices, which in turn increase other costs in an infinite cycle. The second view holds that the aggregate demand for products in the world exceeds supplies of existing resources. These views reflect the belief that inflation is the major factor in causing a recession, because real incomes are reduced and gains in sales drop. This is accompanied by rising unemployment and social unrest.

186

The survival of any firm under inflationary and shortage conditions will depend upon effective marketing strategies that counter or capitalize on the adverse conditions in the marketplace. Also affecting a firm's success in dealing with such adverse conditions is its promptness in recognizing the key changes that are taking place and its capacity to adapt to these changes. Inflationary and shortage conditions naturally present new challenges for those making pricing decisions. As wage demands for high pay continue, and as material costs escalate, some businesses find no other alternative but to pass on such cost increments to final prices. To many firms' dismay, however, they may find out that such a practice has a definite negative impact on volume of scales.

Inflationary and shortage conditions reduce the effectiveness of traditional pricing techniques. The decision to set a price in such an environment is beset by a myriad of challenges, changes, and adjustments that must be dealt with if profits are to be maintained at a satisfactory level. While these conditions and the need for effective response is always present, adverse times such as inflation heighten the critical awareness and appropriate reaction.

Continuous Monitoring of Costs to Protect Profits

A costing practice that was effective prior to the rapid inflationary conditions will no longer be sufficient, owing to the fast pace at which costs change. Dependence on a costing system that is based upon the extrapolation of historical costs can distort the profitability picture. It is necessary, therefore, to develop a costing system capable of identifying changes in the costs of products, product groups, markets, key customers, and operations. Such a system should be capable of tracking and recording the actual flow of expenses within each cost centre. For example, a manufacturing firm needs to be able to monitor material usage, output, direct wages, labour productivity, machine utilization, and any other type of related expense item on a regular basis.

The sophistication of computer technology today can provide a cost monitoring system to reflect daily and monthly cost fluctuations between the current purchase price of every component or material and its last purchase price. These reappraisals of costs can lead to revamping of price lists or the decision to accept lower profit margins on products. Some firms, attempting to foresee cost increases and demand shifts, incorporate a multiplier factor into their base price which can be adjusted periodically. Others have begun using rolling or progressive budgets where extensions are made on a monthly basis to allow for incorporation of current chances in costs and demand.

Use of Information Systems to Monitor Environmental Changes

Economic and marketing intelligence plays a significant role under inflationary conditions. To make the best pricing decision, management needs information on general economic conditions to determine the direction the economy is anticipated to take. Analysing indexes, indicators, measures of economic activities, and prices can help the decision-maker to determine whether to expand, reduce, or diversify operations. Information on anticipated supplies of materials, labour, energy and their costs is also vital as the decision maker adjusts strategies to cope with or capitalize on conditions. Long-run supply conditions may trap the substitution of one component or material for another, or new techniques of processing same.

Companies need to be more sensitive to changes in consumption patterns and spending behaviour. Increasing demands for greater quality, more price consciousness, preference for energy-saving products, and interest in product information and safety as concerns take on greater significance for makers of consumer products and their major suppliers. Flexibility in manufacturing, shorter production runs, and inventory policies such as just-in-time changes in industrial or business-to-business market, and the monitoring of competitive price policies and practices take on special importance during inflationary periods. A close watch on such policies may determine whether the firm's own prices should coincide, supplement, or deviate from competition. The recent rebates by the car industry and, the flurry of changes in airline fares, as well as the shift from promotional discounts to price discounts for grocery products, are all examples of major changes.

Examination of Accounting Procedures

Many firms are adopting accounting procedures that reflect a more realistic picture of profitability. Changes have taken place in depreciation allocation, inventory costing, and budget periods. In addition, more attention is being given to possible tax credits and the opportunities that acquisition provide for tax benefits.

A problem with costing materials is the evaluation method used for stock, particularly with long lead times in manufacturing. Costing stock on the basis of FIFO (first in, first out) is logical, and corresponds with the movement of stock. FIFO, however, does overstate profits during inflation. Using LIFO (last in, first out) has the advantage of charging production with costs which are as near as possible to the current rate. This method eliminates the 'paper profits' that result from higher finished product prices and input costs that are lower than present levels.

Inflationary accounting is concerned with providing an accurate and up-to-date picture of the firm's assets and liability situation. Its function is to produce a realistic evaluation of fixed assets, stocks, and work in progress. The traditional methods of depreciating an asset assumes that a new asset will cost the same as the present one. Under inflationary conditions, the price of a new asset may be much more than the price of the old one. Unless the accounting system shows a true representation of the firm's assets, the profitability picture may be unrealistically high. Buildings, factory sites, equipment, and other fixed assets appreciate rapidly in times of inflation, which necessitates a periodical updating of the value of assets to obtain a more realistic estimate of the return on capital. Ordinarily, budgets of operating activity are drawn up for a period of a year, with the year being divided into quarters. If the budget period is too long, there is a greater chance for inaccuracy because of changing conditions. During inflationary periods it may be easier to predict costs, production, and sales in the short-run using a rolling or progressive budget of short duration.

Absorption or Passing on of Rising Costs

One of the major problems facing the decision-maker is whether to absorb increases in cost with a subsequent drop in gross margins, or pass them on to buyers in terms of higher prices and the risk of losing market share. If prices are raised and competitors do not follow suit, the firm runs the risk of losing ground to competitors. It is also possible that if most or all suppliers act in harmony and raise their prices, the cumulative effect in the whole industry will be a loss of the market as customers switch to alternative materials or seek substitute products. It is also true that firms seeking to keep up with inflation by raising prices are in fact boosting the inflationary trend. What happens is that further price increases fuel in the inflationary trend causing a negative impact upon the economy as a whole. A good example is rising health care costs, which increase health care insurance and the costs of operations for businesses, which in turn must increase prices in selling to the health care industry.

The best decision during inflationary conditions may be to absorb at least a proportion of the cost increases to maintain market position. Industries, particularly those with heavy fixed overheads, may find flexible pricing advantageous. Flexible pricing is the willingness to cut prices aggressively in order to hold market share. Unlike the traditional pricing methods of setting a price that the decision maker believes will provide a desired long-run target-rate-of-return, flexible pricing is a short-run system based on accurate and complete information on the workings of the market and the firm as a supplier to the market. In considering a price increase, marketing considerations such as the severity of competition, and the presence or absence of unused capacity take on paramount importance.

Price Protection Systems

A number of systems can be adopted to protect profits against rising costs. These systems are especially valuable for products which require a long lead time to manufacture. All types of construction and commercial aircraft come to mind as examples. A surcharge is used to incorporate increased costs of primary materials into the price of equipment at delivery. To illustrate, with a weighted index of the wholesale prices for the material under question, cost increases can be reflected in the price.

With open-end prices, no price is quoted until after delivery. The price charged will reflect any changes in material and labour costs that have occurred since quotation. The use of phrases such as 'Price is subject to change without notice', is particularly useful if the firm uses elaborate catalogues or price lists prepared in advance. Employing a multiplier factor into base prices protects the firm's profits and may prove to be a relatively easy method to use. Inflation escalation clauses in price contracts are particularly valuable when the manufacturing cycle requires a long lead time between sale and delivery.

Cost Reduction

Under normal economic conditions, profits can be maintained or increased through price increases, cost reductions, or increased volume, or a combination of two or all three of these. During inflationary periods, however, cost increases may not be fully passed on in final prices, and it is difficult for businesses to increase prices rapidly enough to counter-balance increased costs. Therefore, the utmost attention should be directed to the alternative of cost reduction, particularly if the end-result is to maintain price to protect volume.

Shortages and higher prices for materials and components may be offset in several ways. One way is to shorten the product line by eliminating 'losers' or marginal products so that their materials or components can be utilized efficiently in producing profitable items. Weak products, even though they contribute to a company's profitability, consume a disproportionate share of resources, including management time. If dropped, the profit position of the company will improve because resources can be concentrated on developing and sustaining the rest of the more profitable products which have a greater combined payoff. General Electric's policy to compete only in those markets where their status in the market allows the firm to operate at a given level of profitability is a good example of such a policy.

Another way of improving profitability in a company is to seek out and use lower-cost alternatives, provided that such change will not negatively affect the quality reputation of the product. Many firms have increased their investment in basic research and development to produce substitute materials. Car manufacturers, for example, found more economical substitutes for steel in aluminum, plastics, and rubber.

Simplifying or 'tuning down' the product, altering product design to fit standard components, and reducing model changes are all ways of designing cost savings into the production process. Shifting the marketing emphasis to keeping customers from attracting new customers allows the firm to take advantage of the favourable cost ratio of one dollar to keep a customer as opposed to six dollars, mostly spent in advertising, to attract a new customer.

Contrary to a popular misconception, improving quality leads to lower costs. Motorola has found that improving the quality of the product and production process results in the lowest manufacturing cost.[1] One reason for this is the reduction in so-called hidden plant – the people, the floor space allocation, and the equipment dedicated to fixing things that should have been done right the first time. Estimates are that the hidden plant represents 25 to 35 per cent of total production costs.[2] A second reason is the reduction of the more obscure and ill-defined cost of a lost customer.[3] Finally, there is the effect of quality on a firm's competitive position: the experience of Motorola is that high-quality companies are not just better, but that they also achieve magnitudes of differentiation that can become insurmountable to competition.[4]

In addition, the role of personal selling should be reduced as the company becomes more selective in its choice of customers, thereby limiting their number to the ones with the highest long-term potential. Heavy packaging costs including inner wraps, colourful packaging, outer cartons, and fibre cases, as well as other sales aids should be critically reviewed.

Keeping a Close Watch on Government Policies and Regulations

Governmental policies and regulations become increasingly important during periods of economic turmoil because of their bearing on companies' operations and pricing policies. The effect of government regulations on price may close off the option of the company to price above the anticipated level of cost inflation. The company, for example, may be allowed to increase its prices by only the amount of increase in certain allowable costs such as materials, components, suppliers, or salaries. Allocation of strategic commodities and quantity restrictions can have a direct bearing on the firm's operations. Export controls may reduce the scope of the firm's geographical market and cause a shift in the production or selling of certain commodities. Import controls may open new domestic opportunities and markets for the firm, but environmental controls may mean higher manufacturing costs and reduction in the supply of basic resources.

Regulations may affect the firm directly, as with price controls and guidelines, or indirectly, as with monetary and fiscal policies that reflect upon the demand for the company's products or services. In either case, the pricing executive will need to know the prevailing rules and their possible reflection on his company's operations and be able to anticipate and make contingency plans for possible governmental policies and mandates likely to affect his particular industry, and the economy as a whole.

Centralizing Pricing Decisions

Centralization of pricing allows greater control over pricing, which in turn allows less deviation from a firm's objectives and more rapid response to the vagaries of the marketplace. Centralization in pricing is particularly important if the company follows a strategy of flexible pricing. The decision to cut prices aggressively in following competition, for example, has to be made promptly so as not to lose market share.

Increasing the Emphasis on Public Information

Customers and the public in general resist change and require explanations for shifts in company policies, particularly those involving price. This requires timely explanations of the firm's actions and policies, and alerting the public to changes as far in advance as possible. This dissemination of public information helps to build the image of the firm as a concerned participant in the economy. Advertising, for example, can be used to show end-users and customers how to obtain more use from the product. Firms can avoid resistance to higher prices and gain customer acceptance through advertising campaigns explaining how to make the best use of scarce materials.

Closer Relationships with Resellers

Close supervision over the distribution function through monitoring the movement of goods along the channel, and the communication of policy changes promptly to dealers in order to assure their cooperation, are essential in good times and absolutely mandatory in times of turbulence. During inflation, the handling of price changes to dealers is charged to the salesperson, who must explain to resellers how costs have risen, clarify the ways in which the company has reduced its costs to minimize the price rise, and demonstrate cheaper substitute products available from the company. Counselling by the salesperson is also important in studying the resellers' problems and attempting to advise them on how these problems can be eased. In this manner, product shortages and price increases can be turned into opportunities enabling the salesperson to enhance goodwill by demonstrating to resellers the sensitivity of the company to their problems.

Other areas which should be considered during inflation are the company's policies regarding cooperative advertising allowances, credit terms, price discounts, freight charges, and service policies. Inflation and shortages may present opportunities to negotiate longer-term contracts, secure better payment terms, and offer fewer discounts and services. Attention must also be given to information provided by channel members on consumer and competitive reactions to a company's price or policy changes. Such information is vital in designing appropriate pricing strategies.

Avoiding the Use of Scarcity Tactics

Some manufacturers, during inflation and shortage conditions, are tempted to use the psychology of scarcity to attain higher prices and profits. Psychology of scarcity can be observed in the changing behavioural patterns of purchasers as a result of actual or perceived shortages. Under these conditions, if panic buying ensues, it may create conditions of actual scarcity, driving prices above normal levels. The use of such tactics may prove to be dangerous and can, in the long run, adversely affect inventories, production, sales, and profitability.

A NEED FOR PRICING STRATEGY DURING INFLATION

The adoption of a special pricing policy during periods of shortages and inflation is a vital step to the survival of the firm. Without such a policy, companies are at the mercy of every shortage in the supply of vital materials or at any change in costs. In the absence of an inflationary price policy, companies short of scarce materials will scramble to obtain them at higher prices, with the hope of recovering the higher costs through themselves charging more for their products. The effect of such action may be the loss of volume, or the passage of restrictive governmental legislation designed to curb the inflationary trend.

It is very difficult for many firms during shortages and inflationary conditions to forego the attractive and profitable techniques of demanding what the traffic will bear. The cumulative effect of such actions, however, can endanger the capitalist system itself, causing economic collapse and social unrest. It is important that the need for a pricing plan for individual companies is clear, but it may also be necessary for producers of essential materials to consider the use of an industry-wide collaboration on pricing where such policies are designed to serve the social needs of the economy.

REFERENCES

1. 'The Six Steps to Six Sigma', Motorola Malcolm Baldridge Quality Seminar, 1989, pp. 6–7.
2. Lois Therrien 'The Rival Japan Respects', *Business Week*, 13 December 1989, p. 112.
3. Robert E. Cole 'The Quality Revolution', Production and Operations Management, vol. 1 (1992) p. 119.
4. James A. Belohlav 'Quality, Strategy, and Competitiveness', *California Management Review*, vol. 35 (Spring 1993) pp. 55–67.

15 Pricing in International Markets

> ABB (Asea Brown Boveri) is a company with no geographic centre, no national axe to grind. We are a federation of national companies with a global coordination centre. Are we a Swiss company? Our headquarters is in Zurich, but only 100 professionals work at headquarters and we will not increase that number. Are we a Swedish company? I'm the CEO, and I was born and educated in Sweden. But our headquarters is not in Sweden, and only two of the eight members of our board of directors are Swedes. Perhaps we are an American company. We report our financial results in US dollars, and English is ABB's official language. We conduct all high-level meetings in English. My point is that ABB is none of these things – and all of these things. We are not homeless. We are a company of many homes.
>
> (Percy Barnevik, in 'The Logic of Global Business: An Interview with Percy Barnevik', *Harvard Business Review* (March–April, 1991) p. 92)

For most firms the potential rewards of doing business in international markets are overwhelming. The most compelling reasons for entering the global marketplace are the sheer size of the marketplace and the limitless opportunities present. One of these opportunities is the leveraging of R&D investment. The global marketplace provides opportunities to obtain a full return on investment that is not possible if technology serves only the home market. Expanding internationally also provides the opportunity to improve products and processes by drawing on the resources of many companies and organizations in different parts of the world. Finally, global expansion allows a firm to remain competitive.[1]

The fundamentals of pricing that are useful in pricing products in domestic markets are also of value in pricing products sold in international markets. What is different are the relentless competitive pressures on prices and costs. As an illustration, management at Cummins Engine Company discovered that competitive prices on comparable products from other countries were as much as 30 per cent lower than their present domestic prices. Further, it must be understood that the driving force behind world economic growth is not manufacturing volume, but improving customer value.[2] Change in the international marketplace is accelerating, with companies developing products and bringing them to market at a record pace.

CONSIDERATIONS IN INTERNATIONAL PRICING

Two considerations are paramount in pricing products in international markets. The first is the organizational status of the firm: is it a global company or a multidomestic? The second is: what is the nature of the product being priced? Market factors that go into pricing a high-tech product will be different from those for a culture-bound product.

Global Company versus Multidomestic

A global company markets standardized products worldwide in an effort to capitalize on the commonality of international markets. Laurence Farley, President and CEO of Black & Decker, views globalization as an organizational response to the world becoming more homogeneous, with distinctions between national markets fading and for many products eventually disappearing. A multidomestic company, on the other hand, markets differentiated products in response to local needs and wants. However, it is difficult to classify a company operating in international markets as strictly either global or multidomestic from a practical standpoint. The reason is that a company may standardize some products and not others, or may market a standardized product using a different marketing programme in each country.

The implications of whether a product is standard or an adaption is of vital importance in the pricing decision. Obviously, the same product with the same brand name cannot be sold successfully at different prices in different countries. Just as obviously, the same product under different brand names or different products under the same brand name will have different prices. Thus, the price affixed to a product sold in a particular national market will depend not only upon the cost and demand structures for the product, but also upon the marketing programme. The same skin lotion under different labels and with different prices can be sold to sunbathers in one national market and skiers in another. In that few consumer goods companies market the same products using the same marketing programme worldwide, the job of pricing is one of adaption to the market as part of the marketing program.[3]

Using aspirin as another example, it might be sold worldwide at the same price per tablet, but in differently sized packages, giving the idea of different prices for the same product. In a developing nation, such as one in Latin America where consumers have limited resources, the package might contain only 10 to 15 tablets compared with 100 to 200 in the USA or a country in Western Europe. Carrying the example one step further, it may be possible to price a tablet higher in Latin America and still keep the price of the package within acceptable limits for that national market because of the size of the package.

Nature of the Product

High-tech products are easier to market worldwide than many consumer products where purchase tends to be culturally based. A computer or an item of earth-moving equipment are global products because the benefits from use are identical in every national market. On the other hand, food preparations such as soup, pickles, and frozen dinners tend to be viewed differently in each national market on the basis of cultural norms.

Consumer products used in the home are likely to be more culture-bound than those used outside the home such as cars. Procter & Gamble has successfully developed Pampers disposable diapers, an obvious culturally bound product, as a global product.[4] Figure 15.1 shows the pricing implications for different products arrayed in terms of varying degrees of cultural-based purchasing evaluation and general acceptance of benefits.

At one extreme are culturally bound consumer products used in the home that require adaptive pricing, while at the other are high-tech products with standard prices. In between are industrial products, where more adaptiveness may be needed in pricing, and consumer products used outside the home that can be standardized at least partially. An example of the latter are industrial gloves worn for protective purposes while working in a plant, mining operation, or construction site. A national market might call for different sizes and varying degrees of protection, which in turn translate into different prices.

One exception to this system of classification is when manufacturing and R&D scale economies or efficiencies with the global product create a price spread between the global and national products that is far too great to resist even for the most culture-bound consumer. As a result, even though the important factors of the marketplace indicate adaptive pricing, the competitive edge provided by the substantially lower price possible with a world product means standardization in both product and price. Another exception is the impracticality of adapting products and pricing to each

Figure 15.1   Pricing situations in international markets

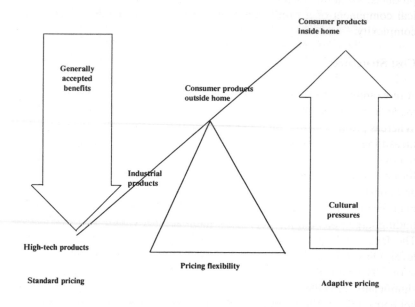

national market. Some national markets may be too small in comparison with other larger national markets to justify the investment in individualizing products. In such cases, a standardized product is developed on the basis of the marketplace parameters of the largest national markets. If possible, flexibility is provided by add-ons that allow for greater acceptance in smaller national markets. As an example, a crane could be standardized for use in steel mills in the USA, Canada, and Western Europe, the largest potential markets. By adding to, replacing, or eliminating components, the same crane could be adapted for use in shipyards in Korea and Japan, and for loading and unloading facilities in Third World nations.

COST AND MARKET STRUCTURES

The dilemma faced by many firms in marketing internationally is that the success initially realized in the domestic market cannot be carried over into the international marketplace intact. The difficult job facing the firm is defining how they are going to compete in international markets. National differences and preferences cannot be ignored if the marketer hopes to be successful, but yet there is the push toward globalization and world-class products. What this means in terms of the pricing decision, already a critical component of a firm's competitive stance, is added significance and complexity.

Cost Structures

A re-examination of cost structures may be called for before a decision is made in regard to the price of a product to be marketed internationally. Whereas profit contribution is useful in evaluating multiple products and in measuring the flexibility possible in pricing, it may not be appropriate for international markets. Several changes may be in order in pricing products for international markets. One of these is to follow the lead of the Japanese, and consider all costs in making the product, with the exception of direct materials and parts, fixed rather than variable. This shifts the emphasis to finding large potential markets and pricing aggressively to secure volume. The Japanese keep the price low until product sales reach the acceptance level. Once this is attained, prices are raised, often through product variations. Typically, the Japanese restrict their efforts to those markets that are significantly affected by economies of scale and the experience curve. Market entry utilizes a low-priced improved product, capturing a large market share, and the generation of substantial profit margins through cost reduction from volume. Typically, these markets are ones with generally accepted features and/or benefits that are not obscured by cultural pressures such as cars, televisions, and stereo equipment.

Besides redefining what is fixed and what is variable in terms of costs, the Japanese identify two phases: (1) entering a market and (2) taking over a market in terms of product acceptance. Espousing a low-price stance at least initially, the Japanese focus on acceptance, which in turn allows increases in price and break-even with a substantial proportion of fixed costs. It is also possible to alter cost structures substantially by making parts and subassemblies of a product in different countries and assembling the final product in yet another. One reason for this is that certain countries offer substantial cost savings in production. Packard Electric, a division of General Motors, for example, has reduced its production costs considerably by shipping parts to Mexico for labour-intensive assembly operations.

Two other factors are important in costing products for international markets. One is that parts and subassemblies usually have lower import duties than finished products. Therefore, it may be possible to postpone final assembly and gain the benefits of this cost reduction. Another possibility is to purchase parts and materials locally and avoid import duties completely. As an example, IBM in 1985 did over $2 billion of business with European subcontractors who supplied components and sub-assemblies to fifteen plants. Decentralizing assembly besides offering the possibilities of cost reduction builds linkages to national markets by emphasizing ties to local economies not only in terms of customers but also in relation to suppliers and employees. It can also provide some flexibility in adapting products to national markets.

Complex Marketing Arrangements

While international marketing has been characterized as a choice between globalization and local adaption, there is a wide array of possible options. It is not unusual for a single international business relationship to involve licensing, partnership, one-way or cross-supply agreements, and elements of cooperation and competition between and among principals.[5] Complex relationships require flexibility and the greater is the flexibility needed, the greater are the pressures on pricing. Flexibility is also needed to cope with collaboration efforts involving other firms, that may be necessary to gain market entry, make connections to do business in foreign markets, or share the substantial investments required.

Pricing structures must be flexible enough to accommodate the numerous and ever-changing ways of bringing a product to market, and yet fulfil the basic goals of the marketer. Imagine, for example, the conflicting demands on a price schedule when a product is sold direct in one country, distributed through local middlemen in yet another, and part of a government-sponsored monopoly in still another. Adding to the confusion is the requirement in many countries that localized production costs be used as partial payment for sold merchandise.

REGULATORY AND POLITICAL ENVIRONMENTS

The legal and political environment in every country in which a firm hopes to do business will impact significantly the pricing decision. The most obvious are tariffs and quotas. More subtle, but frequently more devastating, are government subsidization and protection programmes.

Tariffs and Duties

Tariffs or duties, whether passed on to the customer in the form of a higher price or absorbed as a cost of doing business in an international market, cannot be ignored in making the pricing decision. A tariff or duty is a form of tax that is assessed by product type on the basis of the value or quantity of goods imported into a country. For example, the US Customs Service classifies all imported minivans and sport utility vehicles as trucks, which are taxed at 25 per cent of value versus cars which are taxed at 2.5 per cent. The stated purposes of tariffs are: (1) to protect local industries by increasing the prices of imported products making them less competitive in local markets and (2) to generate revenue. A tariff or duty that is levied on the basis of product value is called an *ad valorem* charge. Suppose for a particular country the *ad valorem* charge is 30 per cent for cars and related subassemblies and parts. Suppose still further that cost of the completely assembled vehicle is $8,000 and the cost of the subassemblies and parts that make it up is $5,000. The question for the importer in this hypothetical situation (Table 15.1) is whether the car can be assembled for less than the difference in delivered costs, or $4,100. In this example, the importer can pay more for local assembly and still benefit. This same type of analysis can be applied to the subassemblies and parts making up the final product.

Tariffs may also be assessed on the basis of some unit of weight or measurement of quantity such as a bushel of grain or a barrel of oil. Quantity duties are usually found where the value of the products concerned varies widely. Regardless of whether the tariff is based on value, quantity, or some combination of both, the net effect is discrimination against imported goods. By raising the cost to the importer, tariffs limit price competitiveness.

Table 15.1   Trade-off of assembly versus subassemblies and parts purchase

Assembly		Subassemblies & parts	
Subassemblies & parts	$ 5,000	Subassemblies & parts	$5,000
Assembly	3,000		
Total cost	$ 8,000	Total cost	$5,000
Tariff (30 per cent)	2,400	Tariff (30 per cent)	1,500
Transportation cost	500	Transportation cost*	300
Total import cost	$10,900	Total import cost	$6,800

*Subassemblies and parts can be packaged more effectively, resulting in lower shipping costs than finished cars.

Other Trade Barriers

While tariffs have come down throughout the world, the use of non-tariff barriers has increased significantly. One of the most frequently used non-financial barriers is the quota. A quota is a limitation on the quantity of certain goods that can be imported during a specific period of time. It can apply to a particular country or to all foreign sources. When the limitation for a particular country is set bilaterally rather than unilaterally, it is called a voluntary restrain agreement. Regardless of whether the purpose is protectionism or the more equitable distribution of a major market among foreign competitors, the net result is reduced volume and higher prices for foreign products. It was estimated, for example, that the average price of a Japanese car import rose by $2,500 under a voluntary restraint agreement between Japan and the USA.

Other non-tariff barriers affecting the volume of products that can be imported into a national market are import licences and boycotts. Import licences are similar to quotas in that the purpose is to limit the quantity of imports. The difference is that licences are issued on a case-by-case basis. Boycotts, on the other hand, are absolute restrictions on imports, or, for that matter, on any form of trade with another country. Countries can boycott trade with other countries or companies that trade with boycotted countries. Arab states, for example, have boycotted Israel and companies that traded with Israel. Standards in such areas as health, packaging, labelling, and safety will in all probability add to the cost of imported products. There is also a good chance that standards will restrict the volume sold in a foreign country. While the purpose of the standard is understandably legitimate, the application of the standard to imported products may not be. For example, cosmetic products missing even one single ingredient from the Japanese government's approved list must be held for a safety test that may take as much as two years to arrange. To add to this problem, foreign companies do not have access to the top official list of 2,500 ingredients approved by the Japanese government.

Content and country-of-origin labelling, as well as safety standards, are common standards for consumer products that can prove restrictive when the foreign country will not accept testing and certification completed outside the country. The latter has been especially troublesome to marketers of appliances, electrical transmission equipment, and hospital equipment. Local content requirements specify a certain percentage of the finished product that must be produced locally to qualify it for sale in a particular country. Mexico, for example, has a local content requirement of 50 per cent of the parts and materials used in an imported car. Cars not meeting this percentage are barred from the Mexican market. Monetary barriers include blocked currency, differential exchange rates to foster or restrict trade in certain products or with certain companies, and exchange permits. One country may block the currency of another by refusing to exchange its currency. By blocking a currency, a nation can effectively restrict imports because currency received for the sale of imported products cannot be redeemed in international financial markets.

A differential exchange rate sets different exchange rates, depending upon the 'desirability' of the imported product. If the import is not desirable (that is, it competes directly with a locally produced product) then the exchange rate will reflect this and reduce the amount of revenue received for a product sold in a foreign country. Suppose, for example, that the imported product and the locally produced product are both priced at 40 units of currency. A differential exchange rate of one dollar for eight units of currency compared with a rate of one dollar for five units of currency translates into a loss of $3 for every product sold in that foreign country. In other words, instead of getting back $8 for every sold product, the importer gets back $5, or nearly 40 per cent less. To rectify this differential exchange rate, the imported product's price would have to be raised to 64 units of currency, a price that would in all probability reduce sales volume. Recent decreases in the value of a dollar relative to foreign currencies have resulted in significant prices for imported products such as cars, wines, and clothing.

Exchange permits are legal permissions to exchange an amount of local currency for the currency of another country. A branch or operating unit of the importing company or a reseller must apply for an exchange permit prior to the actual transfer of products. One possible requirement may be the deposit of funds in a local banks for a period of time. Another provision may be an exchange rate. As with other non-tariff barriers, exchange permits can add to the costs of doing business internationally, which in turn makes the product or products involved less price-competitive or reduces profitability. Specifically, exchange permits interrupt cash flow and subject the importing firm to the risk of changes in the exchange rate.

MONOPOLY PRICING, INFLATION, AND PRICE CONTROL

Within a foreign country, there are a number of price-related restrictions on the flow of products into the marketplace. These restrictions exist in addition to tariff and non-tariff barriers.

Monopoly Pricing

Monopolies exist in foreign countries that control the sale of products in that country. In Japan, for example, the Japan Tobacco and Salt Corporation, a government-approved monopoly, controls a business estimated to be worth $10 billion. Having to market through this monopoly, brands of cigarettes in the USA have been able to gain little more than 1 per cent of the total market. Only 20,000 of the 250,000 stores and 270,000 machines where cigarettes can be sold are approved for US brands. In addition to a tariff of 35 per cent, these brands are priced 60 per cent higher than Japanese brands.

Inflation and Price Control

Where rapidly escalating prices bring inflation and price control as a government response, this presents serious problems for a firm selling in international markets. Once price controls are set in place, the competitive situation is comparable to operating in a regulated industry such as the utilities in the USA. Among the countries that have had price controls in the recent past or still have such arrangements are Argentina, Brazil, Denmark , Finland, France, Greece, the Philippines and Venezuela. The countries that have price restraints on foodstuffs include Honduras (basic foodstuffs), Italy (sugar, bread, some meats, and pasta), Malaysia (rice, milk, sugar, and flour), Peru (essentials foodstuff), the Philippines (rice, repacked sugar, canned or evaporated milk, chicken, and pork), Spain (basic foodstuffs) and Switzerland (milk and eggs).

Price increases may be granted for increases of actual costs. However, there may be some question as to what is a justifiable cost. For example, the costs of working capital may not be an allowable cost. When there is a net or gross margin limitation, it is important to know whether it is absolute or relative. With the latter, for example, purchase of higher-cost materials and parts can actually increase the absolute margin as shown later:

All forms of price control make use of a base period and contain rules on the grouping of products. For example, in France there is little distinction between corn and vegetable oils as compared with the much cheaper soybean and sunflower oils.[6] A company may benefit from a broad grouping of products, but if it does not then it can petition the government for a regrouping or narrowing of the classification. Both price controls and inflation place emphasis on cost analysis and the ability to project the effect of either on cost structures. The pricing decision is not what level prices should be set, but rather whether if the firm can operate profitably given the circumstances.

EXCHANGE RATE FLUCTUATIONS

Today, all major currencies float freely relative to one another. The net result is uncertainty as to the value of currency in a foreign market. It may be one value today, another tomorrow, and still another some time in the future. Obviously, the possibility of added costs from currency fluctuations must be considered in pricing decisions. While it is true that profits over and beyond original estimates can accrue, it is true that substantial losses can also result.

It must be remembered that foreign currency has to be exchanged into dollars, and, between the time the price of a product is set and payment is received, the amount of money involved is subject to exchange-rate fluctuations. For example, suppose the price of a tractor is set at 50,000 units of a currency which at the current exchange-rate of one unit equalling $.20 US would yield $10,000. Suppose still further that 10 tractors are sold during the next three months in the particular national market. The following is a schedule of payments for the 10 tractors.

First month	4 tractors; payment received: 200,000 units
	Exchange Rate: 5 to 1
	Conversion: $40,000
Second month	3 tractors; payment received: 150,000 units
	Exchange Rate: 7.5 to 1
	Conversion: $20,000
Third month	3 tractors; payment received: 150,000 units
	Exchange Rate: 10 to 1
	Conversion: $15,000
Summary	Actual payments received: $75,000, for an average of $7,500 per tractor. Expected payments: $100,000, for an average of $10,000 per tractor. Exchange-rate loss: $25,000, or $2,500 per tractor.

In the above example, it is obvious that the dollar is progressively losing value in this particular national market. A conversion provision in the sales contract would prevent this loss. It may also be possible to anticipate the possible weakening by raising the initial price. If the initial price is set at 65,000 units of foreign currency then the average price in dollars would be only $250 less than the original $10,000, for a total loss of $2,500 compared with $25,000.

FOREIGN TRADE ZONES

Foreign-trade zones are areas of a country set aside for the storage and assembly or processing of imported products without the payment of tariffs and the application of import regulations. Only when the products leave the foreign-trade zone and officially enter a country do import regulations and duties take effect. One major advantage in using a foreign-trade zone is a reduction in the time between shipment of a product into a country and its eventual sale. The shorter is the time period, the less exposed is the importer to fluctuations in price and currency. Ideally, a unit of product will not leave the foreign-trade zone and be imported formally until it is sold.

There are other potential savings in using foreign-trade zones:

1. A reduction in time between formal importation and sale reduces in turn the carrying costs associated with imported products. There is less time between the payment of import tariffs and fees and the recovery of such costs in the sale of the product.
2. It may be less costly to utilize local labour, which may also bring exemption from assessments of value for tariffs.
3. Shipping of unassembled products or products in bulk form is almost always subject to lower shipping rates.
4. Locally produced parts and materials may not be included in the assessments of value for tariffs.

DUMPING

When a firm sells essentially the same product at different prices in various countries to fit the market circumstances in the respective local markets, it may find itself facing charges of dumping. Dumping is defined as selling at a price below the price of the product in the country of origin, or selling below production costs. If found guilty of dumping, the firm is subject to a countervailing duty on the product involved. The duties levied by the EC, for example, have ranged from less than 10 per cent to more than 40 per cent.

There are a number of reasons for dumping. Eastern European countries dumped products at one time to acquire the currency of Western nations. The Japanese have been accused of dumping to secure a foothold in large foreign markets. There is also the possibility, although it is never publicly acknowledged, that dumping is employed by some international competitors to disrupt national markets.

The harshness of economic penalties make dumping or the appearance of dumping a risky pricing strategy for the international marketer. It is vital, therefore, to ensure that there is no dumping or appearance of dumping in any adaptive pricing strategy. Any time the price of a product in a foreign country is less than the price in the country of origin, the international marketer runs the risk of a dumping charge. The size of the market notwithstanding, a lower price signals dumping to many governments. For example, Japanese manufacturers of motorcycles were accused of dumping by Harley-Davidson when the clearance price to move inventories was about 28 per cent below the prices in Japan, France, Italy, and West Germany.

To avoid having to use the price in the country of origin as the base price in any adaptive pricing scheme, international marketers have a number of alternatives. An obvious one is to market different versions of a product in different countries. Another is to take advantage of the possibilities of adding content locally.

COUNTERTRADE, OFFSETS, AND BUYBACKS

Countertrade, offsets, and buybacks are similar to barter in that one product or products is exchanged for another product or products. Some form of barter arrangement is estimated to represent almost one-third of world trade. Countertrade is a barter arrangement where a seller is given a list of products from which to choose for exchange. A buyback refers to the seller of a manufacturing plant taking a specified quantity of the future output of the plant as payment for the plant. Offsets refer to a broad category of non-cash payments for an imported product. As an example, in exchange for purchasing $200 million of telephone switching equipment, the seller is asked to locate a semiconductor plant in the foreign country that will produce $100 million per year of memory devices of which half will be exported.[7]

In pricing products for sale in international markets, marketing management needs to be aware of the substantial effects that these forms of barter have on trade patterns. One obvious effect is that value in terms of currency or price may be replaced by value in terms of other products, which in turn must be sold or used in some way to produce a financial result from the transaction. Another effect of countertrade is the increasing governmental role in dictating conditions for international sales. Increasing governmental involvement means international trade becomes an instrument of national development.

TRANSFER PRICING

Transfer prices are those charged for intracompany movement of goods and service. Transfer pricing decisions are necessary when goods are transferred from one unit of a global or domestic company to another unit in the same company. A significant proportion of world trade today occurs between the parent company and its foreign affiliates.

Examples of Transfer Pricing Schemes

- Transfer prices are at manufacturing cost plus packaging and shipping. R&D costs are distributed to all divisions on the basis of a set formula.
- Transfers to overseas branches are billed at cost plus set markup to cover handling costs and profits.
- Transfer prices are based on competition. For products produced wholly within the company, approximate prices are established by a policy council.
- A surcharge is added to manufacturing costs for all transfers.
- All transfers are priced at market or negotiated between producing and selling divisions.
- Reasonable manufacturing and selling profits are targeted in setting transfer prices to overseas subsidiaries. Adjustments are made to reflect market size implications in various countries.

Companies transferring goods between their units have to be able to justify their transfer prices and explain how they have computed. Firms may manipulate transfer prices to reduce or avoid tariffs and duties as well as currency exchange and regulations. In the USA the Internal Revenue Service (IRS) has the power to review and amend transfer prices to reflect the free market price arrived at by independent buyers and sellers.

There are four generally recognized approaches to transfer pricing. These are: (1) direct cost, (2) direct cost plus standard increment, (3) market price, and (4) 'arm's-length' price. Transfers at cost or cost-plus are based on the assumption that each stage in the movement of the product towards the market must be reimbursed for its functional contribution. Both cost approaches, and in particular cost-plus, can result in prices completely unrelated to competitive circumstances in an international market. As an illustration, suppose a product costs $200 to produce. Given a markup of production of 20 per cent and shipping and tariff costs of $30, the cost to the international sales division is $270. If the competitive price in the international market is $300, the margin of $30 or 10 per cent will be unsatisfactory to the international sales division, even though $70 or 23 per cent is acceptable at the company level.

A market-based transfer pricing system is based on a competitive market price. Instead of beginning with the costs of production and working forward, transfer prices are determined by working backward from the competitive market. The only constraint on price is cost at a functional level. The fourth approach, 'arm's length', sets prices on the basis of what they would be if the product were being sold at this functional level to independent parties. The problem with this is finding such transfer prices for products other than those of a commodity type. Usually 'arm's length' prices are viewed as a range of possible prices rather than a pricing point.

When evaluating transfer prices, the IRS prefers methods of evaluation using an 'arm's-length' approach. In other words, price is established on the basis of comparisons with transactions for similar goods in the open market. In the case of absence of market transactions involving comparable products, cost-plus methods are deemed appropriate by the IRS.

PRICING ALTERNATIVES

For the firm selling in an international market, there are three alternative positions in regard to price. One is a standard pricing policy, another is an adaptive pricing policy, and the third is a combination of both standard and adaptive.

Standard Pricing

This policy requires that a product has the same price anywhere in the world. It is used with globally standardized products and is based on the assumption that distinctions between national markets are fading and that for many products there is no need for distinctions. With economies of scale and learning curve efficiencies, standard pricing can result in lower prices that are hard to resist even for the most culture-bound international customer.

Standard pricing is also commonplace for technology-based products. With a global company, local management seeks to exploit similarities across countries rather than to emphasize differences. Canon, for example, in marketing a personal copier found a difference in paper size between Japan and the USA and Europe. It was decided to omit the feature to handle the larger Japanese paper because it would significantly increase the cost and the complexity of the copier, which had a high degree of price elasticity. Other problems encountered with using standard pricing are the necessary adjustments with tariffs and other trade barriers, and those in not taking advantage of profit opportunities in countries where a higher price is possible.

The question of what the standard price should be is usually answered by analysing competitive conditions in the largest potential markets. Ideally, the standard price will be set at a level that maximizes customer acceptance (minimizes customer resistance and subsequent loss). Practically, the standard price is often the lowest price necessary to remain competitive in a large potential market. If the two largest potential markets are the USA and Western Europe then the lowest competitive price, will be the standard price, even though it could be sold for more in the other large potential market.

Adaptive Pricing

This pricing policy is based on the idea of setting different prices according to the circumstances existing in an international market. By varying the price with market conditions, the firm can avail itself of the profit opportunities in some markets to offset more competitive circumstances in others. It also provides an opportunity to vary price with the other strategic elements in the marketing mix, to solve local problems, and to match up with possible local supply and technological know-how. Transfer systems are difficult to set up when various prices are charged in different countries.

Combination Pricing

This pricing policy assumes that neither a totally global approach nor a customized approach is the most effective. Instead, a standard price for a global product will be used in some international markets, and in others a differential approach will be taken using adaptive pricing. The assumption in using this approach is that every international market is unique, but that a standardized low price may in certain situations overcome market differences. In one international market the price and marketing programme might be the same. In another international market the only difference might be price, while in yet another both price and marketing programme might be different from one regional market to another. The difficulties in using combination pricing are the complexity of the marketing task and the continuous monitoring required for each targetted international market.

REFERENCES

1. Thomas R. Horton 'Winning in the Global Marketplace', a speech delivered to the American Rubber Company, Southbury, Connecticut, 24 October 1985.
2. G. Harlan Carothers Jr. and Mel Adams 'Competitive Advantage Through Customer Value: The Role of Value-based Strategies', in Michael J. Stahl and Gregory M. Bounds (eds), *Competing Globally Through Customer Value*, (New York: Quorum Books, 1991) pp. 32–66.
3. John A. Quelch and Edward J. Hoff 'Customizing Global Marketing', *Harvard Business Review*, vol. **64** (May–June 1986) pp. 59–68.
4. Philip Kotler and Liam Fahey 'The World's Champion Marketers: The Japanese', *The Journal of Business Strategy*, vol. **3** (Summer 1982) pp. 3–13.
5. B. Joseph White 'The Internationalization of Business: One Company's Response', *Executive*, vol. **11** (February 1988), pp. 29–32.
6. Victor H. Frank Jr. 'Living with Price Control Abroad', *Harvard Business Review*, vol. **62** (March–April 1984) pp. 137–142.
7. Stephen S. Cohen and John Zysman 'Countertrade, Offsets, Barter, and Buybacks', *California Management Review*, vol. **28** (Winter 1986) pp. 41–56.

Index